Praise for The Risk Takers

"Don and Renee Martin want to remind you that even in these tough times, the American dream is alive and well. The accomplished entrepreneurs they have interviewed for *The Risk Takers* will teach you, in their own words, how persistence and creativity can lead to success. Trust your gut and read this book!"

—Ken Blanchard, coauthor of *The One Minute Manager®* and *The One Minute Entrepreneur*™

"*The Risk Takers* is a must-read, particularly as our economy goes through its current strains. It is, after all, the entrepreneurs, such as those documented in the book, who will lead our economy out of the darkness and back to the sunshine. It is an easy read, with great lessons throughout."

—James G. Ellis, Dean Marshall School of Business, University of Southern California

"*The Risk Takers* delivers a treasure chest of ideas and strategies that make it an essential tool for those seeking to start or grow their own business. A great read filled with engaging stories of some of America's most successful entrepreneurs."

—Peter V. Ueberroth, "Man of the Year," *Time Magazine* 1984; President and CEO, Los Angeles Olympic Organizing Committee; Former Commissioner of Major League Baseball in U.S.

"What amazing stories of hope, tenacity, and courage by some of America's greatest entrepreneurs. You'll be entertained and inspired by these remarkable men and women who defied conventional wisdom and overcame significant adversity on their way to success. The book will encourage any budding entrepreneur to just start."

—Linda A. Livingstone, Dean and Professor of Management, Graziadio School of Business & Management, Pepperdine University

"*The Risk Takers* tells the story behind the story of some of America's most successful entrepreneurs, from humble beginnings to dreams come true. Renee and Don Martin will surely inspire entrepreneurs at any age or any stage. Wonderful, well-told stories show you how to turn your dream into the American Dream. This book is a must for anyone ready to trust their gut!"

—Harvey Mackay, *New York Times* #1 bestselling author
of *Swim With The Sharks Without Being Eaten Alive*

"Not since Napoleon Hill (*Think and Grow Rich*) has anyone captured the secrets on how real people become successful. A must-read for anybody that has dreams about becoming an outstanding entrepreneur."

—Stephen Alan Odell, Co-Owner & CEO,
Sugar Foods Corporation (Sweet 'N Low®)

"The future belongs to the risk takers, not the security seekers, and these stories will inspire you to take intelligent risks in the directions of your dreams."

—Brian Tracy, *New York Times* bestselling author

"There has never been a time in history that was hungrier for the entrepreneur's creativity and passion to serve others' needs than today. At just the right time, Don Martin has captured the nuts and bolts of how entrepreneurs think and act with stories that inspire and empower those who have dreamed of creating something special. It is a book whose time has come. It should be on the reading list of anyone who is seeking direction for a time of peril such as the opening decade of the 21st Century."

—James R. Wilburn, Dean, School of Public Policy,
Former Dean, Graziadio School of Business and
Management, Pepperdine University

"Don Martin has lived the quintessential American Dream and has written a powerful and inspiring story of entrepreneurship, ingenuity and perseverance. In this post Great Recession era, his timely and enduring advice is more relevant than ever."

—Anil Puri, Dean, Mihaylo College of Business and
Economics, California State University, Fullerton

The Risk Takers

*16 Women and Men Share Their
Entrepreneurial Strategies for Success*

Renee and Don Martin

Vanguard Press
A Member of the Perseus Books Group

Published by Vanguard Press
A Member of the Perseus Books Group

Designed by Joseph Parenteau / Pronto
Set in 11 point ITC New Baskerville

Cataloging-in-Publication data for this book is available from the Library of Congress.
ISBN 13: 978-1-59315-587-2

Vanguard Press books are available at special discounts for bulk purchases in the U.S. by corporations, institutions, and other organizations. For more information, please contact the Special Markets Department at the Perseus Books Group, 2300 Chestnut Street, Suite 200, Philadelphia, PA 19103, or call (800) 810-4145, ext. 5000, or e-mail special.markets@perseusbooks.com.

10 9 8 7 6 5 4 3 2 1

◆CONTENTS◆

"Wherever you see a successful
business, someone once made
a courageous decision."

—Peter F. Drucker, university professor
and author of thirty-nine books, including
*Managing for Results: Economic Tasks
and Risk-taking Decisions* (1964) and
The Effective Executive (1966)

The American Dream

"I believe that entrepreneurs all have sort of the
same soul and that they are self-starters, unafraid,
willing to take risks and accept the consequences.
Sometimes they win, sometimes they lose. But
they are always able to bounce back. Every
entrepreneur I know is cut from the same cloth."
—**Alan Rypinski, founder of Armor All**

Americans are worried. Jobs once viewed as secure now seem vulnerable. Plans for starting a business have been put on the back burner. Unsure how to react to their current reality, most Americans just wait.

We have always been a nation of entrepreneurs, and if we are to rebuild our economy, we must reinvigorate the culture and mind-set that have built that tradition. My wife, Renee, and I wrote *The Risk Takers* because we want to remind readers about the power of the entrepreneurial spirit, the promise of the American Dream. What better way to ignite that spirit than to showcase the inspiring stories of the sixteen remarkable men and women profiled in *The Risk Takers*? These were ordinary men and women who started with very little, opted to strike out on their own, and struggled with disappointment and failure yet managed to overcome adversity and build hugely successful multi-million-dollar companies.

We personally interviewed some of the most successful entrepreneurs in America today. You'll meet the fascinating founders of companies most Americans will recognize, including Amy's Kitchen, Curves,

Geek Squad, Kinko's, Liz Lange Maternity, Paul Mitchell, Spanx, and nine others. They started with just a good idea, defied the conventional wisdom time and again, and trusted their gut when nobody else would. Along the way, they took both great strides and costly missteps, all part of the learning process. Each believed in his or her company and *willed* it to succeed. Together, their stories prove that even in the bleakest of circumstances, inspired business ideas can prevail when a risk-taking entrepreneur has enough faith, drive, and resilience. We wrote *The Risk Takers* to ignite that same spirit and faith in you.

The idea to write my third book came to me shortly after I sold my own business. My personal path toward entrepreneurship had begun more than four decades earlier with a part-time job. As a young man with no money, I'd worked to pay my way toward a college degree by selling insurance. After graduation, I convinced the owner of the tiny, one-man insurance agency to sell me his business. Because I had no funds, he accepted my signed note for $10,000 with the promise to repay him from my future earnings.

Over the next several decades, I built that little agency into an insurance brokerage that generated over $200 million in annual revenue. Then forty years later, I sold my privately held business, The Cal-Surance Companies, to Brown & Brown, a New York Stock Exchange company, for $64.5 million in cash.

Shortly after, I was having a discussion with one of my best friends and a member of my board of advisors. He asked, "Now that you've sold the company, what are your plans?" I knew I didn't want to start another business. I had just spent forty years running one and needed a change. My friend said to me, "Don, you're a hammer looking for a nail. With your energy level, if you don't find something meaningful, you'll drive Renee crazy." I realized he was right and told myself something would present itself.

A few weeks later, I stopped by to visit with my daughter and her husband one Saturday. Nick, my son-in-law, had just turned thirty and happened to be hosting several of his business-school fraternity brothers that day. Just a few years removed from graduate school, they had all begun careers of their own. By way of introducing me, Nick told them about the recent sale of my company, and they started to ply me with questions and wanted to hear my story.

I told them how I'd grown up in poverty in a small town in the Ohio Valley, where most of the men worked either in the coal mines or the steel mills, and how my business journey had culminated in the company's sale. Nick's friends loved the story—a small-town kid with nothing goes on to hit the big time. But instead of finding inspiration from my success, they lamented that a rags-to-riches story like mine was no longer possible in today's economy. In their eyes, the opportunities that I had as a young man simply weren't available to them. They saw my anything-is-possible tale as a relic of a bygone era. It was as though they believed that the great days of America's trailblazing innovation and dominance were long gone, and I was lucky to have been a part of that.

When I returned home, I told Renee about their response to my story. Nick's friends were all bright, educated young men. Their potential for success was unlimited—if only they believed that. Both Renee and I were deeply troubled by their gloomy perception and forecast that our rags-to-riches entrepreneurship was no longer possible. We both knew that our own success was rooted in a spirit of optimism that allowed us to dream bigger and push ourselves further.

That same sense of optimism had driven me to move to California, enroll in college, learn the insurance business, and start my own company—even though I had barely a dime to my name. That same optimism had also prompted Renee's parents to emigrate from the Ukraine to America, enduring that long ocean voyage in the ship's steerage. Renee carried on the tradition when she moved from her family's Ohio home to California and became a successful real estate broker in the hypercompetitive Los Angeles market.

Renee was always just as driven and ambitious as I was. After working as a high-volume real estate broker for Coldwell Banker, she launched her own business specializing in handling sales for high-end residential developers. In the early 1980s, when interest rates spiraled out of control and the real estate market tumbled, she sought the advice of an occupational counselor at the University of California, Los Angeles. Renee's test results pointed to a career in public relations, and she shifted her focus to selling ideas instead of houses.

By the 1980s, my insurance business was thriving. That gave Renee the freedom to pursue jobs that sparked an altruistic passion in her, jobs that allowed her to make a difference in the community—even if the salary was considerably less than what she'd earned in real estate. Over the next several years, she held a number of positions that showcased her communications and problem-solving skills. Her employers included such organizations as the American Cancer Society and the Children's Bureau of Los Angeles. She worked as a rape counselor at Cedars-Sinai Medical Center and as a child advocate for Court-Appointed Special Advocates.

Despite the demands of her own career, Renee always found time to act as a sounding board for me. She was my secret weapon, my behind-the-scenes muse and collaborator. The Cal-Surance Companies stayed a few steps ahead of competitors by developing new specialized products and services. That was my strong suit. But I always brainstormed with Renee before proposing new ideas to my board of advisers. Working together, we could always take a good idea and make it even better. Renee was also my human resources guru/safety net. Before hiring someone new to a major company position, I'd always arrange a dinner, with the spouses invited. Renee inevitably found a way to draw out the job candidate's personality in a way that I couldn't in a traditional job interview. She was the consummate judge of character, too.

Our entry into the publishing world came quite by accident in the early 1990s. After a friend was suddenly widowed, Renee and I offered to help her get her financial affairs in order. Like many women, our friend had always deferred money-related matters to her husband and remained in the dark about the family finances—which left her vulnerable in many ways, as we came to learn.

Realizing that many women find themselves in a similar predicament following a death or divorce, Renee and I decided to take what we'd learned from the experience and organize a presentation titled *The Survival Guide for Women*. We made the presentation to a group of business people and their spouses one day. The talk included some practical advice on how women could get their own credit ratings, borrow money, deal with a cash emergency, and so forth. The response to this talk was overwhelmingly positive. Later, a radio talk show host asked us to appear on his program, and the station was flooded with requests for our book—the only problem being that we didn't yet have one. So, as there was clearly a need, we decided to write *The Survival Guide for Women*, which was published in 1991, and Renee and I embarked on a book-publishing side business. A couple years later, we collaborated again on *TeamThink*, a book exploring how sports-management concepts can be applied to the business world.

After *TeamThink*, we hadn't really felt compelled to write another book. I guess you can probably figure out what happened next. After my encounter with Nick's friends, I kept mulling over our conversation and what it meant in the broader context of our country's future. Then, a few weeks later, I had an epiphany and broached my idea with Renee. "We're going to write another book," I declared. I proceeded to elaborate passionately on the need for this book. When I had finished, she looked me in the eye and asked, "When do we start?"

Why the Entrepreneurial Spirit Is So Important *Now*

We both believe that, as a nation, we need to remind ourselves of who we are. Sure, we face daunting challenges today, but we have a brilliant and enduring base. We must tap into that brand of hope that's uniquely American, that "can do" spirit that gathers strength during challenging times. We believe the entrepreneurs we interviewed for this book personify that spirit.

It's never been easy to start your own business and steer it through all the inevitable potholes to ultimate success—not in any economy or any era. It's easier to romanticize the past, bemoan the present, and let fear of failure prevail—but business opportunities present themselves in any economy.

You may be surprised to learn that several successful businesses that still endure and thrive today were established during the Great Depression. Included among them are Ocean Spray Cranberries, Yellow Book USA, and Hewlett-Packard. Bill Hewlett and Dave Packard, both engineers, self-funded their business in a rented garage in the mid-1930s. By 1939, the Hewlett-Packard Company had produced its first product—a sound-test device sold to Disney Studios, another Depression-era innovator.

As the stories in this book demonstrate, an entrepreneur's level of commitment and willingness to buck convention often outweigh all other factors in determining whether a business ultimately succeeds or fails. Successful entrepreneurs fully believe in themselves and their ideas and will work their butts off to prove that faith justified. Naysayers' predictions of failure just fuel their passion to succeed. It's the same competitive drive and confidence you see in the world's most accomplished athletes.

Renee and I aren't career journalists. We didn't write this book to further our own careers. We're entrepreneurs who have already realized our dreams and are now eager to inspire others to pursue theirs. We hope the stories of these sixteen entrepreneurs will help provide that spark of inspiration and convince you that your dream of running your very own business is indeed attainable. Perhaps you've already started your own business but want more guidance on how to be successful. Why not learn from those who've been there and done that?

Conventional wisdom might tell you that working in the corporate world is less risky, especially during times of economic instability. But corporate job security has proven an illusion. Given recent headlines, there are no guarantees that either your employer or the pension plan it promises will be there tomorrow or next year or at any point down the road. Why place your career and future in the hands of others? *You* are supremely more qualified to make decisions in your own best interest. You can create your own job, your own career, your own American Dream.

In fact, you might be especially well suited for entrepreneurship. Studies suggest that's particularly true for many members of Generation Y—the children of baby boomers—who are now in their twenties. They want to build in a kind of work/life balance that their parents never had. They desire a more free-flowing, collaborative work environment. They're willing to take risks to customize a career that's right for them. Does that sound like you?

Why *These* Sixteen Entrepreneurs' Stories Are Worth Reading

In planning the book, we decided to personally interview men and women who, when they started out, weren't that different from you. The entrepreneurs we selected and interviewed came from a range of backgrounds and work in different fields and in different regions of the country. Some launched their business while they were still in college; others became entrepreneurs in middle age. Some built their business from the ground up; others acquired and reinvented an existing company to make it their own. The criteria we established were these:

- The entrepreneur started with very little cash. (Most of our book's entrepreneurs launched their business with less than $10,000.)
- The entrepreneur struggled with failures and overcame adversity.
- The entrepreneur's story isn't just inspiring or motivational—it's entertaining.

After two years and many traveled miles, we now feel privileged to have met the incredible men and women who spoke to us with openness and candor. They shared their stories with the honest hope that they would bring something of value to aspiring entrepreneurs. We think they do and hope you'll agree.

The entrepreneurs whose fascinating stories we tell here include:

- **Gary Heavin**, founder and CEO of **Curves International**, the world's largest fitness franchise company. He found an overlooked customer niche of forty- to seventy-year-old women who felt intimidated by large, snazzy gyms with all their frills and spandex-clad patrons. Curves, which caters to women only, has 10,000 franchises worldwide—7,000 of which are in the United States.
- **Linda Alvarado**, founder and CEO of **Alvarado Construction**. In a male-dominated industry in which most Hispanics are viewed only as laborers, she ignored the naysayers, became a general contractor, and built the largest Hispanic-owned construction company in the United States. She also became the first Hispanic owner of a Major League Baseball team.
- **Paul Orfalea**, founder and former CEO of **Kinko's**, the onetime retail leader in copying, printing, and binding services. Struggling to get through college because of his undiagnosed attention deficit hyperactivity disorder and dyslexia, Paul decided he needed to run his own business to ensure his own job

security. He grew a one-hundred-square-foot copy shop into a company with sales of $1.5 billion a year, which FedEx eventually bought for $2.4 billion.

- **Liz Lange**, founder of **Liz Lange Maternity**, the leading design firm of maternity fashions in the United States. Her designs changed the look of maternity clothes for every pregnant woman in the country. In addition to her upscale line sold in boutiques, she designs an affordably priced line sold at Target stores. In late 2007, Liz sold a majority stake in her company to Bluestar Alliance for an estimated $50 to $60 million.
- **Robert Stephens**, founder of **Geek Squad**, North America's leading technology-support company serving owners of home computers and home-theater systems. Without big bucks, he built his company's brand using ingenuity and chutzpah. In 2002, he sold Geek Squad to Best Buy for millions.
- **Barbara Corcoran**, founder and former chairperson of **The Corcoran Group**, a $5 billion residential real estate company based in New York City, and founder of the prestigious *Corcoran Report*, the real estate bible for New York City. Labeled as stupid by her teacher when she was in the second grade, Barbara struggled with dyslexia as a child. But the learning disability sharpened her creative skills, and she became a masterful marketer as an entrepreneur. In 2001 she sold her company to real estate conglomerate NRT for $66 million.
- **David L. Steward**, founder and CEO of **World Wide Technology Inc.**, the nation's largest African American–owned company. Subjected to prejudice and segregation as a youth, David learned all about maintaining optimism in the face of adversity at an early age—a strength that ultimately served him well as an entrepreneur in the information technology industry. Starting on a shoestring in 1990, he built a privately held, billion-dollar company that provides technology solutions to companies in many industries.
- **Maxine Clark**, founder and chairperson of **Build-A-Bear Workshop Inc.**, a retailer specializing in customer-made teddy bears and other stuffed animals. She reinvented the teddy bear as an entertainment commodity that reached $468 million in total

sales in 2008. The company operates more than four hundred stores in the United States, Puerto Rico, Canada, the United Kingdom, Ireland, and France. There are also franchise stores abroad.

- **John Paul DeJoria**, cofounder and chairman of **John Paul Mitchell Systems**, maker of Paul Mitchell–branded hair and beauty products. The company has annual salon retail sales of over $900 million. John Paul is also the cofounder of the spirit company that produces Patrón tequila. He went from broke and sleeping in his car to owning several businesses and residences, including a home in Hawaii.

- **Sara Blakely**, founder and president of **Spanx**, a body-shaping hosiery manufacturer that offers more than 150 styles and generates $350 million in annual sales. Told she was crazy when she first tried to manufacture her footless pantyhose design, she has transformed the hosiery industry.

- **Andy Berliner**, cofounder and CEO of **Amy's Kitchen**, a leading producer of organic frozen foods distributed in health-food stores and supermarkets. He identified a growing trend in America's eating habits and pounced on it. Since its launch in 1987, the company has grown an average of 20 percent each year. Annual sales top $270 million.

- **Joe Liemandt**, cofounder and CEO of **Trilogy Inc.**, a company that pioneered development of product-configuration software systems in the early 1990s. Just as he was entering his senior year at the prestigious Stanford University, he blew off his degree to pursue a dream and was worth an estimated $500 million before his thirtieth birthday.

- **Mal Mixon**, chairman and CEO of **Invacare**, the world's leading manufacturer and distributor of wheelchairs and home-health-care products. He was thirty-nine years old when he decided to quit his secure corporate job and purchase a struggling business in need of an overhaul. Since acquiring Invacare in 1979, he has led the company to grow its annual sales from $19 million to $1.8 billion.

- **Tova Borgnine**, founder of **Tova Corporation**, a multi-million-dollar direct-marketing beauty-products company whose line includes best-selling fragrances and skin-care products. Speaking no English when she and her mother emigrated from Norway to the United States, Tova grew up as a housekeeper's daughter. After working as a makeup artist, she eventually launched her own brand of beauty products, which she personally helped develop. In 2002 she sold her brand to cable TV's QVC network for an eight-figure price tag, but she remains the brand's spokeswoman.

- **Florine Mark**, founder and CEO of **The WW Group**, the largest Weight Watchers franchisee in the United States. As a struggling mother with five children, Florine parlayed her own personal weight-loss success into a thriving business. In 2003, she sold 75 percent of her franchises back to Weight Watchers International for $181.5 million but remains the system's biggest franchisee in the nation.

- **Don Martin**, founder and former CEO of **The Cal-Surance Companies**. I tell my own story—how I built a global insurance brokerage, which generated over $200 million in sales, from one tiny strip-mall insurance office. Cal-Surance fetched $64.5 million when I sold the business.

How This Book Can Help *You* in Your Business

When we began working on *The Risk Takers*, we had no plan to write a business how-to book. Our goal was to motivate and inspire. However, after we had interviewed our first dozen or so entrepreneurs and written their stories, something surprising happened. After reading through all of the completed chapters one day, Renee came into my office with a look of excitement on her face. "Don," she said, "it's uncanny—I never focused on it until now, but so many of the traits that contributed to each one's success are evident in *all* of our entrepreneurs." She started to enumerate the shared traits she'd identified and cited examples of where they appeared in each entrepreneur's story. I realized she was onto something incredible and totally unexpected. All I could say was, "Wow! You're right!"

These traits had revealed themselves. They had not been preconceived, so we were truly surprised, yet delighted, by the important bond all these entrepreneurs shared. We highlight these common traits, which we now believe contributed strongly to these men and women's successes, in each chapter and present them together in our final chapter, "Strategies for Success." It can't be a coincidence that so many of these characteristics crop up in the stories of these successful entrepreneurs.

In *The Risk Takers*, you'll meet contemporary entrepreneurs who, in most cases, had little more than a great idea and faith in themselves when they first started their businesses. They ignored the naysayers. They persevered despite setbacks and disappointments. They set out to create a thriving business and made it happen. So can you. You can reclaim the American Dream if you're willing to embrace it and work harder than you have ever worked before. We hope the following stories will give you that hope, that belief, and that inspiration. We just want to give you a push in the right direction. Isn't it time you got your business started?

—Don Martin

CHAPTER 2

Gary Heavin *(Courtesy of Curves International)*

Gary Heavin

Cofounder and CEO, Curves International

"I learned that I didn't have to repeat the same mistakes. I learned that failure doesn't taint you unless you let it."

—Gary Heavin

A Texan through and through, multimillionaire Gary Heavin feels more comfortable wearing cowboy boots than Bruno Maglis. He's an evangelical Christian who speaks freely about the time he spent in jail years ago and how that experience changed his life forever. He pilots his own Learjet and owns a ranch near George W. Bush's spread in Crawford, Texas. He publicly supports pro-life groups without worrying about his controversial stance's impact on public relations or the bottom line. He's a take-me-or-leave-me kind of guy with an independent streak as wide as the Rio Grande River. And, along with his wife, Diane, he founded the Curves International franchise company, one of the biggest entrepreneurial success stories of the past quarter century.

Starting a Business with $10,000

Gary doesn't really look the part of someone who leads a fitness empire. He's slim but not muscle-bound, with thinning sandy-brown hair and a closely trimmed mustache. The fifty-five-year-old could more readily pass for an oil-rig worker or truck driver. In fact, those are two of the blue-collar jobs he held during his stint in college, before he entered the fitness business.

Curves was launched in 1992, when Gary and his wife of two years, Diane, took a huge risk and spent their entire $10,000 in savings to open a women's fitness center in Harlingen, Texas. The idea for the business was simple but *bucked conventional wisdom*: Curves would cater to middle-aged and elderly women who needed a safe, nonthreatening place to unlearn a lifetime of unhealthy habits and finally get in good physical shape with a regimen of exercise and a balanced diet. Gary recognized this was an *underserved niche* in the fitness industry.

But to stay solvent, Gary and Diane needed to sell at least one hundred gym memberships in the first three months. A skilled marketer (with ten years' experience in newspaper advertising and marketing),

---

Curves catered to middle-aged and elderly women who needed a safe, nonthreatening place to unlearn a lifetime of unhealthy habits and finally get in good physical shape with a regimen of exercise and a balanced diet. Gary recognized this was an *underserved niche* in the fitness industry. Curves targets a demographic that competitors have written off or cast aside.

Diane met that goal in just one week. Within three years, the couple operated two Curves clubs, and earnings topped $250,000. Within a decade of Curves's launch, the company's revenue hit the $2 billion mark. Yes, that's *billion*. Today, Curves is the world's largest fitness franchise and the sixth largest franchise company of any kind, according to *Entrepreneur* magazine.

"We never borrowed money to build Curves," Gary says. "It's a debt-free company. Nor did we take on any investors. What that meant was we were free to 'do the right thing' as we made decisions. We didn't have to worry about quarterly profit reports or stockholders."

Learning from Past Mistakes

Gary's entrepreneurial story shows how far a dream can soar with the right combination of innovation, calculated risk, and faith. But his story also illustrates how taking the wrong risks can doom a healthy business, triggering a reversal of fortune that can lead to the depths of personal despair. In the business world, fearless risk taking can lead to ruin, and it can lead to redemption. In Gary's case, it has led to both.

"The real reason I'm successful is because of persistence," Gary says. "I kept getting back up. And every time I got back up, I had new information. If I made a mistake, I'd never forget it. I'd get back up, and I'd apply the lesson."

Curves wasn't Gary's first fitness business. In the mid-1970s, while just twenty, Gary ran out of money for tuition and quit college, abandoning his plans to one day become a doctor. Instead, he joined his brother David in launching a women's gym called Women's World of Fitness. The business thrived, and they began opening additional locations with amenities like tanning beds and saunas. Within ten years of its launch, the company had fourteen locations. "By the time I was twenty-six, I had a $1 million financial statement," Gary says.

But to offset the expense of those extra amenities and the additional square footage needed to accommodate them, the brothers opted to open the gyms up to men as well—a misstep from which the business never recovered. It resulted in a loss of comfort for many of their longtime female clients, who dropped their memberships, and the company started losing money. Accustomed to living large, the two brothers didn't heed all the signals and change course in time to cut their losses. Having turned their backs on the feature that had made their business unique in the first place, they had adopted a growth strategy that alienated existing customers.

Losses continued to pile up, and bankruptcy followed in 1986. Gary lost everything: his marriage, his house, his private plane, his cars, his self-respect. He was $5 million in debt. After missing child-support payments, Gary was sentenced to three months in the Cameron County Jail in Brownsville. He wasn't just a failed businessman; he was officially a deadbeat dad.

But that time alone in jail changed his life. He studied the Bible and became a born-again Christian. Upon his release from jail, Gary was eager to begin his new life and launch a new business. "I learned that I didn't have to repeat the same mistakes," Gary says. "I learned that failure doesn't taint you unless you let it."

———————◄◦►———————

"We never borrowed money to build Curves.
It's a debt-free company. Nor did we take
on any investors. What that meant was we
were free to 'do the right thing' as we made
decisions. We didn't have to worry about
quarterly profit reports or stockholders."

———————～———————

Starting Over by Focusing on an Underserved Market

Gary *wouldn't let adversity defeat him.* First, he took the steps to rebuild his life, working as a fitness-equipment salesman and gym consultant. Then, with the help of his second wife, Diane, Gary launched Curves. Despite his past mistakes, he *trusted his gut* that his new business could see long-term success because it tapped an *underserved niche.* "I knew the pain of failure, but I'm ambitious, and I had faith," he says.

Gary had remarried shortly before serving his jail sentence. "It's kind of a neat thing that we married then because he knew that I really loved him," Diane recalls. "He didn't have a lot of material things." It was Diane who came up with the Curves name and logo.

With Curves, Gary wasn't just out to build a profitable business. He truly wanted to help overweight women change their lifestyles so that they could lead happier, healthier, and longer lives. The inspiration behind Curves was Gary's mother, Doris Heavin, who had died of a stroke when Gary was just thirteen. She had spent a lifetime battling obesity, depression, and high blood pressure. "She had just turned forty and died in her sleep," Gary recalls. "My two little brothers and I found her. It was a real traumatic experience."

Many of Curves's early clients reminded Gary of his mother. In a moment of self-reflection, he remembered his youthful dreams of someday becoming a doctor. He realized that his desire to heal women was rooted in his regret about his mother's health problems and premature death. "I had the epiphany that what my life had been about was healing women because of my mother," he says. "And that was what my destiny was going to be."

───────────◄○►───────────

"The real reason I'm successful is because of persistence. I kept getting back up. And every time I got back up, I had new information. If I made a mistake, I'd never forget it. I'd get back up, and I'd apply the lesson."

───────────

Expanding the Business by Selling Franchises

With Curves's initial success, Gary and Diane realized how emotionally rewarding the business was. They wanted to make Curves accessible to more women without assuming a great financial risk. Gary still had memories of his previous attempts at business expansion. He and Diane arrived at a solution: selling Curves franchises.

They decided to test their plan in Paris, Texas. "I ran a $250 ad in the paper announcing that a Curves franchise would be coming to town and that a representative would be there on a Thursday to interview prospects," Gary recalls. The interviews were held at the restaurant in the local Holiday Inn. At the time, Curves was far from a national household name. Nonetheless, the company had enjoyed regional success, and eight people showed up. Sipping iced tea in one of the restaurant booths, Gary talked to the franchisee prospects and

—◄○►—

One mistake Gary had made in an earlier business
was turning his back on the feature that made the
business unique in the first place and adopting a
growth strategy that alienated existing customers.

—◄◡◡►—

tried to get a sense of whether they were right for the job. Not only
did their financial resources need to pass muster, but they needed to
understand Curves's business goals and philosophy of helping women
change their lives.

About eight glasses of iced tea later, Gary wrapped up the final
interview. He decided three of the candidates had what he was looking for and told them to weigh carefully whether the investment was
right for them before calling him back on Tuesday morning. One of
those candidates, Stephanie Armstrong, wasted no time. Her 6:30
a.m. phone call the following Tuesday roused Gary from a sound
sleep, but her enthusiasm convinced him that she was the right person to help launch Curves's franchise system. Gary's hunch proved
on the mark. Armstrong's Paris franchise opened in 1995 and is still
going strong.

> In 2001, *The Guinness Book of
> World Records* listed Curves as the
> world's largest fitness franchise.

The franchising approach placed Curves's expansion in the
hands of entrepreneurs rather than company-employed managers.
Entrepreneurs have a greater stake in a business's success, which
becomes a personal mission. Gary contrasts Curves's franchise approach with the Starbucks model, in which locations are corporate
owned. "Their managers are required to make a pretty good cup of
coffee, and I think you can train thousands of managers to perform
that task," Gary says. "But our people who open these Curves, they're
charged with taking these women and equipping them to become

healthy and fit, to stick with their diet and to change their lives. It's a heck of a responsibility, and it's all about relationships, training, and follow through."

―――――――――――◄○►―――――――――――

The franchising approach placed Curves's expansion in the hands of entrepreneurs rather than company-employed managers. Entrepreneurs have a greater stake in a business's success, which becomes a personal mission.

―――――――――――⌇―――――――――――

Keeping Prices Low—for Franchisees and Other Aspects of the Business

During the franchise system's infancy, Gary would load the exercise equipment onto an open-bed trailer and haul it to franchisees with his pickup truck. After crossing dusty Texas plains and hill country, he would often find himself scraping a layer of bug guts off the equipment after reaching his destination. Meanwhile, Diane created marketing and training materials. She also designed Curves T-shirts and water bottles to help the brand *get noticed without expensive advertising*.

Gary's franchising strategy was first to establish a presence in small towns before moving into more populous urban areas. When a franchisee's membership peaked, Curves would typically sell another franchise, often to a member, who would open in the next available market. Each franchise was given ample opportunity to reach its full potential.

The company carefully studied potential customer demand in a given area, based on population demographics, competition, and proximity to other Curves locations. During the company's early growth spurt, Gary resisted the temptation to raise franchise prices. Instead, he focused on attracting the best-qualified, most devoted franchisees. His criteria for aspiring franchisees included the three *P*s: pride (in their skills, their business, and themselves), people skills, and passion. "I kept the price low and sacrificed profit to keep the opportunity open to a much wider range of people," he explains. "We ended up selling 95 percent of our franchises in America at $19,900.

Gary's franchising strategy was first to
establish a presence in small towns before
moving into more populous urban areas.

Only later did we raise the price. I see myself as a creator of opportunities, and that's a good testament to how we did that."

Gary also adopted a franchise system model all his own. Instead of charging a monthly royalty based on a percentage of the franchisee's total income, he charged a fixed amount of $395. This *bucked conventional wisdom*: No major franchise company had ever done that, but Gary was determined to avoid the mistakes of other franchisors. He didn't want franchise fees to represent a disincentive for franchisee growth. He *exploited his competitors' weakness*—their systems for calculating franchise fees—*and made it his strength.*

"I saw franchisees for other companies working harder, making more money, and then having to give more of it to the franchisor," he says. "They resented that. It ended up harming the relationship between the very best franchisees and the franchisor."

During the company's early growth spurt,
Gary resisted the temptation to raise franchise
prices. Instead, he focused on attracting the
best-qualified, most devoted franchisees.

This risky strategy paid off and helped strengthen Gary's relationship with his best-performing franchisees. Moreover, the Curves brand was *getting noticed by franchisee prospects without expensive advertising.* "Franchisees ended up shouting from the rooftops how well they were doing and how they loved this franchise system because there was no penalty for doing well," he says. "Our franchise sales skyrocketed, and we ended up making far more money in the end because we didn't have to spend a lot of money on advertising and marketing to sell new franchises. Our franchisees did that by word of mouth. Everybody won."

Only recently did Gary change his franchisee fee structure. Today, the monthly royalty fee is 5 percent of total income, capped at $795. "The reason why I did that was because there were actually people in small communities that were paying $395—the same as people in large communities—and I wanted the smaller community franchisees to get a break," he says. "Now if you're in a small community of 5,000 people or so and you've got one or two hundred members, you might pay as little as $195, and the larger communities that support a larger membership pay a bit more."

———————◄○►———————

He didn't want franchise fees to represent a disincentive for franchisee growth. He *exploited his competitors' weakness*—their systems for calculating franchise fees—*and made it his strength.*

———————

Enormous and Rapid Growth

Curves sold its six thousandth franchise after just seven years. Compare that to McDonald's, which took twenty-five years to reach that milestone, or Subway, which took twenty-six years.

In January 2007, Gary imposed a moratorium on new American franchises and began focusing more on international markets. He didn't want to oversaturate the market, with U.S. franchises competing against each other for members.

Today, Curves has more than 10,000 franchise locations in sixty-nine countries. About 6,300 of these franchises are in the United States, and the value of a franchise has climbed steadily over the years. By 2007, the initial franchise investment, when bought through corporate rather than franchisee resale, was in the range of $38,425 to $53,450.

A Different Type of Fitness Center

Curves's corporate headquarters provides each Curves franchisee with training, advertising support, and the right to use the brand name. Because Curves members follow a prerecorded voice during workouts, franchisees don't have to assume the cost of hiring fitness instructors. They can operate with a small part-time staff. Commercial leasing costs are minimal as well. A Curves location can operate in a space as small as 1,000 to 2,000 square feet. In comparison, multipurpose gyms can require up to 40,000 square feet.

> In 2008, *Entrepreneur* magazine named Curves the number six global franchise.

As a result, you're more likely to find Curves locations in rural, sparsely populated towns, where having a traditional gym location might not make economic sense. To borrow an old baseball idiom, you could say that Curves franchisees can *hit 'em where they ain't* because of their modest operational costs. Today, there's 1 Curves for every 1.5 McDonald's. More than 4 million women belong to Curves clubs. In the United States, Curves memberships cost about $40 a month on average.

Curves applies a no-frills approach, *bucking the conventional wisdom.* There's no sauna, no swimming pool, no basketball court, and no juice bar. When you visit a Curves location, you don't really feel like you're in a gym. The facility basically comprises one big room with about ten pieces of weightlifting equipment spread out in a circle. The walls

---

◄○►

"Franchisees ended up [telling everyone] how well they were doing and how they loved this franchise system because there was no penalty for doing well. . . . We ended up making far more money in the end because we didn't have to spend a lot of money on advertising and marketing to sell new franchises. Our franchisees did that by word of mouth. Everybody won."

HOW CURVES HAS GROWN

Year	Number of Locations
1992	First Curves for Women opens in Harlingen, Texas
1995	First Curves for Women franchise center opens in Paris, Texas
1996	44 locations
1997	247 locations
1998	537 locations
1999	860 locations First one opens in Canada
2000	1,258 locations First one opens in Spain
2001	2,221 locations First one opens in Mexico
2002	5,000 locations worldwide First ones in England, Portugal, and Wales
2003	6,733 locations worldwide First ones open in Brazil, Chile, Dominican Republic, Guatemala, Ireland, Italy, New Zealand, Northern Ireland, Peru, Puerto Rico, Scotland, and the Virgin Islands
2004	8,500 locations First ones open in Argentina, Australia, Bahamas, Bermuda, Cayman Islands, Colombia, Costa Rica, Cyprus, Ecuador, El Salvador, France, Guam, Honduras, Netherlands, and Panama
2005	9,500 locations First ones open in Barbados, Bolivia, Germany, Greece, Iceland, Japan, Nicaragua, South Africa, and Venezuela
2006	10,038 locations in 51 countries First ones open in Denmark, Egypt, Hong Kong, Hungary, Israel, Jamaica, Korea, Namibia, Norway, and Sweden
2007	10,269 locations in 63 countries First ones open in Kuwait, Lebanon, Morocco, Saint Lucia, Singapore, Swaziland, Switzerland, Taiwan, Turkey, and Vietnam
2008	Nearly 10,000 locations in 69 countries First ones open in Bahrain, Belgium, Botswana, Channel Islands, Jordan, Malta, Qatar, Saudi Arabia, Slovakia, and the Ukraine
2009	Nearly 10,000 locations in 73 countries First ones open in Bulgaria and Senegal

Source: "Curves: Timeline and Success Statistics," Curves, April 2009, http://news.curves.com/images/20003/Media_Timeline_4–2009.pdf.

aren't covered with mirrors either. You won't find any fitness-obsessed twenty-five-year-old Barbie dolls wearing $300 skintight "active-wear." Nor will you find sweaty jocks grunting with every lunge to get Barbie's attention from across the room. You won't find any men period.

> Curves applies a no-frills approach, *bucking the conventional wisdom.* There's no sauna, no swimming pool, no basketball court, and no juice bar. When you visit a Curves location, you don't really feel like you're in a gym.

You *will* find women, mostly in their fifties and sixties, wearing T-shirts and shorts or sweats. The thirty-minute workout combines strength training and cardiovascular activity through hydraulic resistance. Up-tempo music helps club members keep up the pace, but there is no pressure to outlift, outrun, or outlast anyone else in the room. And members feel secure in knowing that if they struggle with that weight machine, nobody will roll her eyes. Members encourage each other. These women know they will never qualify for an Olympic event; they just want to get into shape. Most come three times a week. Curves appeals to many women who just wouldn't feel comfortable at a traditional gym. The company's weight-management program is specifically designed to raise women's metabolic rate so they burn more calories.

When visiting Curves locations, Gary is still often reminded of his mother during encounters with gym members. Her memory continues to provide inspiration. Sometimes he even imagines what it would be like to have a conversation with her today. "I let her know

In 2009, *Health* magazine named Curves one of America's healthiest gyms.

that the tragedy of her death is now helping millions of people, and she smiles," he says.

Gary took a huge risk by creating a workout facility totally different from the "traditional gym." Curves has succeeded because Gary found an *underserved niche* in the broader fitness market. In essence, Curves targets a demographic that competitors have written off or cast aside.

"In this particular part of my industry—fitness centers for women—I became the best at it," Gary says. "That's one of the keys to success—you become very, very good at some small part of something. You're a specialist, not a generalist."

---◄○►---

Risk taking is also about embracing change.
Businesses that avoid change will inevitably stagnate.
Change takes you out of your comfort zone, but
how else can a business grow? "I think people
like me learn to *like* feeling uncomfortable. In fact,
we get comfortable with being uncomfortable."

Partnering with Like-Minded Companies

Gary continues to *reinvent his company*, finding new ways to expand the Curves brand and promote its message of fitness and health. In 2006, Curves partnered with Destiny Health, a Chicago-based company, in a program that offers plan members 50 percent off their enrollment fees at Curves. Destiny Health develops wellness-based health-care plans that balance health insurance coverage with incentives that reward healthy behavior. Curves has also worked with major health insurance companies like Blue Cross and Blue Shield to provide wellness-program benefits.

A partnership with the American Association of Retired Persons has made Curves membership available through that association. "Everybody knows that if you exercise a few times a week, you lower your health-care costs by 50 percent," Gary says. "Another way of looking at it is that for every dollar you spend on wellness, you save as much as $5 on illness."

In 2009, the American Association
of Franchisees and Dealers
announced Curves was its
"Franchisor of the Year."

In 2007, Curves partnered with General Mills to launch weight-management food products, including granola bars and cereals. Gary's readiness to expand Curves's reach through partnerships proves that risk taking remains a major part of the company's agenda.

When asked to define risk, Gary responds, "Weighing those factors that would allow for success against those that would allow for failure." Then, he adds, you factor in your experience level and ability to forecast a likely outcome.

◄◊►

"I'm not afraid of losing my money or my business. I'm going to wake up every day and do the right thing. And if I were to lose everything I own, I'd just rebuild again."

Risk taking is also about embracing change. Businesses that avoid change will inevitably stagnate. Change takes you out of your comfort zone, but how else can a business grow? "I think people like me learn to *like* feeling uncomfortable," Gary concludes. "In fact, we get comfortable with being uncomfortable."

Meanwhile, Gary continues to write best-selling books, including *Curves: Permanent Results without Permanent Dieting*, *Curves on the Go*, and *Curves Fitness and Weight Management Program*. Gary remains focused on finding new ways for Curves to reach more women.

"I'm proud that I've created an opportunity for 4 million women to find their way into the gym, many of them for the first time," Gary says. "Our sisters, our mothers, and our grandmothers now have an opportunity to start taking care of themselves and to avoid disease."

And, he adds, he's also created an "entrepreneurial opportunity for thousands of women to own their own business, provide for their families, and make a difference in their communities. So whether it's the entrepreneurial opportunities or the health opportunities I've been able to create, those are the things I'm most proud of."

Curves's success owes much to Gary's willingness to take high-stakes risks, despite the disappointment of past failures. "I'm not afraid of losing my money or my business," he says. "I'm going to wake up every day and do the right thing. And if I were to lose everything I own, I'd just rebuild again."

⌐∿⌐

STRATEGIES FOR SUCCESS

♦ Gary Heavin saw opportunity in an *underserved niche*: out-of-shape older women who wanted to exercise but felt unwelcome amid young, fit bodies in traditional gym and health-club settings.

♦ His first fitness club for women failed when he opened it to men, changing the factor that had made it unique. He fell into a downward spiral of debt and inability to meet child-support obligations that led to jail time. But he *resolved not to let adversity defeat him.*

♦ He *trusted his gut* that a women-only exercise studio was a good idea, and he decided to expand the idea by offering franchises to owner/managers who he believed could build the relationships he felt were essential in such a business.

♦ Rather than concentrate on pricing issues, he focused on finding the most committed franchisees, and he charged them a flat fee instead of a percentage of income. *Bucking conventional wisdom,* he made the fee structure Curves's strength. He felt the percentage system was a disincentive to growing the business, and he was proven correct when satisfied franchisees encouraged others to come aboard.

♦ His model—small, no-frills operations—worked even in sparsely populated areas that couldn't support more elaborate setups, so his franchisees could *hit 'em where others ain't.*

♦ Distributing T-shirts and water bottles with the company logo, combined with positive word-of-mouth reports, *drew the company notice without expensive advertising.* And Gary continues to *reinvent the business* by partnering with food companies, health insurers, and others who target the same customers Gary's company serves.

Linda Alvarado at the 2008 Democratic National Convention
held at the Pepsi Center in Denver, Colorado
(Photo courtesy of Alvarado Construction, Inc.)

Linda Alvarado

Founder and CEO, Alvarado Construction

"One of the great myths is that all great careers
are planned. But sometimes accidental careers,
or opportunities, are presented in your way."

—Linda Alavarado

When Barack Obama accepted the Democratic Party nomination
at Denver's Invesco Field in the summer of 2008, more than 84,000
cheering supporters in the stadium stands—and millions watching
on TV around the world—knew they were witnessing history. Here

was the first African American presidential candidate to accept a major party nomination for the nation's highest office. Linda Alvarado saw that and much more. She saw the perfect symbol for her American Dream, the culmination of a life spent working to succeed in the construction industry. Her business, Alvarado Construction—the first major American construction company founded and headed by a woman—was the general contractor on the team that had built Invesco Field at Mile High years earlier. Alvarado Construction was also the lead construction manager that, in five short weeks, had transformed Denver's Pepsi Center for the 2008 convention at which Obama had been nominated the night before.

"It was like the American Dream," Linda says of her company's role in the history-making event. "This wasn't just about politics—that's not what was so overwhelming. It was about a Hispanic woman-owned firm, Alvarado Construction, being the lead construction manager and general contractor for the convention, serving multiple clients—the Democratic National Committee, the owners of the Pepsi Center, and the city of Denver—making sure that everything went perfectly. It was incredible, unbelievable. It took an incredible amount of work to do everything, from design through construction, and managing hundreds of people working 24/7 to complete the work ahead of schedule."

That meant transforming Pepsi Center luxury suites into broadcast booths, running miles of cable, removing 5,000 seats and installing a giant stage and podium, installing additional lighting and heating, ventilation, and air-conditioning units, and adding 164,000 square feet of office space. There were countless meetings with a multitude of agencies, including Homeland Security and the Secret

---

◆◇◆

Alvarado Construction is the first major
American construction company founded
and headed by a woman; Linda is also the first
woman and the first Hispanic to buy a major
professional sports team in the United States.

Service. The list goes on and on. The Pepsi Center also had to be restored to its original condition within fifteen days following the convention to accommodate a scheduled sports event.

Overcoming Prejudice and Financial Obstacles

So how did a Hispanic woman who grew up in a house without indoor plumbing find herself in that position? As a risk-taking entrepreneur, Linda Alvarado hasn't just *bucked conventional wisdom*; she's shattered long-standing stereotypes with a will that refuses to be thwarted. The modest construction business she founded in the mid-1970s eventually grew into an industry giant, constructing office buildings, stadiums, and convention centers. In 1992, she banded with six other Denver entrepreneurs to buy an expansion team that became the Colorado Rockies Baseball Club. Linda isn't just the first American woman to head a major construction firm; she's also the first woman and the first Hispanic to buy a major professional sports team in the United States.

––––––––––––––––⟨○⟩––––––––––––––––

Linda's parents stressed that the true value of
work stems not from "building a bank account
[but from] building your character and giving
back some of what you earn to help others." And
growing up with five brothers, she says, created a
"competitive environment [that] taught me about
teamwork and the importance of taking risks."

––––––––––––––––⟨ᴠ⟩––––––––––––––––

Linda's work ethic and competitive drive—along with her faith in overcoming prejudice and financial obstacles—are rooted in her upbringing. She was born Linda Martinez in 1951 in Albuquerque, New Mexico—the only girl in a family of six children. Though Linda's father, Luther, worked hard to provide for his family, they were poor and struggled to make ends meet. When Linda was born, the family lived in a cramped three-room adobe house that Linda's father and his brothers had built. The home had neither heating nor indoor plumbing. Linda's mother, Lily, took in ironing to earn extra cash.

Linda Alvarado with her parents, Luther and Lily Martinez, in front of their adobe home in Albuquerque, New Mexico (*Photo courtesy of Alvarado Construction, Inc.*)

Despite the family's financial struggles, the home wasn't the least bit dreary. Linda's parents made certain of that. "My parents were very, very positive people," Linda recalls. "They believed that helping others was an important part of life—that was in their DNA and religious beliefs. Even when we were little, my mother had us get involved with organizations to help others in need. And for my mother, it wasn't good enough just to be a member. *Anybody* can be a member. She said we needed to also be a leader to demonstrate our commitment."

When Linda and her younger brother started their own neighborhood yard-work business, their parents stressed that the true value of work isn't measured solely in dollars and cents. "My parents would say, 'This is not about building a bank account. This is about building your character and giving back some of what you earn to help others,'" Linda remembers. Her parents also expected their children to excel in school. The kids in the Martinez household were often called upon to explain what they'd learned in the classroom earlier that day. And report cards were taken very seriously.

It wasn't always easy growing up with five brothers, but that family dynamic did teach Linda how to be assertive—out of necessity. "The competitive environment with my brothers taught me about teamwork and the importance of taking risks," she says. Linda and her five brothers also shared their dad's love of sports. "My father played recreational baseball and would take us to watch the games as young children," Linda says. "As we grew older, we began playing baseball, basketball, soccer, football, and other sports. And when you have six kids, you have a team!"

While attending Sandia High School, Linda was a member of the girls' basketball, track, soccer, softball, and volleyball teams. As a student athlete, her natural leadership skills emerged. She was president of the Girls Sports Club and captain of the girls' softball team. Despite the demands of competitive sports, she still managed to keep her grades high. Her mother excused Linda from most of the household chores so that she'd have plenty of time for school assignments and to prepare for tests. "That was her gift to me," Linda says of her mother. "She did the housework so that I could study."

Loving Getting Her Hands Dirty

In her senior year, Linda earned an academic scholarship to Pomona College, a private liberal arts college in Claremont, California, and planned to major in economics. But that's where she first became intrigued by the construction industry—quite by accident. It all started when she set out to land a part-time job and checked out the college job-opportunity board. There were three jobs posted for work on campus: a food-service job at the cafeteria, a book-stacking job at the library, and a grounds-keeping job tending the campus landscaping. To Linda, this was a no-brainer, and she decided to apply for the grounds-keeping position. The hiring supervisor, however, was incredulous.

"I showed up, and the supervisor asked me, 'What are you doing here?' I said that I needed a job," Linda recounts. "And he says, 'Don't you understand that girls do food service and boys do landscaping?' He suggested that I get counseling from my advisor."

But Linda had grown up in a family that never imposed limits on her because of her ethnicity or gender. Her parents had always encouraged her to excel in sports and pursue any field that interested her. Her father had even let her do some tinkering under the hood of his car. The supervisor's notion that she couldn't handle the demands of the landscaping job—and that she was better suited for dishing up meatloaf and mashed potatoes in the cafeteria line—didn't sit well with Linda. "I wasn't trying to be obstinate or to change the rules," Linda explains. "I just didn't want to work in the cafeteria, and I was already spending a lot of time in the library studying."

Undeterred, she returned to restate her case to the supervisor. But this time she tried persuading him with a little bit of humor—a tactic she'd picked up from her mother. When he launched into his belittling speech about the job's physical demands under the scorching sun—and how no pretty girl like her could handle the work—Linda had a retort at the ready. "I said, 'Let me get this right. I'm going to get a great tan. I don't have to go to the gym anymore. I get to wear Levis every day. I get to work with all these single men. And you actually *pay* me to do this?'"

The strategy worked. He gave her a chance, confident that a day on the job would prove him right anyway. But he wasn't right. Linda loved working in the gardens and getting her hands dirty, despite the unwelcoming attitudes of some male coworkers. "One of the great myths is that all great careers are planned," Linda says. "But sometimes accidental careers, or opportunities, are presented in your way."

During college, she took a job with a commercial development company in California. The only female employee, she again encountered resistance in a male-dominated industry—especially among some construction crew members. "The outdoor restrooms were quite an experience," she remembers of that time. "There were no federal laws requiring separate restrooms. Why would they need them, right? So I'd find drawings there of myself in various stages of undress. Some were nice; some were not so nice."

Creatures of habit, the restroom-wall artists typically used the color-coded pens assigned to their respective trades. Interestingly, the electricians were much more respectful in their renderings than workers in some of the other trades. Linda took it all in stride, focusing on what she loved about the job.

"What you may appear to be to other people is important, but we should be careful that we don't get caught up in conventional thinking and eliminate ourselves and say, 'I can't do that,'" Linda says. A little coworker ridicule wasn't going to send her fleeing to a more traditional workplace for a woman. "I would smile and try to think positively that my hair really did look great in one of the drawings!"

———————————◄○►———————————

"Although Hispanics have always worked on construction sites, we were stereotypically viewed as laborers and craftsmen, not as company owners. And if any women were on construction sites at all, it was as secretaries. . . . So it's not how other people see us, but more important, how we perceive ourselves in trying to achieve our goals."

———————————✿———————————

Learning the Business and Thinking Big

Linda also had the good fortune of being assigned to assist an office engineer who valued a round of golf a lot more than he valued a long day's work. When he realized how competent and detail-oriented Linda was, he started piling mounds of his paperwork on her desk so that he could head to the golf course. Soon, despite the prevailing gender bias in the office, Linda was accompanying the engineer, superintendent, and architects on walk-throughs, reviewing work progress, and calculating the percentage of project completion for billing purposes. She was learning the construction business from a management perspective. "It was intriguing to learn how the design process and the construction phase come together to complete a project," she explains.

Linda enrolled in construction-related classes to learn how to read blueprints and to estimate and bid on projects. Moreover, she learned about computer-based critical-path-method scheduling. It was the first generation of computer scheduling used by the construction industry. The technique calculates a project's minimum completion time as well as the possible start and finish times for its different activities. A project model is constructed that takes into account all of the activities needed to finish the overall project, the time required to complete each activity, and all the dependencies among them. Any delay in an activity on the "critical path" directly affects the project completion date. Mastering that software gave Linda a competitive advantage. Most scheduling methods in use at the time were still linear, using bar charts, with limited detail on the connections among the various project activities.

"That skill, which many men didn't have at that time, helped me develop somewhat of a niche in the industry," she says.

Her career path was taking shape, despite all the obstacles in her way. Linda *wouldn't accept the limits others tried to impose on her.*

"Although Hispanics have always worked on construction sites, we were stereotypically viewed as laborers and craftsmen, not as company owners," Linda says. "And if any women were on construction sites at all, it was as secretaries in the job-site trailers. So it's not how other people see us, but more important, how we perceive ourselves in trying to achieve our goals."

Going Out on Her Own

Linda's goal was to own a construction company one day. Remembering her mother's advice to start small but think big, she developed a written business plan and applied for a small start-up business loan at six different banks. They all turned her down. Clearly, the loan officers didn't think a woman could run a successful construction company. When she discussed her disappointment and frustration with her parents, they bravely offered, without being asked, to help Linda finance the business by taking out a mortgage on their family home.

"They gave me the money as a gift, not as a loan. That demonstrated how much they believed in me," Linda says. "I've repaid the money but I'll never be able to repay them for what they did." The financial risk her parents assumed also gave Linda extra motivation to ensure her company's success. "I knew if I did not succeed, they could lose everything," she says.

They gave Linda $2,500—barely enough to *just start*, and in 1976, she founded her own firm. During the company's infancy, she quickly learned that her business had to pay its dues to earn a place in the construction industry. Her company first specialized in simple concrete curb, gutter, and sidewalk projects. Her employees were a band of "crazy risk takers like me," she says. "It was kind of a youthful entre-preneurial adventure."

Linda became a master negotiator to get work from general contractors. Her concessions often got creative. For example, to help her cash flow, she might offer a lower labor cost if the contractor agreed to purchase the concrete. Her creative bartering often nabbed the job assignment while making the client feel like he was getting a great deal.

Linda has been honored twice as the U.S. Hispanic Chamber of Commerce Business Woman of the Year. *Hispanic Business Magazine* has named her one of the "100 Most Influential Hispanics in America."

To avoid being ruled out based on gender bias, Linda began to sign bids with her first initial instead of her first name. Before long, the company started to win small contracts with municipal transportation agencies to construct passenger bus shelters. In fact, the firm built about 350 bus shelters during one stretch to increase cash flow and develop a track record. When asked which construction project she's most proud of, without hesitation Linda surprisingly answers, "The bus shelters. While only ten feet in length and three feet wide, they demonstrated to

One of the bus shelters built by Linda Alvarado's firm
(Photo courtesy of Alvarado Construction, Inc.)

me that I could build a structure and get paid for it, as opposed to just installing curbs, gutters, and sidewalks."

Linda then found herself in a better position to approach former employers and potential clients to solicit some direct sales and market her company. "First and foremost, I had to sell my credibility," Linda says. "No one had ever seen or heard of a woman contractor. People needed to meet me to make sure I was not crazy and I knew what I was talking about and had the ability to do the work."

During this time, Linda married Robert Alvarado, a cement finisher born in East Los Angeles who grew up in Long Beach. On one of their first dates, they went to an LA Dodgers game—perhaps foreshadowing her eventual status as a baseball team owner.

By 1978, Alvarado Construction had been incorporated. Linda was advancing through the different classifications of commercial licensing requirements for general building contractors. That meant navigating through—and gaining a full grasp of—the tangle of federal, state, and local building codes and procedures in effect. As she earned each additional license, she qualified her company for more construction work classifications. She was positioning Alvarado Construction to offer the full range of commercial development and construction services—from project concept through design, construction, and ongoing facility-management services.

Relocating Required Building a New Client Base—from Scratch

Robert, Linda's husband, had always wanted to be in the restaurant business. So when an opportunity presented itself for him to buy a restaurant in Denver, they decided to make the move—which meant Linda had to start all over again in establishing a reputation and client base for her company. She quickly took steps to plant roots in her new hometown. Like she'd done when she was a young girl, she volunteered for service organizations, including the League of United Latin American Citizens, and she served on the board of the Colorado Boy Scout Council, the Children's Museum, the Tennyson Center for Children, and other nonprofit organizations. She was also one of the founders and the first woman chairman of the Denver Hispanic Chamber of Commerce. In the process, Linda met and formed friendships with some of the city's most influential business and civic leaders. Those contacts helped propel Alvarado Construction further into the big leagues of the regional construction industry. Using the cutting-edge project scheduling and management techniques she'd mastered, Linda gained a reputation for completing projects on budget and on time.

"In Colorado it was in many ways easier to gain access to the higher level of decision makers, compared to California," Linda explains. Potential clients were more readily accessible, and there was a strong sense of community in Denver. Many of her new clients actually had already met her, so she found she no longer needed to expend as much energy to instill confidence in those wary of hiring a Hispanic female general contractor. She also educated herself about federal procurement procedures and started meeting with government officials. She *got her business noticed without expensive advertising*.

Diversifying from Construction to Retail Development

In the mid-1980s, Linda entered the fast-food franchise business when she and her husband identified an area where they could *hit 'em where they ain't*. At the time, major commercial and residential developers had virtually abandoned investing in Denver's inner-city neighborhoods, leading to bargain-basement prices for commercially zoned properties there. The couple decided to develop a retail shopping center in one of those inner-city neighborhoods and to anchor the project with a fast-food restaurant in which she could become a franchisee.

"But when we went to all the large, quick-service restaurant companies—McDonald's, Wendy's, Burger King, and Dairy Queen— they all turned us down," Linda says. As a last resort, Linda set up a meeting in California with Taco Bell executives. PepsiCo Inc. had acquired Taco Bell from an entrepreneur, Glenn Bell, just a few years earlier, and upper management was eager to broaden the brand's footprint. When Linda pointed out that a Taco Bell in her shopping center would face no competition, the executives decided to schedule a trip to the area to take a look for themselves.

Although the project's sales prospects won the Taco Bell executives over, they wanted the restaurant to operate not as a franchise but as one of their corporately owned Taco Bells. As the property owners, however, Linda and Robert held all the cards and ultimately acquired their franchise. As predicted, the Taco Bell location did phenomenally well, outperforming all the other businesses in the retail center. "I learned a valuable lesson," Linda says. "She who controls the land controls the deal. I subsequently sold the shopping center but kept the restaurant which had become the most valuable asset."

With that deal, the couple established a solid relationship with PepsiCo and over the years continued to build new restaurants and acquire additional franchises from the company. In 1997, PepsiCo exited the restaurant business, selling some locations and spinning others off into a new company—today known as Yum! Brands Inc. Linda and Robert remain major Yum! Brands franchisees, operating scores of Taco Bell, KFC, Pizza Hut, and Long John Silver's locations. Robert handles the day-to-day restaurant operations, while Linda assumes responsibility for finance, site selection, development, construction, and franchise relations. It's been a very lucrative business, largely because of the couple's savvy in picking locations.

———————◄○►———————

Linda gives local kids tours of the stadium
and Colorado Rockies team facilities, and
sometimes they stop at her office, where she
points to her desk and says, "The job you want
to aim for is to be an executive manager or
to be the owner of your own company."

————————————————

Putting Up Money for a Major League Baseball Team

Meanwhile, Alvarado Construction established itself as one of the fastest-growing commercial construction firms in the Denver area. The company built the Colorado Convention Center, Concourse B at Stapleton International Airport, and a nine-story office building for U.S. West Communications in Inverness Park.

In the early 1990s, a small group of business investors trying to win a new Major League Baseball expansion team for Denver approached Linda. That group included Peter Coors—someone she

The Colorado Convention Center expansion
(Photo courtesy of Alvarado Construction, Inc.)

knew through her charitable work and construction at the Coors
Brewery. When the businessmen asked her to join their consortium,
she agreed. The stakes were high, but she *trusted her gut*. All the investors had to put up their own money for a bid deposit and include an
additional $100 million in financial commitments with the proposal
submission. The deposit was mostly nonrefundable if they didn't win
the bid.

"This was about supporting the city of Denver and getting into
the big leagues," she says. "It was also about risk taking. If the city was
not selected, we'd lose our deposits. And if Denver was selected, of
course, we'd have to write even bigger checks. But it was phenomenal
in many ways. First of all, I'd played softball as a catcher like my dad.
And baseball is a sport in which Latinos excel. It's a sport that shows
diversity in action, a sport that shows that when people are given a
level playing field and the rules are the same for everyone, anyone
can succeed."

In early 1992, Linda was elated when she first heard the news
that the group's bid had been accepted. "It was the first time in history that a woman, not through marriage but as an independent entrepreneur, had become an owner of a major league franchise," she
says. She was also the first Hispanic—male or female—to own a Major
League Baseball team.

When the Colorado Rockies settled in town, she not only loved
rooting for her team but also enjoyed giving local kids tours of the
stadium and team facilities—something she still does. "I take them to
the broadcast booths and talk to them about careers in broadcasting
and journalism, and to the Rockies offices to learn about sales and

marketing, and in the dugout to talk about careers in sports," she explains. "We give them game tickets above the dugout where they tell me that they believe that only the mayor or very important people sit and I say to them, 'Someday you'll be here, too.'"

Linda with the Colorado Rockies Ownership Group
(Photo courtesy of Alvarado Construction, Inc.)

Another stop on the tour is sometimes her own office, where she points to her desk and says, "The job you want to aim for is to be an executive manager or to be the owner of your own company." Linda hopes to inspire young people to believe they, too, can become entrepreneurs. She relishes encouraging young people, particularly young Latinas, that they have the ability to achieve their dreams.

Linda cherished her new role as a baseball team owner. Instead of turning to the business section of the morning paper first, she started reading the sports section first. Meanwhile, Alvarado Construction was thriving more than ever. Life was good in the Mile High City.

Dealing with Tragedy, Criticism, and Stress

And then tragedy struck. It happened in 1992 while Alvarado Construction was acting as general contractor for the new nine-story airport office building at the new Denver International Airport site. Two ironworkers employed by Anderson Steel Erectors Inc. were killed at the job site after a column fell and the men plummeted thirty-five feet. Platte River Steel Company, one of Alvarado's subcontractors on the project, had actually hired Anderson Steel Erectors. Though an Occupational Safety and Health Administration investigation ultimately cleared Alvarado Construction of any culpability in the accident, Linda's company immediately came under harsh media scrutiny.

Alvarado Construction had never before, nor has it since, had a fatal accident at a job site in all its years of doing business. In fact, Alvarado Construction has received several safety awards from the Army Corps of Engineers and other agencies for its safe work practices.

Although the company was cleared of any wrongdoing related to the fatal accident, Linda realized she needed to rebuild her reputation and prove herself all over again. Some of her most outspoken critics seemed to be exploiting the tragedy, appealing to lingering stereotypes and pandering to prejudices to call into question the qualifications and capabilities of women and minorities. It was an intensely stressful time for Linda, both personally and professionally.

Meanwhile, the new Denver International Airport project, which had been fraught with millions of dollars in massive cost overruns and significant schedule delays even before Alvarado began construction of the office building, was shut down by the city during the investigation and fell even further behind schedule. That fueled more criticism. When the contract was completed and the building was turned over to the city of Denver in mid-1993, the Department of Aviation disputed the final billing and withheld payment. That placed Alvarado Construction in the difficult position of having to use its own cash to pay its subcontractors.

Alvarado provided mountains of documentation supporting the company's claims, hired a scheduling expert to analyze delays, and participated in a series of lengthy negotiations. But the company and Department of Aviation didn't finally reach a settlement for two long years. Throughout this trying chapter in the life of her business, Linda persevered and *never let adversity defeat her.*

"I had a great team of people working for me who believed in our company," Linda says. "It took us some time, but we came back." That's an understatement. Linda has been honored twice as the U.S. Hispanic Chamber of Commerce Business Woman of the Year. *Hispanic Business Magazine* has named her one of the "100 Most Influential Hispanics in America." In 2001, she received the prestigious Horatio Alger Award during a ceremony in Washington, D.C. That

Linda Alvarado visits a construction site *(Photo courtesy of Alvarado Construction, Inc.)*

same year her company was a partner in the general contracting team building Invesco Field at Mile High Stadium, home to the Denver Broncos National Football League team. She didn't know at the time, of course, what role that venue would ultimately play in American history. Meanwhile, Linda continues to make history in the still male-dominated construction industry.

"While my career may still be viewed as nontraditional, I view my path as one that will hopefully open doors of opportunity for other women and people of color to pursue. As in the poem by Robert Frost, 'I took the road less traveled and that has made all the difference,'" Linda says.

꒰∞꒱

STRATEGIES FOR SUCCESS

♦ Linda grew up in a family that never imposed limits on her because of her gender. She readily *bucked conventional wisdom* and pursued a career in the male-dominated construction industry. Despite the resistance she encountered, she *trusted her gut* that her talent and commitment would ultimately overcome any gender or racial bias in her way.

♦ While working for a commercial development company, Linda drew ridicule from male coworkers who disapproved of women working in construction. But she *wouldn't let adversity defeat her* and focused instead on what she loved about the job.

♦ After *just starting* Alvarado Construction with financial help from her parents, Linda initially established a track record for her company by targeting a niche, the construction of bus shelters.

♦ Linda *exploited her competitors' weakness*—accurate scheduling—by offering her clients an advanced form of computer-based scheduling *and made that her strength*.

♦ Within only a few years of starting her business, Linda earned additional commercial licenses that qualified her company for more classifications of construction work. That enabled her to *reinvent her company* so that it offered the full range of commercial development and construction services—from project concept through design, construction, and ongoing facility management.

♦ After moving her business from California to Colorado, Linda volunteered for several Denver-based service organizations. In the process, she formed friendships with some of the most powerful local business and government leaders. As a result, Alvarado Construction *got noticed without expensive advertising*.

♦ In the mid-1980s, Linda teamed with her husband, Robert, to open fast-food franchise businesses in Denver's inner-city neighborhoods, *hitting 'em where they ain't*.

♦ While Alvarado Construction acted as general contractor for an office-building project at Denver International Airport, two ironworkers hired and employed by a subcontractor were killed in a tragic accident at the work site. Though the Occupational Safety and Health Administration cleared Alvarado Construction of any culpability for the accident, the company came under harsh media scrutiny, and final payments were initially withheld. During this trying time, Linda again *wouldn't let adversity defeat her.* She gradually reestablished her company's stellar reputation and eventually began attracting even more prestigious construction projects.

CHAPTER 4

Paul Orfalea *(Photo by Alice Williams Photography)*

Paul Orfalea

Founder and Former CEO, Kinko's

"Your attitude will define your altitude. If you think
you can, you will. If you think you can't, you won't."

—Paul Orfalea

As a kid, he was a perpetually poor student. He flunked the second grade because he couldn't grasp the alphabet. School administrators even suspected he was retarded. As a teenager, he couldn't hold a job for long, even when his boss was a family member. So just how did Paul Orfalea manage to launch and oversee a company that would eventually fetch $2.4 billion?

A Business Idea Spawned by an Opportunity Seen Firsthand

The idea to open his own photocopy store first came to Kinko's founder Paul Orfalea while he was a senior at the University of Southern California (USC) in 1970. His study group had just completed a major term paper for a business class, so Paul made the trek to the campus copy center to make photocopies. Since he hadn't really helped write or research the paper—reading and writing weren't his fortes—handling the photocopying was the least Paul could do for his team. It was supposed to be a mundane task. But when he stepped inside the center, Paul was instantly struck by the flurry of activity.

Students weren't the only ones rushing to make copies before an impending deadline. There were also legal aides rifling through stacks of documents, frantically copying a page at a time. They happened to be working on the infamous Charles Manson murder trial—a case that had the local media transfixed. What had Paul transfixed, however, was the sense of urgency that gripped the university copy center. These people *really* needed their photocopies—and *now*. While others at the center saw long lines and a ticking clock, Paul saw a lucrative business opportunity. By chance, he had discovered an *underserved niche*.

---◄○►---

"I don't believe in hard work. I believe in hard worrying, hard thinking into your soul, and understanding. Most people surrender themselves to being busy. Being busy is very intoxicating—you don't have to come to grips with who you are. I was never busy. I was always with my anxiety, and that puts you in the moment so you always know to seize opportunity."

Having worried about his future after graduation, Paul had a hunch that launching his own photocopy business might be the answer. His mind began racing. Before he had even finished making all the term-paper copies, he ran to class and told his best friend Danny, a member of his study group, about his business idea. Danny was incensed. Paul had done it again. Given a simple task, he nearly always got distracted. Instead of having the term-paper copies *in hand*, Paul came to class with an ambitious business plan *in mind*. As Danny knew all too well, Paul's attention to detail was as brittle as a potato chip.

––––––––––◄O►––––––––––

What transfixed Paul was the urgency that gripped
the university copy center. These people *really*
needed their photocopies—and *now*. While
others saw long lines and a ticking clock, Paul
saw a lucrative business opportunity. By chance,
he had discovered an *underserved niche*.

––––––––––⚬––––––––––

At the time, Paul and his friends didn't know that Paul would eventually be diagnosed with attention deficit hyperactivity disorder (ADHD) and dyslexia. In the 1960s and 1970s, the public didn't know much about so-called learning disabilities. Neither did the schools. As a child, Paul had been forced to repeat the second grade because of his struggles with learning the alphabet. In the third grade, he was even sent to a school for the mentally retarded—until he scored 130 on an IQ test and was returned to the public school system. Despite these setbacks, Paul *never let adversity or failure defeat him*. He just became more and more adept at accentuating his strengths—creative problem solving and collaborating with and motivating others, for example—and masking his weaknesses. This was one tenacious young man, as demonstrated by his decision to attend college and his commitment to someday starting his own business.

But his inattention to details was no secret to his friends and family—or his business-course study group. That's not to say Paul couldn't maintain focus on big-picture goals. Within just a couple of months of his copy-center epiphany, he discovered the need for a copy center near the University of California, Santa Barbara (UCSB) campus and decided to *just start*. He located and rented a tiny storefront in Isla Vista, near UCSB, for the business site. The location wasn't ideal, considering Isla Vista was 106 miles away from the USC campus where Paul was a student—not exactly close enough to drop by between classes. But Paul's girlfriend at the time attended UCSB, and he knew how much local students and faculty members needed a photocopy center. The lack of competition allowed him to *hit 'em where they ain't*. Paul's instincts told him this was the right time and place to launch his business, so that's what he did. He *trusted his gut*.

Early Family Support and an Unconventional Approach to Business

Paul was raised in a Lebanese American family of entrepreneurs. His father ran his own women's clothing company in downtown Los Angeles. His grandmother ran a clothing store in LA's Fairfax District. The family always assumed Paul would someday start his own business, despite his struggles in school. "My parents never looked at my report card," Paul remembers. "It was, 'Honey, are you saving your money?' So I always knew I'd have my own business."

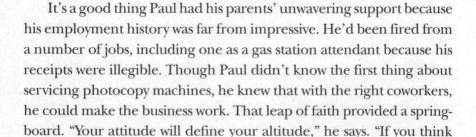

He knew how much local students and faculty members needed a copy center. The lack of competition allowed him to *hit 'em where they ain't*. Paul's instincts told him this was the right time and place to launch his business, so that's what he did. He *trusted his gut*.

It's a good thing Paul had his parents' unwavering support because his employment history was far from impressive. He'd been fired from a number of jobs, including one as a gas station attendant because his receipts were illegible. Though Paul didn't know the first thing about servicing photocopy machines, he knew that with the right coworkers, he could make the business work. That leap of faith provided a springboard. "Your attitude will define your altitude," he says. "If you think you can, you will. If you think you can't, you won't."

After his father cosigned on a $5,000 bank loan, Paul leased a photocopy machine from Xerox for $1,000 a month and dubbed his new business Kinko's. Kinko was one of Paul's nicknames, inspired by his kinky blond hair. Other nicknames included Brillo Pad and Carpethead—you get the idea.

No market studies, no written business plan, no problem: Kinko's opened for business in 1970 in a one-hundred-square-foot space attached to Carlos's Hamburgers and charged four cents per copy. To ensure his business caught the eye of Carlos's customers and anyone else sauntering by, Paul placed a sandwich-board sign out front. He asked an artist friend to add some design touches to the outdoor wall where Kinko's customer-service window was located. The result was a mural featuring mermaidlike women donning bikini tops. How this hole-in-the-wall eyesore of a business evolved into a retail giant worth $2 billion per year is one of the most unlikely, fascinating entrepreneurial Cinderella stories of our time.

The first Kinko's store in Santa Barbara, California
(Courtesy of the FedEx Kinko's archive)

College and municipal libraries had copy
machines, but they were costly to use and
often poorly maintained, and there was nearly
always a waiting line. Kinko's provided a quicker,
lower-cost alternative, with a laid-back vibe
geared toward the academic world. Paul was
exploiting his competitors' weaknesses—wait
times and cost—*and made those his strengths.*

Paul established his unconventional managerial style from the outset. Because he was still a student at USC, he worked at Kinko's only two days a week. During those two days, he rarely worked behind the store counter; that kind of drudgery just couldn't hold his attention. Instead, he went out prospecting for clients. He handed out flyers on the UCSB campus and stuffed them in faculty mailboxes (without authorization); he even hawked pens and pencils in front of the store. He *saved his bucks and got the company noticed without expensive advertising.*

"I put my notebooks and pens on the sidewalk, and I sold $2,000 worth of notebooks and pens the first day," Paul says.

Within four months of opening the first store, Kinko's had made enough money to pay off the bank loan Paul's father had cosigned. When the store added a new Xerox machine to handle the workload, Paul's team had to operate it outdoors using an extension cord because the store was so small and the copier was so bulky.

The second Kinko's store was even smaller
than the first: It was a converted dumpster
stall attached to a restaurant. The rent was
enticingly cheap—a mere $80 a month.

Paul had come up with the right idea at the right time. Keep in mind, this was the early 1970s—long before the era of personal computers and desktop printers. Students and faculty wrote on typewriters. Carbon copies were still in use, but not at all practical for authors prone to typos and white-out fixes. College and municipal libraries had photocopy machines, but they were costly to use and often poorly maintained, and there was nearly always a waiting line. Kinko's provided a quicker, lower-cost alternative—with a laid-back vibe geared toward the academic world. Paul was *exploiting his competitors' weaknesses*—wait times and cost—*and made those his strengths.*

During the company's infancy, Paul also managed—just barely—to graduate from USC. How did he accomplish that feat? "There are three rules," Paul explains. "Always register for more credits than you need, so you can drop the hardest course. Find the easy professors—generally, where the football players are, that's where you want to be. And apply to start in the second semester since their standards aren't as high then."

Expanding to New Locations

The next year, Paul decided to spend a few months backpacking in Europe to take a break. He trusted his coworkers that much. During that trip he eventually grew bored, spent all his money, and found time to mull over ideas for company expansion. He returned revitalized and inspired and opened a second store near the University of California, Irvine. The second store, even smaller than the first, was a converted dumpster stall attached to a restaurant. The rent was enticingly cheap—a mere $80 a month.

He trusted his employees implicitly, often deferring operational decisions to them. That left him free to focus on the broader picture: overall growth strategy, product expansion, customer service, and employee motivation.

Paul's early growth strategy—opening stores near colleges or universities—was crucial to Kinko's success because it guaranteed a robust customer base and a source of capable part-time workers. Experience soon taught Paul that the largest, most prestigious universities represented the best business prospects. After all, faculty

First Kinko's coworkers in the early 1970s (Paul Orfalea,
top right) *(Courtesy of the FedEx Kinko's archive)*

members and grad students at these universities were more likely
to engage in major research projects, which required plenty of
documentation. Lots of documentation meant lots of photocopying
and binding. Kinko's custom publishing services became especially
popular with professors. Again, he was taking advantage of an *underserved niche.*

"The secret to life is to look like a Republican. You
don't have to be one, but you should look like one."

An Open and Trusting Company Culture

The Kinko's success story couldn't have happened without Paul Orfalea, aka Kinko, at the helm. Paul was the antithesis of the archetypal
work-consumed business leader, *bucking conventional wisdom* at every
turn. He trusted his employees implicitly, often deferring operational

decisions to them. That left him free to focus on the broader picture: overall growth strategy, product expansion, customer service, and employee motivation.

Paul enjoyed vacations and took them often. He abhorred staff reports and meetings, preferring one-on-one communication either face-to-face or on the phone. Even after Kinko's became a household name, Paul's desk remained devoid of any paperwork, files, or even a computer. Instead of spending hours in his office, like big-time CEOs are expected to do, Paul was typically out visiting one of his stores. He loved to chat with store managers and customers to learn first-hand what worked so that those practices could be implemented in other stores. "I always wanted to know why the top 10 percent were performing," he says. "I didn't worry about the bottom 10 percent—I could always send somebody out to do something about that."

Paul Orfalea helps clean one of the stores *(Courtesy of Adrianna Foss)*

Paul's management style was unconventional by necessity. He had a great mind for business, but that mind seemed to operate in a parallel universe. To this day, however, Paul views his so-called learning disabilities as his primary strengths as a business leader. From the time Paul was a child, his reading problems required him to rely on others' help. He became skilled at verbal communication and forging strong, lasting friendships and partnerships. He learned to work with and trust others. "If you're lucky enough to have my skill sets, you become very trusting of other people," Paul says. "You think anybody else can do it better."

As a result, as a business owner, he was more skilled at identifying and nurturing the strengths of colleagues, delegating responsibilities, marketing to clients one on one, and fostering a productive and upbeat work environment. By leaving the day-to-day operations to others, Paul was free to tap his creative mind to set a course for the company's long-term growth and success. His restlessness and anxiety fueled his creativity. "I don't believe in hard work," he says. "I believe in hard worrying, hard thinking into your soul, and understanding. Most people surrender themselves to being busy. Being busy is very intoxicating—you don't have to come to grips with who you are. I was never busy. I was always with my anxiety, and that puts you in the moment so you always know to seize opportunity."

Paul's early growth strategy—opening stores near colleges or universities—was crucial to Kinko's success because it guaranteed a robust customer base and a source of capable part-time workers.

During an interview, trying to get Paul to focus on one subject, or one question, at a time is like trying to catch a butterfly while you're wearing winter mittens. You just can't do it—and, ultimately, why would you want to? Paul's train of thought veers this way and that, in fits and spurts—and then bigger spurts. His rapid-fire observations may still be a half step behind his racing mind, but his gift for gab is engaging. He's got a boyish, boundless energy. It's easy to understand why so many talented people joined the ranks of Kinko's when its future was still uncertain. Paul is a risk taker with a penchant for convincing others to take risks alongside him. "My secret to managing people is work with competent people and get the hell out of the way," he says.

Paul believed that his biggest competitive advantage was his staff. If he could make Kinko's a great place to work and nurture workers' best qualities, he was convinced the business would thrive. He set out to make employees feel like "empowered entrepreneurs," literally giving everyone a stake in the company's success. Partners, managers, and sales staff all shared in the profits of their stores. Employees were designated as "coworkers." They didn't work *for* Paul; they worked *with* him. "Our workers got asked their opinions all the time, which is very fulfilling for them," he says.

<o>

He loved to chat with store managers and customers to learn firsthand what worked so that those practices could be implemented in other stores. "I always wanted to know why the top 10 percent were performing. I didn't worry about the bottom 10 percent—I could always send somebody out to do something about that."

In those early years, the work environment was casual, fun, and open to experimentation. Work attire in the summer months was often cutoff jeans and flip-flops. Coworkers sometimes brought their pets to the store. After a long day's work, they'd often share a few beers together and just hang out. As the business grew, so did the family of coworkers, which became closer. Paul also enlisted a real family member, his cousin Denny, to open a Kinko's location in downtown Los Angeles in the summer of 1973.

Early on, managers received a whopping 25 percent of their store's profits. Later, Paul expanded the profit-sharing system, giving each manager 15 percent of the store's profits and splitting the 10 percent among the store's coworkers. The goal was to keep everyone highly motivated and personally invested in Kinko's success. It worked. Employee turnover stayed low; morale stayed high. And exceptional employees stayed put because Kinko's gave them "a fraction of the action." Paul's willingness to share company control and profits with others represented a huge risk on his part. Essentially, he was gambling on the company's long-term success.

He was more skilled at identifying and nurturing the
strengths of colleagues, delegating responsibilities,
marketing to clients one on one, and fostering
a productive and upbeat work environment. By
leaving the day-to-day operations to others, Paul
was free to tap his creative mind to set a course
for the company's long-term growth and success.

Paul made a point of regularly reminding Kinko's staff members that their work wasn't just about making money. They were also making a contribution to society and playing a role in some of the most important events in people's lives. Kinko's coworkers photocopied résumés to help customers get jobs. They photocopied first-time novels and screenplays for aspiring writers. They copied photos of missing children to help their parents locate them. They printed wedding invitations, birth announcements, and death announcements. They reproduced works of art. Paul knew the value of reminding coworkers of this. It helped give everyone a sense of fulfillment and fostered a connection to the community.

"My biggest challenge at Kinko's was we had to go from a culture based on things to a culture based on people," Paul says. "What really built Kinko's were caring employees who humanized all the machines." Paul made certain each store appeared orderly and uncluttered. "My job was to make people comfortable, to do everything calmly," he says.

He set out to make employees feel like "empowered
entrepreneurs": partners, managers, and sales
staff all shared in the profits of their stores. The
goal was to keep everyone highly motivated and
personally invested in Kinko's success. It worked.
Employee turnover stayed low; morale stayed high.
And exceptional employees stayed put because
Kinko's gave them "a fraction of the action."

One of Paul's strongest skills was recruiting worthy business partners. If convinced that someone could contribute to Kinko's success, he was aggressive—and at times relentless—in his efforts to convince that person to come onboard. One such partner was Tim Stancliffe, whom Paul eventually enlisted to open the company's first out-of-state location in Boulder, Colorado, in late 1975. Again, Kinko's set up shop in modest quarters and relied on guerrilla marketing techniques to drum up business.

Paul typically required partners to make at least a $2,000 initial investment. He saw a potential partner's inability to come up with the $2,000 as a red flag. If the candidate lived from paycheck to paycheck and never saved money, he probably wouldn't be cautious enough with a store's profits either, Paul reasoned.

Paul and another longtime partner—his cousin Denny, for example—would hand over 40 percent of the store to the new partner and keep 60 percent (30 percent each) for themselves. If the new partner fell short of expectations, then Paul and Denny still had the option to buy him out.

Paul's reading problems required him to rely on others' help. He became skilled at verbal communication and forging strong, lasting friendships and partnerships. He learned to work with and trust others.

Expanding via More Locations and More Services to Meet New Customer Needs

Kinko's opened additional Southern California stores in Fullerton, Van Nuys, San Luis Obispo, Westminster, and San Diego. That first San Diego store represented a departure and milestone of sorts—its eight-hundred-square-foot size was eight times that of the Isla Vista store and cost about $10,000 to open. By 1975, Kinko's had twenty-four stores throughout California, a number that more than *tripled* in the next four years alone. In 1980, Kinko's had eighty stores, each located near a college campus.

Just five years or so later, however, that profile changed dramatically. Kinko's started attracting swarms of small-business customers (another *underserved niche*), fueling an unprecedented growth spurt. Now with hundreds of locations, Kinko's was bringing high-end reprographics technology, once accessible to only major corporations, to the masses. In the mid-1980s, Paul opted to add desktop publishing services to the mix, giving customers the option of using in-store Apple computers for an hourly fee. He had *spotted a new trend*—desktop publishing—*and pounced.*

Paul is a risk taker with a penchant for convincing others to take risks with him. "My secret to managing people is work with competent people and get the hell out of the way."

By this point, Paul knew it was time to develop a more uniform, professional look for Kinko's. The company had outgrown its bohemian image. "The secret to life is to look like a Republican," he says. "You don't have to be one, but you should look like one." No more shorts and no more flip-flops. Coworkers began wearing professional-looking slacks, shirts, and aprons. The latter emphasized the service nature of the business. The Kinko's logo got a facelift, too. Paul's wife, Natalie, came up with the idea that the *i* in Kinko's would have a red dot.

By 1990, Kinko's had 450 stores, many in suburbs and business districts catering to small businesses. During the ensuing decade, Kinko's added high-quality color copiers, high-volume laser printers, fax machines, and even videoconferencing capabilities at many stores. Paul continually *reinvented the company* by introducing new services. The decade's phenomenal growth in home-based businesses—the telecommuting craze—provided a major boost, too.

Despite the company's explosive growth, Kinko's organizational structure remained flat. There was no corporate hierarchy like that seen in other organizations of comparable size. Paul was intent on maintaining Kinko's democratic structure, *bucking conventional wisdom.*

By the mid-1990s, the original partners were all middle-aged. Some started thinking about early retirement; others needed an influx of cash to send their kids to college. They decided it was time to consider taking Kinko's public and selling a controlling stake in the company.

In 1995, annual revenues topped $1.5 billion, with Kinko's comprising 127 partnerships. That's when the partners assembled a small team, which included Paul, to begin interviewing private equity and venture capital firms. Because Kinko's unconventional structure was a major stumbling block in attracting prospective buyers and investors, the team decided to merge all 127 independent partnerships to form a single C corporation.

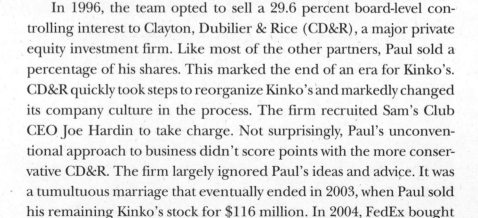

Paul typically required partners to make at least a $2,000 initial investment. He saw a potential partner's inability to come up with the $2,000 as a red flag. If the candidate lived from paycheck to paycheck and never saved money, he probably wouldn't be cautious enough with a store's profits either.

In 1996, the team opted to sell a 29.6 percent board-level controlling interest to Clayton, Dubilier & Rice (CD&R), a major private equity investment firm. Like most of the other partners, Paul sold a percentage of his shares. This marked the end of an era for Kinko's. CD&R quickly took steps to reorganize Kinko's and markedly changed its company culture in the process. The firm recruited Sam's Club CEO Joe Hardin to take charge. Not surprisingly, Paul's unconventional approach to business didn't score points with the more conservative CD&R. The firm largely ignored Paul's ideas and advice. It was a tumultuous marriage that eventually ended in 2003, when Paul sold his remaining Kinko's stock for $116 million. In 2004, FedEx bought Kinko's for $2.4 billion. FedEx later changed the name—first to FedEx Kinko's, then to FedEx Office.

Paul now teaches college business courses and oversees real estate ventures. He also devotes much of his time to the Orfalea Foundations, two nonprofit groups he launched that focus on four primary areas: education, early care, critical community needs, and youth development. The foundations—the Orfalea Family Foundation and the Orfalea Fund—support nonprofit programs that further Paul's vision to "promote healthy development and build skills for success in learning and in life." One priority is to assist children grappling with the same kinds of learning challenges that Paul faced as a youth. Another is to make preschool more accessible to underprivileged children. Twice a year, the foundations review funding applications and issue grant awards to deserving nonprofit groups and projects. The Orfalea Family Foundation also sponsors an annual three-day conference for directors of child development and early-care centers in California's tri-county region of Santa Barbara, Ventura, and San Luis Obispo. The Orfalea Fund works closely with the Santa Barbara Foundation, which has helped finance a range of local charitable projects since 1928.

> Despite the company's explosive growth,
> Kinko's organizational structure remained flat.
> There was no corporate hierarchy like that seen
> in other organizations of comparable size. Paul
> was intent on maintaining Kinko's democratic
> structure, *bucking conventional wisdom*.

Paul's freedom from the rigors of corporate politics has allowed him to focus on giving back to the community in which Kinko's began nearly four decades ago. And the money he made from selling the business gives him the freedom to support a broad spectrum of charitable endeavors aimed at helping kids and families.

The company's current state isn't really on his radar anymore. Paul today views the company "like an ex-girlfriend. It's best not to hear anything about her," he says. "If she's not doing well, you're sad. But if she's doing great, that doesn't make you feel good either."

These days, Paul has plenty else to occupy his one-of-a-kind mind.

STRATEGIES FOR SUCCESS

♦ At a crowded campus copy center where not just students but local lawyers were vying for assistance, Paul Orfalea discovered an *underserved niche* that sparked a business idea.

♦ As a youngster with undiagnosed ADHD, Paul had encountered many academic hurdles, but he *never let adversity or failure defeat him.*

♦ His impulsive behavior became a boon when he decided to *just start* by opening a copy center in a college town that lacked one—*hitting 'em where they ain't.*

♦ He continued to expand Kinko's in college towns. There, potential employees abounded, and students and professors writing papers and documenting research formed an ongoing *underserved niche.*

♦ Paul *exploited his competitors' weaknesses*—price and speed of service—*and made them his strengths.*

♦ Initially, he knew nothing about servicing the machines and had no business plan, but he *trusted his gut.* His ADHD, which made him averse to staying at a desk, again proved a plus. He found offbeat, creative ways to get publicity, which helped him *save his bucks and get noticed without expensive advertising.*

♦ He eventually opened stores to reach a new customer segment, small businesses (another *underserved niche*); he *spotted a new trend*—desktop publishing—*and pounced on it,* adding in-store Apple computers for customer use; and he expanded Kinko's to offer so many new services, like videoconferencing, that he *reinvented his company.*

Liz Lange *(Photo by Patrick McMullan Company, Courtesy of Liz Lange)*

Liz Lange

Founder, Liz Lange Maternity

"No matter what anyone says, if you think you

have a good idea, you probably do."

—Liz Lange

Growing up on New York City's Upper East Side in the 1970s and 1980s, Liz Lange always had a passion for fashion. As a little girl, she loved donning dresses designed by fashion pioneer Florence Eiseman.

As a teenager, Liz considered her Fiorucci jeans collection a source of pride. But a *career* in fashion wasn't something young Liz ever envisioned for herself—at least not until one day in 1994 when she had an epiphany of sorts at the age of twenty-four.

Without that revelatory moment, she might never have pursued a career in the fashion industry. And she might never have launched her own maternity clothing line a few years later—a business she eventually sold for an estimated $50 to $60 million.

Finding a New Career, Unexpectedly

In 1994, Liz had recently met Stephen DiGeronimo, a young, struggling, but talented fashion designer, through a mutual friend. One day, she visited DiGeronimo at his cramped workroom in a seedy section of New York's Garment District to check out his latest designs. She was hoping to find a bargain.

> "Labor of Love: Maternity Wear Is Suddenly Chic, Thanks to Designer Liz Lange"
> —*Good Housekeeping*

Liz, a native New Yorker, had never before ventured to this section of town. To her surprise, it nonetheless felt like home. The moment Liz set foot in DiGeronimo's tiny one-room studio, she had a visceral response. "I just felt this connection, like *I have to be here.* I just *have* to be a part of this," Liz explains.

The creative energy inside was palpable. This was a new world to her. A mannequin stood in the room, wearing a garment in mid-construction. Books and design sketches were strewn across tables, with fabric rolls and samples scattered about. The room was charged with a frenetic but beautiful disorder.

In this one-room world a designer could hatch a fresh idea for a new garment, sit down and sketch the design, and oversee its creation one stitch at a time. For Liz, this was the ultimate creative outlet, and she felt like something was tugging at her to join that world.

───────────◄○►───────────

The moment Liz stepped foot in DiGeronimo's
tiny one-room studio, she had a visceral
response. "I just felt this connection, like *I have
to be here*. I just *have* to be a part of this."
The creative energy inside was palpable.

───────────～○～───────────

Taking a Chance on a New Job—Even Without Pay

This abrupt shift in her career goals was unanticipated; she'd already charted a career path in the field of writing. A recent graduate of Brown University, Liz had earned a degree in comparative literature and landed a position at *Vogue* magazine, working as an editorial assistant. It seemed like the perfect entry-level job for her, one that meshed her love for both writing and fashion. She figured she would work as a writer until she married and started raising a family. But those plans had suddenly faded to black.

> **"Expansion Plan: Liz Lange
> Wows Celebs with Frump-
> Free Maternity Wear"**
> —*People* magazine

Liz begged DiGeronimo for a job. He couldn't afford to give her a salary, but that didn't stop her. "I said, 'That's fine, you don't have to pay me. I just need to be here,'" Liz recalls. "I begged him to let me be his apprentice. So I left my job at *Vogue*."

She *trusted her gut* and plunged headfirst into the fashion industry. As Liz knows, trusting your gut can open doors you haven't yet begun to imagine. Even today, nearly two decades later, Liz recounts that day's events with the same youthful enthusiasm that swept over her then. In her mind, the choice was easy; she didn't view it as a risk. "If you're not enjoying what you're doing on some level, then what's the point?" she says. "I really do believe we all only go around once. I wanted to love whatever it was I did."

―――――――――◄○►―――――――――

Liz begged her friend for a job. He couldn't afford to give her a salary, but that didn't stop her. "I said, 'That's fine, you don't have to pay me. I just need to be here.' I begged him to let me be his apprentice. So I left my job at *Vogue*."

―――――――――〰―――――――――

In her job at *Vogue*, she spent her time assisting one of the editors, writing short reviews and blurbs, and attending New York social events, where she coached the magazine's photographers on what to shoot. She was far removed from the creative trenches of the fashion industry. Too far removed, in her view.

> **"New Clothing Lines Emerging for Sophisticated Expectant Moms"**
> —*Naples* (FL) *Daily News*

After joining DiGeronimo's company as an unpaid apprentice, Liz immersed herself in the business, learning its every aspect. She also persuaded DiGeronimo to launch a more affordably priced line of contemporary sportswear that could be sold through department stores.

"I became the fit model. I became the fabric finder," she says. "I sourced all the fabrics and found what I thought would make cute dresses. I found the best showroom for our sales representatives who sold the DiGeronimo line to department stores."

Eventually, Liz's devotion was rewarded. She became a partner in the business. Liz's persistence proved invaluable time and again— whether she was negotiating fabric prices or marketing the brand. "I basically did everything," she says. "We even had a fashion show, and I was the one who cajoled the models into working for free. Stephen actually did all the real designing, but another partner and I did everything else out of necessity. There were just the three of us."

———————————◄◦►———————————

"If you're not enjoying what you're doing on some level, then what's the point? I really do believe we all only go around once. I wanted to love whatever it was I did."

———————————※———————————

Discovering a New Market from Customers Who Can't Find What They Want

As a young, fashion-conscious New Yorker, Liz also served as a one-woman, in-house focus group. She embodied the company's target customer and provided insight into what those customers wanted. So did Liz's friends, most of whom shared her love of fashion. And sometimes, those friends visited Liz at work, hoping for the chance to buy one of DiGeronimo's new designs at a wholesale price.

> ### "9 Months in Style"
> ### —*New York Times*

In their twenties and thirties, some of these female pals happened to be pregnant. To Liz's surprise, her pregnant friends were just as eager to try on DiGeronimo's new designs as her friends who weren't pregnant. Liz was perplexed.

"I'd say, 'What are you doing here? You're pregnant. I know you want to save some money here, but that's crazy. You need to go to a maternity store.' But no matter who they were, they'd always have the same answer: 'You don't understand. There's nothing out there. There's nothing out there,'" Liz recounts.

Liz also noticed that her pregnant friends showed up at the studio wearing nonmaternity clothes that were a few sizes too big to accommodate their expanding bellies. They couldn't bring themselves to wear real maternity clothes. A pregnant fashionista is still a fashionista, after all.

Though DiGeronimo didn't design maternity wear, Liz's pregnant friends always managed to wiggle their way into his new dresses made with stretch fabrics. "The DiGeronimo dresses weren't really cut right for a pregnant woman, so it would barely work," Liz says. "But because they were squeezed into them, I noticed that they looked so much thinner and cuter and better. I had to agree with them that it made sense for them to wear nonmaternity clothing."

At the time, stretch fabrics were new to the fashion industry, and DiGeronimo had just begun incorporating them into his designs. These garments had the give to accommodate Liz's friends' ballooning bellies without looking oversized or sloppy. The clothes provided a fitted, chic look, and that meant her pregnant friends felt more attractive and self-assured.

———————————◄○►———————————

Liz immersed herself in the business, learning its every aspect. "I became the fit model . . . I sourced all the fabrics [for] what I thought would make cute dresses. I found the best showroom for our sales representatives. . . . I basically did everything."

———————————————————————

Going Out on Her Own When Her Boss Nixed Her Ideas

That's when Liz got a big idea: DiGeronimo would launch a maternity line using stretch fabrics. Fashion-conscious expectant mothers could trade in the circus-tent look for haute couture. She presented her idea to DiGeronimo—who promptly nixed it. Maternity clothing had never been a big moneymaker, and he wanted no part of that category.

"I said, 'We'll make a mint. It's genius. And we won't have to change anything we're doing. We just have to make sure that every fabric we use has stretch in it.' But he didn't get it—which I totally understand. He did not want to do it. Nobody did," Liz remembers.

––––––––––––––––◄○►––––––––––––––––

"It wasn't because I had a burning desire to be an entrepreneur or because I thought the idea would make lots of money. It was because I was in love with the idea, and I just really wanted to do it."

––––––––––––––––◦––––––––––––––––

Nevertheless, she couldn't let go of the idea. She asked her pregnant friends. Their response was lukewarm; they said they didn't want to spend that much money on maternity clothes. She queried merchandise buyers at high-end department stores, asking whether they would be interested in a fitted, high-fashion maternity line. They pooh-poohed the idea as well, saying there was no money in retailing maternity clothes.

"Some of them said, 'Women don't care what they look like when they're pregnant. It's a short period of time,'" Liz remembers. "Everyone gave me reasons why it was a bad idea."

> ## "Oh Baby! How Chic"
> ### —Women's Wear Daily

But Liz couldn't shake her belief that she'd come up with a great idea. At night, after work, she found herself sketching potential designs and choosing the right fabrics for them. Her husband of just a year, Jeffrey Lange, could see what was coming: She was readying the launch of her own maternity-clothing business.

"I left Stephen [DiGeronimo] because I felt that if I didn't do the maternity idea and saw someone else do it, I just wouldn't be able to forgive myself," Liz says. "It wasn't because I had a burning desire to be an entrepreneur or because I thought the idea would make lots of money. It was because I was in love with the idea, and I just really wanted to do it."

So, in 1997 Liz *just started* her business, against the advice of others, and set out to develop a new line of maternity clothing that *bucked conventional wisdom.* She *trusted her gut* that if pregnant women saw how flattering her maternity clothes looked on them, they would in fact be willing to pay extra.

She had discovered an *underserved niche*—high-fashion maternity clothes—but the concept was so foreign to the industry that nobody took her seriously yet. "No one ever thinks anything is a good idea until someone else does it," Liz explains. "You can never get any positive reinforcement."

She borrowed less than $25,000 from family and started calling garment factories, trying to find one willing to construct her maternity designs in tiny volumes. Without the promise of high-volume orders, one factory after another rejected her. Because her parents made it clear they wouldn't loan her another dime, she knew she was racing against the clock and soldiered on.

> "Not Frumpy but Chic: Retailers
> Cater to Stylish Expectant Set"
> —*Crain's New York Business*

"I pounded the pavement on Eighth Avenue [in Manhattan's Garment District], visiting factory after factory, until I finally found one that was willing to work with me the way I wanted," Liz says. "I'd designed eight essential pieces you need when you're pregnant, and the factory would make one of each design. I could fax them orders each night, and they would complete each order within a two-week window."

<o>

"Customers and investors will never have your
vision for the product because they can't
touch it and feel it in advance. It's your job to
follow your instincts, prop yourself up, and
trust that if you build it, they will come."

Liz gave the factory her general designs, and the staff there created the patterns. She chose high-quality Italian stretch fabrics for the garments, which were all in solid colors with no frilly baby-themed details. The designs were clean and sophisticated. One of the most expensive outfits was a cashmere twin set.

Competitors in the maternity category offered designs that were ill fitting, dull, and uninspired in comparison. Liz *exploited her competitors' weakness and made it her strength.* Her boldly creative, yet tasteful and sophisticated, designs were also fitted—they accommodated the pregnancy without trying to hide it.

> "No one ever thinks anything is a good idea until someone else does it. You can never get any positive reinforcement."

Do-It-Yourself Often Required Doing It All

In the early days, Liz was continually juggling a plethora of roles. She even acted as her line's fit model, though she wasn't pregnant. At her request, the factory made her a body suit with a pillowed belly and a padded bra to simulate a pregnancy. When she tried on one of her garments wearing the baby-bump suit, she could give the factory seamstresses specific directions on how to improve the fit and look. It was a collaborative relationship that worked—even though Liz had little technical knowledge of sewing. "I became very close to the people at that factory," she says. "After a while, they understood me."

> **"Pregnancy Chic: Red Hot Fit"**
> —*Redbook*

Liz rented a tiny, windowless office space on East Sixty-first Street that doubled as a showroom. It was a one-woman operation at the beginning, so she did it all, including answering phones. Marketing took place at a grassroots level. She invited pregnant acquaintances and friends to see her designs, then urged them to spread the word to their pregnant friends and family—and they obliged. When an order arrived from the factory, Liz would box it up and deliver it to the customer personally.

————————————— ◄◊► —————————————

Without the promise of high-volume orders, one factory after another rejected her. "I pounded the pavement on Eighth Avenue, visiting factory after factory, until I finally found one that was willing to work with me the way I wanted."

————————————— ⸎ —————————————

"Honestly, at the beginning it was sort of slow, but not as slow as one would imagine because these women came and then started telling other women."

Aggressive Publicity and Celebrity Endorsements Help Sales

Liz *saved her bucks and got noticed without expensive advertising*. She checked the mastheads of newspapers and women's magazines and contacted countless editors to entice them to check out her new maternity clothes. At first they were reluctant, but Liz's persistence paid off.

> ## "Finding Mother Lode of Fashion"
> ### *—Crain's New York Business*

"I was very aggressive," she says. "I would say, 'You *have* to see them.' And truthfully, I would usually get an appointment."

Liz also knew the power of celebrity endorsement in the fashion world. She contacted the personal assistants of pregnant celebrities and offered to dress their clients for high-profile events, like award shows, in exchange for a plug. Soon celebrities such as Cindy Crawford, Gwyneth Paltrow, Elle Macpherson, and Kelly Ripa were being photographed wearing Liz's designs and singing their praises. They showed the world it was possible to be pregnant and glamorous at the same time.

Because Liz's maternity clothes were so different from others on the market, the press took notice. Within a month or so after the launch, her line had already warranted a write-up in the *New York Times*. A couple of months later, *Vogue* ran a blurb calling Liz the "Michael Kors of maternity." In her eyes, that was high praise indeed, because Kors had long been one of her favorite designers. A few months later, *In Style* ran a feature story on Liz's line. The media coverage fueled sales. "Once these press pieces started to come out, that opened the flood gates, and my phone was always ringing," she says. Orders streamed in from clients as far away as France and Indonesia.

Competitors in the maternity category offered designs that were ill fitting, dull, and uninspired in comparison. Liz *exploited her competitors' weakness and made it her strength*. Her designs were boldly creative yet tasteful and sophisticated.

Lack of Experience Brings on a Setback

The company's sales were soaring—and then trouble struck. Liz's lack of inventory-management experience came to light and threatened the business's survival. She misread demand during the holiday season and heavily overstocked inventory—a mistake that reflected her lack of market research and long-term business planning. In a sense, Liz had been flying by the seat of her stretch-fabric pants, succeeding on the strength of her business idea and work ethic. But that wasn't enough anymore.

"It really should have put us under, but we survived it," Liz says of that period's inventory debacle. The company held a series of warehouse sales, struggling to make ends meet over the course of one tumultuous year. Little by little, Liz pulled the company out of the hole.

In retrospect, Liz acknowledges that her lack of a comprehensive business plan placed the company at risk for such a management

> ## "A Woman's World: From Power Dressing to Maternity Chic, Pregnant and Still Looking Swell"
> *—International Herald Tribune*

misstep. On the other hand, she recognizes that someone with an MBA and years of business experience probably would never have green-lighted her business idea in the first place—it was too untested. Conventional wisdom dictated that chic fashion and pregnancy just didn't mix. Regardless, Liz found a way to keep the company afloat during a rough stretch. She didn't panic, and she *didn't let adversity or failure defeat her.*

———————————————◄○►———————————————

It was a one-woman operation at the beginning, so she did it all, including answering phones. Marketing took place at the grassroots level. She invited pregnant acquaintances and friends to see her designs, then urged them to spread the word to their pregnant friends and family—and they obliged. When an order arrived from the factory, Liz boxed it and delivered it personally.

———————————————✧———————————————

Expanding the Business: More Locations, Licensing Deals, New Product Lines

Liz also became more intimately acquainted with her clients' needs after she and her husband learned she was pregnant with their son Gus. At last, she could wear her own designs. She eventually hired an assistant during that pregnancy. In 1999, she also launched a Web site and published a biannual catalog to spur mail-order sales.

Before long, the business outgrew its office space, and in February 1999, Liz moved operations to a second-floor shop on Lexington Avenue and hired more help. But she'd hardly had time to unpack

─────────────◄○►─────────────

She checked the mastheads of newspapers and
women's magazines and contacted countless
editors to entice them to check out her new
maternity clothes. At first they were reluctant, but
Liz's persistence paid off. "I was very aggressive,"
she says. "I would say, 'You *have* to see them.' And
truthfully, I would usually get an appointment."

─────────────ᗧ─────────────

the moving boxes before that site became woefully too small as well.
Liz responded quickly, acquiring ground-level retail space at Seventy-
fifth Street and Madison Avenue as well. Liz Lange Maternity finally
had a real honest-to-goodness boutique visible from the street. That
same year, 2000, she got pregnant again, with daughter Alice, and she
opened a second store in Beverly Hills. The following year, the company moved into real corporate office space—finally—and Liz signed
an exclusive five-year licensing deal with Nike.

> ## "Liz Lange's 'Sexy and Cool'
> ## Maternity Line Draws Notice"
> ## —*The Record* (New Jersey)

By this time, Liz's maternity line had inspired a host of copycat
maternity designers. The brand's control of the high-fashion/fit-
ted maternity niche—a niche that Liz invented—was diminishing
somewhat.

Liz's high profile as a celebrity designer also meant she got plenty
of letters and e-mails from the public. Some of the correspondence
came from pregnant women frustrated that Liz's clothes were out of
their price range. That's when Liz decided it was time to *reinvent the
company* and offer a secondary, discount version of her line.

"So I approached Target, and Target loved the idea," she says. "In
2002, we rolled out Liz Lange Maternity for Target, a diffusion label
that's much, much, much less expensive."

Under the licensing agreement, Target has exclusive rights to the Liz Lange Maternity for Target brand and its designs. "I employ a whole team of designers that does nothing but design for Target," Liz says. "Target does the manufacturing and distribution to its own stores."

The brand was such a hit with Target shoppers that in 2006 the Liz Lange Maternity for Target line became the only maternity product sold at Target's 1,500 stores nationwide.

◄○►

> She contacted the personal assistants of pregnant celebrities and offered to dress their clients for high-profile events, like award shows, in exchange for a plug. "Once these press pieces started to come out, that opened the flood gates, and my phone was always ringing."

The original upscale line, Liz Lange Maternity, continued to be sold at her boutiques and high-end department stores. But Liz's deal with Target broadened the brand's reach tremendously. Meanwhile, in 2002, she opened a third store on Long Island and even found time to author a book titled *Liz Lange's Maternity Style: How to Look Fabulous During the Most Fashion-Challenged Time*. As a celebrity designer and entrepreneur, Liz has always found ways to keep her brand in the spotlight, cement her stature as the preeminent authority on maternity fashion, and reinvent her brand to expand its customer base and reflect shifts in the marketplace.

In 2006, Liz introduced yet another new concept: postpartum pieces designed to make brand-new moms look trimmer until they have a chance to take off the extra weight they've gained. This new category, dubbed the fourth-trimester concept, was uncharted fashion territory to be sure. But Liz has never shied away from treading such ground. Back in 1997, everyone she knew in the industry advised her not to launch Liz Lange Maternity. Fortunately, she had more faith in her gut instincts than in that professional advice.

"Customers and investors will never have your vision for the product because they can't touch it and feel it in advance," Liz explains.

"It's your job to follow your instincts, prop yourself up, and trust that if you build it, they will come."

Liz Lange made fashion industry history because she *trusted her gut*.

---◄○►---

The brand was such a hit with Target shoppers that in 2006 the Liz Lange Maternity for Target line became the only maternity product sold at Target's 1,500 stores nationwide.

In late 2007, Liz sold Liz Lange Maternity to Bluestar Alliance for an estimated $50 to $60 million. However, she remains involved with the company creatively. Eventually, she expects the Liz Lange brand to evolve further and move into new product categories. "I love that we are a maternity brand," she says. "And that will always be where my heart is, where my roots are. But I really do think that we are much more than that. Our brand really resonates with women, and I think it could develop into more of a lifestyle brand and move into so many other areas."

For example, the future may see the Liz Lange brand offering beauty products or baby clothes—anything is possible. The advice Liz offers aspiring entrepreneurs is the creed she still lives by: "No matter what anyone says, if you think you have a good idea, you probably do. Don't let anyone tell you it can't be done."

STRATEGIES FOR SUCCESS

♦ Deciding to *trust her gut* and make a career shift into the fashion design world, Liz Lange was so determined to *just start* that she agreed to work for nothing. Her instinct was rewarded when she became a partner in the business.

♦ Pregnant but fashion-conscious friends complained that there were no designs for them. Recognizing an *underserved niche*, Liz took advantage of new stretchable fabrics to design a haute couture maternity line.

♦ Even though her friends said the clothes would cost more than they would be willing to pay and department store buyers said customers didn't care about fashion when they were pregnant, Liz again *trusted her gut, bucked the conventional wisdom,* borrowed money from her family, and tried to find a factory that would agree to work with a small-volume operation.

♦ She pursued fashion editors to spread the word about her designs, then supplied her clothes to high-profile, expectant celebrities to *get noticed without expensive advertising.* Authoring a book also helped increase her exposure at no cost.

♦ Although her lack of inventory-management expertise caused a setback, she *didn't let adversity defeat her* and managed to forge ahead.

♦ She *reinvented her company* by partnering with Target to offer a less expensive line that was hugely successful and led to her becoming the huge chain's exclusive maternity-wear supplier. Having sold the company, she's still actively involved. Among the many ideas she's developed to expand the brand is a post-partum "fourth-trimester" line, a totally new concept.

Robert Stephens

Founder, Geek Squad

"Advertising is a tax you pay on having an
unremarkable brand, and training is a tax you
pay for having an uninspired internal culture."

—**Robert Stephens**

When Robert Stephens launched Geek Squad back in 1994, the cash-strapped college student had just $200 to invest in his business, leaving no budget for advertising. But he *trusted his gut* that he could generate enough word-of-mouth referrals to make his computer tech-support company profitable. His business plan went something like this: Hire a few friends who know their way around a motherboard, dress them kind of like 1960s police detectives or Apollo-era NASA engineers (white shirt, black clip-on tie), dispatch them to the homes of customers at their wits' end due to a misbehaving computer, and make customers' computer nightmares go away for a flat rate.

The company started as a way for the University of Minnesota student to earn some extra cash, but Geek Squad ultimately evolved into an operation that today employs 20,000 people and brings in more than $1 billion annually. Though Robert remains Geek Squad's founder and "chief inspector," he sold the company to retail giant Best Buy in 2002.

An Early Talent for Fixing Things Leads to a Great Business Idea

Robert grew up in Chicago, the youngest of seven children. His mother was a homemaker, and his father worked as a systems analyst with Allstate after retiring from the navy. Even as a kid, Robert showed signs of his gift for mechanics and troubleshooting. In those days, however, the focus was on cars, not computers.

"My brother, who's eleven years older than I am, was a mechanic as a teenager," Robert recalls. "Every night, he used to bring carburetors from Volkswagen Beetles home from the shop where he worked because I would take things apart. He'd pay me a buck to rebuild carburetors. So while everybody was sitting around after dinner, watching TV, I'd be sitting at the coffee table with a screwdriver, taking carburetors apart."

Before long, he moved from cars to other contraptions and gained a reputation as the neighborhood fix-it kid. If someone's television was on the blink, Robert could fix it. If a neighbor's lawnmower was sputtering instead of cutting, Robert was the one to make the repair.

Seeing an Opportunity to Meet an Untapped Market Need

In high school, Robert's inquisitive nature and creativity also fueled his interest in the arts. After graduation, he began attending the Art

―◇―

Most home computer users had limited technical knowledge. If their hard drives crashed or their monitors flickered ominously, they were thrown into a state of panic. Robert saw opportunity in this *underserved niche*.

Institute of Chicago on scholarship. But he found himself logging more hours in the computer lab than anywhere else in the institute. He was naturally drawn to the business world, despite his initial resistance. So he decided to change course and pursue a degree in computer science at the University of Minnesota instead.

"Art clearly has a higher purpose to it—human endeavor, excellence, and all that stuff," Robert notes. "Business isn't looked upon as something lofty, yet that is what I was good at."

When he headed to Minnesota, he had no money and no place to live. But that didn't stop him. After enrolling in classes at the University of Minnesota, he eventually landed a part-time job at the university's Human Factors Research Lab (which explored the design of human-machine systems) through a referral from a roommate. That's where he learned about the Internet.

> **"Geek Squad Puts Fun into Computer Repair: Novel Marketing Program, Good Service Are Helping Company to Grow Rapidly"**
> —*Star Tribune: Newspaper of the Twin Cities*

It was the early 1990s. Apple had already introduced the Macintosh, and Microsoft had introduced Windows. Students were using computers in their dorms to write papers. More and more people were using computers at home for e-mail, to catch up on work from the office, and to keep spreadsheets on personal investments and household budgets. But most of these home computer users had limited technical knowledge. If their hard drives crashed or their monitors flickered ominously, they were thrown into a state of panic. Robert saw opportunity in this *underserved niche*. To earn extra money in his senior year, he started making computer-repair house calls. Before long, he got his friends involved in his burgeoning business. That marked the beginnings of Geek Squad.

———————————◄○►———————————

Robert recognized the importance of avoiding the
pitfalls that have historically made service calls such
a dreaded nuisance for consumers. Robert removed
the "flake factor" from the service-call experience. He
exploited his competitors' weakness—the level of
professionalism—*and made it his company's strength.*

———————————◅◦▻———————————

Creating a Quirky and Memorable Company Image

From its inception, Geek Squad drew upon Robert's strengths as a creative but practical thinker. The geek marketing concept and tongue-in-check image reflected his vivid imagination and ability to look at the big picture. At the same time, his aptitude for computer science and attention to detail propelled the service side of the business. As Robert sees it, he finally found a way for his left-brain and right-brain functions to make peace. "Really, Geek Squad is my answer to art versus commerce," he says.

But in the category of risk taking—a right-brain function—his right brain clearly dominates the left. Why else would he start a company with just $200?

The idea for the retrocop theme came to Robert while he was relaxing at home, watching old TV reruns. "I was watching *Dragnet* one night—you know, the TV show from the sixties with Joe Friday," Robert explains. "Their car pulls up, there's a frantic person at home, a crime has been committed, and they have to investigate. That's exactly like a house call. I show up, and they're all freaked out, saying, 'It's over there! It won't behave!' So I'm like, 'Step away from the computer, ma'am.' I saw a lot of parallels."

That realization prompted Robert to adopt the Joe Friday–style uniforms (sans Joe's ever-present jacket). Geek Squad employees weren't known as service reps; they were henceforth known as agents. The investigating-cop motif not only helped Geek Squad's branding and marketing efforts but gave customers an analogy they could easily identify with, Robert says. And the company was *getting noticed without expensive advertising.*

Geek Squad uniforms also drew inspiration from the NASA engineers portrayed in *Apollo 13*, one of Robert's favorite films. "The tie, the short-sleeved white shirt—it all enforces an image of humility," Robert says.

————————————◀◉▶————————————

When Robert bought the first company car, he dubbed it the Geekmobile and painted a giant Geek Squad logo on the door panels. That moving billboard *got the company noticed without expensive advertising.*

————————————⚐————————————

Providing What Customers Wanted and Desperately Needed

But all that would have been just an empty gimmick if Geek Squad's service standards hadn't exceeded its competitors'. Robert recognized the importance of avoiding the pitfalls that have historically made service calls such a dreaded nuisance for consumers. *Bucking conventional wisdom,* he enforced stringent standards. Unlike the cable TV guy, the Geek Squad agent showed up not just on time but five minutes early. Unlike the plumber, he paid attention to personal hygiene and dressed neatly. Unlike the house painter, the Geek Squad agent bothered to wipe his feet before setting foot in the house—he even offered to take his shoes off on the front porch. And unlike the general contractor, Geek Squad *always* returned phone calls promptly.

In short, Robert removed the "flake factor" from the service-call experience. He *exploited his competitors' weakness*—the level of professionalism—*and made it his company's strength.* His Geek Squad agents weren't smelly, messy, unreliable, or creepy. They didn't spew out unintelligible jargon to justify an extra charge. Nor did they talk down to clients. They spoke like real human beings and treated customers with genuine respect. That's because Robert has always had a knack for viewing the customer experience from the perspective of the customer.

---◄○►---

> Robert also courted local newspapers to get free
> publicity. "The best press you ever get is the local
> newspaper, the local coverage. It's the longest
> lasting. It generates the most direct business."

One of the earliest incarnations of Geek Squad actually dressed more like SWAT team members than 1960s-era detectives or NASA engineers. That was Robert's way of paying homage to one of his favorite TV shows from the 1970s, *S.W.A.T.*, which chronicled the adventures of the Los Angeles Police Department's Special Weapons and Tactics unit. But those uniforms did nothing to calm customers who were already stressed out by computer mishaps. In that one instance, Robert's enterprising spirit kind of backfired.

> ### "Revenge of the Nerds"
> —*St. Paul Pioneer Press*

"I'd fixed this ice cream company's computers, but they couldn't pay their bill," Robert explains. "So I said I'd take two of their ice cream trucks. I painted them black because I always wanted my own SWAT truck. Then I put people in black jumpsuits with black combat boots and black fanny-packs so that they could whip out a floppy disk at a moment's notice. But the problem was, it scared the crap out of the customers." Obviously, that wasn't the reaction Robert sought, so he changed the design of the Geek Squad's uniforms and vehicles.

Unconventional Advertising: The Company Car

When Robert bought the first company car, a 1958 French-manufactured Simca Aronde, he dubbed it the Geekmobile and painted a giant Geek Squad logo on the door panels. Robert could hardly believe the car's marketing impact. That moving billboard really *got the company noticed without expensive advertising.*

"People would come up to me and say, 'Hey, your cars are everywhere'—and I only had one," Robert recalls. "So we started playing around with the idea of vehicles as advertising."

Since Robert knew affluent people were more likely to own a computer and use his company's services, the Geekmobile tended to cruise upscale neighborhoods. Robert even drove to downtown Minneapolis and circled the local orchestra hall just as the crowd emptied out. They were a captive audience for his four-wheeled commercial.

> ## "Enterprise—Who You Gonna Call?"
> ## —*Newsweek*

"What happens is the rich people walk out in their fur coats, waiting for the line of limousines to pick them up," Robert explains. "And all they see is my car pass by. I call that 'time-release marketing' because they may not have a computer problem now, but they may remember me at some point."

Robert's hunch was right again. The cruising-logo strategy paid dividends. Geek Squad started fielding customer calls from some of the wealthiest neighborhoods in the Twin Cities area. Having no advertising budget wasn't holding the company back one bit.

"Advertising is a tax you pay on having an unremarkable brand, and training is a tax you pay for having an uninspired internal culture," Robert says.

One night, while Robert was parked in front of the orchestra hall, waiting for the departing crowd to cue his cruising routine, his cell phone suddenly rang. It was one of his employees.

"Dude, you're on TV," his friend said. "Look to your left."

A local TV news station was using a live feed of downtown as a backdrop for its news anchors. The Geekmobile, in all its self-promotional glory, just happened to be in the video frame. Realizing the potential payoff, Robert began parking in that same spot every night during the newscast. When the station changed the camera angle, he'd move the car to reenter the frame. No pivoting camera mount could outmaneuver Robert and his Geekmobile.

Years later, even after Geek Squad became a huge success, Robert continued to dream up quirky marketing techniques. The most bizarre might be the shoe logo. Robert ordered employee shoes with the Geek Squad logo imprinted in reverse on the shoe soles. So when employees walked on sand, mud, snow, or dirt, they might leave a visible imprint of the Geek Squad logo behind.

"I can't tell you to this day how much revenue we've derived from that," Robert says. He pauses a beat. "Frankly, I don't care," he admits. "I've probably got more mileage out of the story than anything else."

Robert also courted local newspapers to get free publicity. "Ultimately, the best press you ever get is the local newspaper, the local coverage," he says. "It's the longest lasting. It generates the most direct business."

─────────────────◄○►─────────────────

Robert was convinced that an alliance with a major retailer—Best Buy—represented Geek Squad's best shot for continued growth. He didn't want to pursue the IPO route. "Anybody can be king of the puddle, but to jump into the ocean where there are bigger fish than you, that's risky." The sale to Best Buy unleashed growth potential that Robert couldn't have matched alone.

─────────────────────────────────────

Expanding to Keep Up with Increased Demand

During the company's first year (1994), it operated with just three or four employees. In its first eight months, the company made $100,000 in billing. By the second year, however, the staff had to expand to keep pace with the service calls. By then, Robert had stopped going to classes because of the demands of his business. "I knew this business was going to work, and I knew that we were going to be better than anybody else because most people in the service business aren't as obsessive as I am," Robert says. "That's just a fact." And the company continued to do well. In its third year, the Geek Squad's annual revenues approached $500,000, with fourteen employees.

> **"Geek Squad: Cool Tech Support"**
> —*Chicago Sun-Times*

Robert even saw the company image and uniforms as catalysts for maintaining quality standards. "The Geekmobile and the uniforms are props that allow the employees to play a character, a role," Robert says. "They bring themselves to the role, but they also get to become this person, this idealized version of themselves, and realize the power of that and tap into that. A lot of companies try to mandate via memo, versus inspiration. But inspiration is very powerful."

◄○►

The investigating-cop motif not only helped
Geek Squad's branding and marketing efforts
but gave customers an analogy they could easily
identify with. And the company was getting
noticed without expensive advertising.

Pursuing a Partnership

In 2000, only six years after he started the company, Robert approached Best Buy's corporate offices in Minneapolis to propose a partnership. He was confident the two companies would complement each other. Best Buy was one of the nation's biggest computer retailers. A partnership with Geek Squad would add luster to Best Buy's extended warranty and service offers at the time of a computer purchase. Plus, Robert respected the brand. "A lot of the people I was hiring used to work at Best Buy, so I knew they had good people," Robert explains. "They probably just hadn't figured out that service is a profit center, not a cost center."

Robert was convinced that such an alliance with a major retailer represented Geek Squad's best shot for continued growth. He didn't want to pursue the initial public offering (IPO) route. Geek Squad was at a crossroads of sorts, so he knew he needed to make a strategic decision soon.

"Finally, I said, 'If I IPO Geek Squad, Wall Street will tear me apart because we're never going to grow as fast as they like,'" he explains. "'I need to partner with somebody who needs to differentiate themselves.'"

It was an ideal match. Best Buy sold the computers, and Geek Squad installed their software and maintained them. Again, Robert and his expanding staff ratcheted up company operations. Having a staff full of computer wizards helped—by 2000, his staff ranged from thirty-five to fifty-five techs.

"We went from paper-based scheduling to computer scheduling and eventually to Web-based scheduling," Robert says. "Being geeks, we built most of that ourselves."

The tremendous growth that followed spurred a number of offers for the company, but Robert resisted. In 2002, though, he finally sold Geek Squad to Best Buy—the most difficult decision he's ever made.

"I felt at that moment, that was the best decision," he says. "All my friends said I shouldn't do it, that it was selling out. But actually, I felt it would have been selling out not to do it. Anybody can be king of the puddle, but to jump into the ocean where there are bigger fish than you, that's risky. It was risky handing over my baby, but it's proven to be so good, even eight years later."

> **"Get Me the Geeks!"**
> —*60 Minutes*

At the time of the sale, Geek Squad had fifty-five agents on staff. Today, it has about 20,000. Geek Squad Volkswagen Bugs are a common sight on roads across America. The roving billboard strategy is still alive.

Continuing Growth and Expansion

In recent years, Geek Squad has reinvented itself, expanding its services to home-theater systems. It has also launched a twenty-four-hour hotline and Web-based service to address computer operating system and software problems remotely. Moreover, Geek Squad has gone international, launching operations in the United Kingdom, China, Spain, Mexico, and Canada. Best Buy and Geek Squad are also exploring expansion into Turkey.

The sale to Best Buy unleashed growth potential that Robert couldn't have matched alone, and he remains a strong voice in the company's decision making as Geek Squad's "chief inspector." Nonetheless, at times Robert, given his rough-around-the-edges guerrilla marketing background, doesn't exactly see eye to eye with his corporate boss. For example, a few years ago, California Highway Patrol (CHP) officers started ticketing Geekmobile drivers because the vehicles were painted black and white. In the view of the CHP, they looked too much like police cars. When Robert heard about this, he had a good laugh.

He also saw the issue as a potential marketing bonanza. He could have a little fun with the conflict by spinning it as a "The Man versus the Geek" drama, and the press would lap it up. But before he had a chance to cue up the opening notes to "I Fought the Law and the Law Won," Best Buy's corporate lawyers squelched the plan. Best Buy wanted no part in milking the controversy. "I let Best Buy talk me into backing down," Robert admits.

Robert may no longer have total control over Geek Squad, but his focus remains the same as when he was sole owner: maintaining high quality standards through personnel. "I want to attract new people and constantly innovate without sacrificing quality," Robert says. "That all comes down to talent; it comes down to people. Geek Squad is essentially a squad of geeks working together. That will always be our biggest challenge. That's what it's been for fifteen years, and it will continue to be for another hundred."

He continually looks for ways to measure customer satisfaction and to improve and simplify processes. He even makes a point of reviewing all Geek Squad mentions in online blogs to identify and resolve problem areas. Today, he might exert less power over Geek Squad than when he owned it, but the brand's influence in the marketplace has ballooned. As a true-blue geek, Robert isn't as concerned with power anyway.

"Geeks have no interest in power. The only power we're interested in is low-power consumption and longer battery life and low prices so we can stay up later at night," Robert deadpans. "Geeks may inherit the earth, but they have no desire to rule it."

STRATEGIES FOR SUCCESS

- ♦ An art student turned computer science major, mechanically gifted Robert noticed that more students and business professionals were using computers for tasks at home. But if they ran into a technical problem, they were totally flummoxed and at a loss for what to do. Recognizing an *underserved niche*, he *hit where they ain't* by becoming a repair person—and making house calls.

- ♦ The old *Dragnet* police show inspired him to build a team of repair people dressed as "agents." Wearing dorky, but oh-so-humble short-sleeved-shirt-and-tie outfits, they responded promptly to calls for help, eventually driving around in company cars with a distinctive logo. Robert even had the logo imprinted on the soles of his employees' shoes so that they would leave it on sand or dirt trails. By means of such attention getters, he *got his company noticed without expensive advertising.*

- ♦ *Exploiting his competitors' weaknesses*—other repair people were often condescending, unreliable, and unprofessional—he developed strengths that were just the opposite. His staff made house calls and built a reputation for being helpful, attentive, and service oriented.

- ♦ *Defying the conventional wisdom*, he decided to partner as a service provider with a national retailer rather than go the IPO route. Although Robert now plays a less prominent role in operations, Geek Squad continues to reinvent itself, adding new services (like home-theater installation) and establishing an overseas presence.

CHAPTER 7

Barbara Corcoran *(Courtesy of Barbara Corcoran Inc.)*

Barbara Corcoran

Founder and Former Chairperson,
The Corcoran Group

"I was never afraid to be different and got
to where I was by being myself."

—Barbara Corcoran

A cowboy hat might have covered her signature platinum-blond pixie cut, but Barbara Corcoran's beaming smile and twinkling blue eyes left no doubt that this was no stunt double. Dressed in a buckskin miniskirt, fringed top, and cowboy boots, the real estate icon had decided to cap off her own going-away party with a Wild West flourish worthy of Annie Oakley. The Corcoran Group founder—also known as the Queen of New York Real Estate—hoisted her slender 5' 6" frame onto a white horse and rode off as her former employees bid her good-bye and good luck. Nobody stepped in the path of the horse, which she had rented for $1,000, so there was no reason for Barbara to reach for the toy pistol tucked under a red garter belt—or to flash her gold sheriff's badge.

Barbara Corcoran bids farewell to the Corcoran Group in 2005. *(Courtesy of Barbara Corcoran Inc.)*

At fifty-six, Barbara was leaving behind the company she founded in 1978 and eventually sold in 2001 to real estate conglomerate NRT for $66 million. Under her leadership, The Corcoran Group's annual closings had reached $5 billion with a payroll numbering 2,150. After the sale, she stayed on as company chair but left the day-to-day operations to her protégés. In 2005, she departed for good to spend more time with her husband and two children. She also planned to launch a new television production company. In the era of reality TV, what else would a larger-than-life real estate mogul do after reaching the pinnacle of success?

Dealing with Dyslexia Developed a Creative Imagination

Barbara rose to the highest levels of success in the hypercompetitive world of New York real estate, despite a lifelong struggle with dyslexia. This was the same Barbara Corcoran who earned straight Ds in school, the girl whom Sister Stella Marie labeled as "stupid" in the second grade. And this was the same Barbara Corcoran who, as a young girl, generally found solace either by listening to her mother's encouraging, homespun advice or by retreating into her own vivid imagination. Those two sources of childhood comfort would ultimately serve her well as a businesswoman. She *never let adversity or failure defeat her.*

Barbara rose to the highest levels of success in the hypercompetitive world of New York real estate, despite a lifelong struggle with dyslexia.

Like many dyslexics, in her youth, Barbara relied on her imagination to get through life without solid reading skills. The burden of hiding her learning disability from others—and the challenge of living her life without the benefit of reading—forced her to rely more on her creative powers. She became adept at finding innovative solutions to complicated problems, often on the fly. She also became a student of human behavior, developing an advanced understanding of what motivates people. Barbara credits her mother for identifying these gifts and helping to cultivate them early in her life. Her mother called her the "Imagination Child."

Her imagination also created a sanctuary from the real world, in which she felt like an outsider, and allowed her to dream of future adventures. "I always had a great movie show going on and could imagine things better than the other kids," Barbara says. "It was the downside and upside. The older I got, the more I focused on the upside, thank God."

Barbara tends to think in images rather than words. Even as a fledgling entrepreneur, she could visualize a business plan in greater detail than others, making her better equipped to execute it. She also felt less constrained by conventional thinking and assumed risks more readily, since she viewed the business world from the perspective of an outsider. Ultimately, her power to visualize helped her map out her own success story. She pioneered new ways to market real estate, using the Internet and publicity campaigns, and changed the way New York's real estate industry does business. Competitors couldn't match her promotional savvy and zest for success.

Barbara grew up in Edgewater, New Jersey, near the Palisades Amusement Park—best known for its outdoor saltwater pool, its tasty french fries (soaked in malt vinegar), and such adrenaline-pumping attractions as a roller coaster and a bobsled ride. Her family lived in the house directly under the massive *L* in the flickering Palisades Amusement Park sign. She shared a room with five sisters on the ground floor, which her family occupied. Her four brothers shared the back room, while her parents—Florence and Ed—slept in the living room on a black vinyl convertible sofa. Her Uncle Herbie and Aunt Ethel occupied the top floor, along with their two daughters, while Nana Henwood lived in the front of the second floor.

Barbara relied on her imagination and found innovative solutions to complicated problems. She also felt less constrained by conventional thinking and assumed risks more readily since she viewed the business world from the perspective of an outsider.

Barbara was the second-oldest child, so it's not surprising that most childhood memories include a pregnant mom—a pregnant but perpetually in motion wrangler of her brood. Despite all the demands on her time and attention, Florence Corcoran had a penchant for recognizing her kids' strengths and helping to nurture them. In Barbara's case, that strength was her imagination.

Starting Young with No Experience, Using an Apartment for an Office

By age twenty-four, Barbara had held twenty-two jobs. Her boyfriend had stirred her interest in real estate when he shared stories about his various real estate development deals in New Jersey. He also encouraged her to leave behind the familiar and safe confines of Edgewater and move to New York City. As extra incentive, he offered to foot the bill for a week at the Barbizon Hotel for Women while she searched for an affordable apartment. Against the advice of her family, Barbara agreed. This was a chance to strike out on her own—a risk she assumed with both trepidation and excitement.

She quickly landed a receptionist job with Giffuni Brothers, a company that owned and managed several apartment buildings in Manhattan and Brooklyn. She then rented an apartment near work with two roommates. To earn extra money, she started working weekends for a brokerage firm owned by her boss's son. She took the real estate exam and began showing residential properties in Manhattan. "The first weekend, by renting two apartments at commissions around $330 each, I earned three times as much as I had in three weeks as a receptionist," she says. "And it was a lot more fun than sitting behind a desk."

Barbara's company's first headquarters was her apartment. She figured, "There'd be virtually no overhead. I created my makeshift office on the sofa that one of my roommates had borrowed from her parents."

After just a few months, Barbara's boyfriend gave her $1,000 to start a real estate company, dubbed Corcoran-Simone. The company's headquarters: Barbara's apartment. "There'd be virtually no overhead. I created my makeshift office on the sofa that one of my roommates had borrowed from her parents," recalls Barbara.

Her former boss, Joseph Giffuni, pledged to pay her a whole month's rent as commission if she found a renter for one of his apartments. She selected the cheapest one-bedroom on the list. When she spread open the classified section of the *New York Times* and scanned the ads of the competition, she knew she needed an attention grabber. She convinced Giffuni to put up a wall dividing the long living room into two separate rooms and placed a tiny classified ad: "One Bedroom + Den $340." The strategy paid off, and Barbara rented her first apartment. More important, she so impressed Giffuni with her ingenuity that he gave her several more of his apartments.

———————————◄○►———————————

"Good salesmanship is nothing more than maximizing the positive and minimizing the negative. Although your competition might offer something you can't match, that doesn't matter. What matters is that you identify and play up what you've got."

———————————ᘻ———————————

"I'm a great marketer. I'm great at bullshit," Barbara admits with a wry smile. "Good salesmanship is nothing more than maximizing the positive and minimizing the negative. Although your competition might offer something you can't match, that doesn't matter. What matters is that you identify and play up what you've got."

From her earliest days in the real estate business, Barbara had a knack for drawing attention to assets and away from weaknesses—whether the object of attention was a high-priced property or her company.

Recognizing the Need to Create a High-Profile Image

Barbara also knew the value of projecting the right image to gain clients' trust. After she received the check from Giffuni, she decided to invest in her wardrobe. If she was going to become a successful real estate broker, she needed to dress the part. She used her $340 commission check to buy the most glamorous fur-collared coat she could find at Bergdorf Goodman on Fifth Avenue. "Was it smart? No. Did it work? Yes," Barbara says of the purchase.

Her new coat became her signature piece, and she never took it off on the job. She felt it was important that her company project an image of luxury and prestige. When she ordered her business cards, she requested the same typeface that Tiffany used. She chose gray ink instead of the usual black. "Perception creates reality," Barbara explains.

Before long, so many clients were coming to her apartment (posing as an office) that her landlord became suspicious. Convinced she was a prostitute, he sent her an eviction notice. When she met with him to challenge the eviction, she not only convinced him that she wasn't a prostitute but persuaded him to let her try to rent one of his long-vacant apartments. After she found a renter for the unit, the landlord became a regular client as well.

Barbara soon began focusing on marketing strategies, delegating sales to employees. She realized early in her career that her greatest strength was her creativity. She was no number cruncher. "I still can't read a financial statement," she admits.

————————◄◦►————————

She used her first $340 commission check to buy the most glamorous fur-collared coat she could find. "Was it smart? No. Did it work? Yes." It was important that her company project an image of luxury and prestige.

————————————————

Going Out on Her Own

After about five years, in 1978, Barbara mustered enough courage to *just start* her very own company, The Corcoran Group. After dividing the previous company's assets and fourteen sales staff members with her ex-boyfriend, Barbara leased office space three flights up in the same building.

"I had nothing to lose and nowhere to go but up," she says. "So I didn't see it as a risk. I was like a dumb kid jumping off the end of the diving board. How do you know what a belly flop feels like if you've never done it, right?"

With her share of the assets, which was less than $15,000, Barbara leased enough office equipment to get The Corcoran Group up and running. Determined to succeed, she thought about how organized her mother had to be to run a household with ten children, and she decided to implement a new set of organizational processes for her new company. She made a list of everything that didn't work at the earlier office and thought up ways to bolster work efficiency as well as employee morale. Her solutions *bucked the conventional wisdom*: Monday morning staff breakfasts, color-coded listing cards to easily identify apartment sizes, and cash incentives for agents who wrote detailed property descriptions.

She realized early in her career that her greatest strength was her creativity. She was no number cruncher. "I still can't read a financial statement," she admits.

Most important perhaps, Barbara also rewrote the existing commission request form, adding a number of questions for sales agents to answer so the company could compile detailed demographic information on clients. Barbara realized that the more the company knew about its clients, the better positioned it would be to negotiate with them. Such data allowed the company to compile statistics to help identify the very latest market trends and the most effective marketing strategies—major advantages over the competition. Sales agents were forthcoming with these details because they couldn't get paid commissions otherwise. Barbara *exploited her competitors' weakness*—market research—*and made it her strength.*

After five years, Barbara mustered enough courage to start her very own company. "I had nothing to lose and nowhere to go but up. So I didn't see it as a risk. I was like a dumb kid jumping off the end of the diving board. How do you know what a belly flop feels like if you've never done it, right?"

A Keen Eye for Market Trends— Ahead of the Competition

Eventually, The Corcoran Group delved further into market research, which helped the firm respond more quickly to changes in the marketplace. For example, the company was able to predict a surge in demand for apartments on the West Side in 1979. Data culled from the forms suggested that well-heeled couples in their thirties found this area increasingly attractive. Many of these buyers had grown up in affluent families on the East Side. Barbara had *spotted a trend and pounced.*

She decided to open a major office in the area to take full advantage of the heightened demand. Since these neighborhoods had historically lagged behind in property values, her competitors seemed perplexed by her extra attention to the West Side. Even her own advisors warned her not to open the office. But she *trusted her gut* and did it anyway. In effect, she was positioning her company to *hit 'em where they ain't.*

"We were also the first firm to see the downtown corridor as a potential residential market," she says. "It became the hippest market in the city. They all said, 'Don't go downtown. It's too early.' And they were right. It was too early by a year. But by the time my competitors woke up to the fact that downtown was a virgin market, I had firm footing. And they never caught up with us."

---◀○▶---

Barbara realized that the more the company knew about its customers, the better positioned it would be to negotiate with them. Barbara *exploited her competitors' weakness*—market research—*and made it her strength.*

Using Creative Sales and Advertising Techniques to Get Customers' Attention

The early 1980s, however, were trying times for New York's real estate industry. Interest rates skyrocketed, and sales were sluggish. The Corcoran Group's mounting debt and dearth of sales threatened to shutter the business. Barbara needed a quick influx of cash but had no money left for advertising. While racking her brain for a creative solution, she found inspiration in a childhood memory. As a young girl, she had once seen ten people argue over the chance to buy three purebred puppies at a neighbor's house. Her mother pointed out that the neighbor had the good sense to invite all the prospective buyers over at the same time to create a competitive environment.

> "The sixteen years I spent working with Barbara Corcoran were invaluable, as she taught me how important it is to pick the right people and how to treat your employees in a positive and effective way."
> —Pam Liebman, president and CEO, The Corcoran Group

Barbara decided to stage a "one-day sale." She took a huge risk and put eighty-eight apartments of varying quality and size on the market, all at the same price. She told her staff they were having a "private sale" and asked them to invite their family, friends, and clients. It was a sales gimmick that created a sense of urgency. Within an hour and a half, Barbara had sold all eighty-eight, netting a $1.2 million profit. The money allowed the company to expand at a time when business was slow and her competitors were laying low. When the real estate recession hit, The Corcoran Group was ranked seventeenth or eighteenth in the market. By the time the recession lifted, the firm was ranked number four.

Rewarding and Motivating Employees as Her Company Grew

Though Barbara had little patience with nonproductive workers—she routinely fired about one-third of her staff every six months—she made sure committed employees were generously rewarded. "Whatever I had to do—whether it was taking them out for fun, canceling meetings, taking them on trips—I treated them as my loved children," she says. "I had a massage therapist in every office. I had manicurists. I had shoeshine people. I had free lunches and a fully packed refrigerator."

How to Get Noticed Without Advertising: Innovative Marketing

Meanwhile, Barbara continued to develop a range of innovative ways to market the company and build the Corcoran brand. Her methods were often unconventional, but she knew the value of *trusting her gut.* "I've found that all innovation is built on a leap of faith and a prayer, using money you shouldn't have spent in the first place, and that waiting to spend money on a good idea is the business equivalent of saving the good china for Sunday," she says.

One way Barbara got The Corcoran Group *noticed without expensive advertising* was by publishing a popular newsletter about New York residential real estate trends, *The Corcoran Report.* Barbara recognized that local newspaper reporters had few resources to draw upon when writing about New York's residential real estate trends— a void she was more than willing to fill. So in 1981, she drew on a very limited pool of her own company's sales (eleven apartments for a six-month period) to compile a list of statistics on average apartment price and average room price for that period. She then mailed off a copy of her statistic-filled newsletter to every reporter with a byline in that day's *New York Times.*

> "Barbara's word is gold. It's never felt like she's my boss."
> —Carrie Chang, vice president and director of the international division of The Corcoran Group

To her shock, the *Times* used an item in that first report as the basis for a short article. The headline was "Study Shows Co-op Prices Nearly Quintupled." The article cited Barbara as the source of the research. Suddenly, she was a real estate authority worthy of being

> "Barbara always made you feel you were very important to her, and because of that, you wanted to do well for her. She really wanted to hear what you had to say, and she actually incorporated it into the business."
> —Norma Hirsh, one of Barbara's original employees who is now an executive vice president at Insignia/Douglas Elliman

quoted in the *New York Times*. Needless to say, The Corcoran Group's research methods eventually grew much more sophisticated, ensuring a long-term stream of local publicity. But Barbara initially took a chance on research because the company basically had no credibility to lose. The brand was little known at that stage. *The Corcoran Report* helped change that.

Barbara decided to stage a "one-day sale." She took a huge risk and put eighty-eight apartments of varying quality and size on the market, all at the same price. It was a sales gimmick that created a sense of urgency. Within an hour and a half, Barbara had sold all eighty-eight, netting a $1.2 million profit.

"The *New York Times* story put me squarely in the middle of the Manhattan real estate game, playing it by my rules," Corcoran says. She realized that writers need statistics to give credence to their business articles, so she found a way to calculate those numbers. Barbara knew that advertising alone could never buy her the credibility that article did, so *The Corcoran Report* became a priority. The one-page stat sheet came out every six months, and reporters came to rely on it. Barbara proved that statistics are the slam dunk of all publicity.

The Corcoran Report became the industry bible and a research resource that media outlets like the *New York Times* and *Wall Street Journal* regularly cited. Such high-profile publicity lent the Corcoran brand credibility and prestige without the expense of advertising—and drew plenty of attention to the brand. Media outlets regularly cited *The Corcoran Report* because they trusted its research. Barbara insisted on a high level of accuracy and objectivity. The report didn't spin the truth to place The Corcoran Group in a positive light. It was real research, not a puffy marketing piece. "I couldn't imagine the growth of the business without that honesty," Barbara says. The publication played such a role in the company's growth that she credits it for about two-thirds of the $66 million she fetched for The Corcoran Group.

---◄○►---

One way Barbara got The Corcoran Group *noticed without expensive advertising* was by publishing a popular newsletter about New York residential real estate trends, *The Corcoran Report*. She realized that writers need statistics to give credence to their business articles, so she found a way to calculate those numbers.

Savvy Publicity: Getting Media Attention by Commenting on the Competition

Time and again, throughout her career, Barbara has demonstrated her skills as a master marketer. She always finds new ways to *save her bucks and get her company noticed without expensive advertising*. When New York society was abuzz because a pregnant Madonna was shopping for an apartment, Corcoran provided the press with a checklist of what the pop singer's requirements for her dream digs were. Four TV stations interviewed Barbara. Never mind that Madonna wasn't a Corcoran client. The Corcoran Group got more publicity mileage out of the story than the firm that actually did have Madonna as a client. That firm had to respect its client's privacy and keep mum.

"I became so good at creating publicity that people always thought we were bigger than we were," Barbara says. With the Madonna story, she also proved the value of two time-tested means for generating publicity: making news on rumors or hearsay and making news with your competitor's sales. On multiple occasions, Barbara also used her imagination to come up with other attention-grabbing story ideas that spotlighted the company and contributed to building the company's brand.

---◄○►---

She *trusted her gut* that the Internet had marketing potential for her company and the real estate market. This was 1993—five years before her competitors even had Web sites.

Taking a Risk on a New Way of Marketing

The Corcoran Group also pioneered using the Internet to market real estate. But that career highlight actually resulted from a marketing ploy gone awry. In 1993, Barbara thought it would be a good idea to promote the company's properties using videotapes. "We had a photographer go and shoot every property we had—73 properties," Barbara remembers. "It was very expensive to do and I put them all on videotape—East Side, West Side, Downtown—and told my brokers to hand them out."

The salespeople, however, were less than enthusiastic. They didn't want their clients to watch the tapes, fall in love with a property represented by a different broker, and give their business to that broker instead. As a result, the tapes piled up and gathered dust. The "Homes on Tape" project, financed with $71,000 in after-tax profit, figured to be an expensive mistake.

When Barbara came home feeling despondent over that big white elephant, she found her husband, Bill Higgins, a former FBI agent and navy reserves captain, brimming with excitement over a demonstration he'd seen. Just returned from three weeks with the U.S. Navy in South Korea, Bill explained how he had played war games on a computer on this new thing called the Internet. Her interest piqued, Barbara asked if the Internet was only available to the navy. Bill explained that anyone with a computer and an Internet connection could use it anywhere, anytime to exchange information. That's when Barbara's reliable imagination kicked in. She *trusted her gut* that the Internet had marketing potential for her company and the real estate market.

Barbara quickly took steps to launch The Corcoran Group's Web site and hired a technician to scan images from the videotapes to post online. The strategy worked, exceeding all expectations. This was 1993—five years before her competitors even had Web sites. "I just threw [the pictures] on the Internet and had my first Internet sale that week," Barbara says. The company launched Corcoran.com in an effort to make up for a mistake and, in the process, discovered a lucrative, untapped marketing channel for real estate sales. Today, Corcoran.com averages a sale a day. Sometimes clients make the purchase solely based on on-screen images and descriptions.

––––––––––––––◄○►––––––––––––––

"I became so good at creating publicity that people always thought we were bigger than we were." Barbara also used two time-tested means for generating publicity: making news on rumors or hearsay and making news with your competitor's sales.

––––––––––––––〰––––––––––––––

Barbara also promoted the Corcoran brand by making appearances on television news and talk shows, offering simple advice about buying and selling real estate. Her infectious energy made her a natural for such consumer-oriented segments.

Creating a Brand That Outlives the Company

Over the years, Barbara skillfully used the media to build The Corcoran Group brand and rightfully earn the nickname Queen of New York Real Estate. Media provided a means of promoting her real estate business. But today, she's using her real estate knowledge as a means of launching a career in media. Barbara is the real estate contributor for NBC's *Today* and CNBC, and she is a columnist for the *Daily News*, *More* magazine, and *Redbook*. Her ultimate goal is to develop her own TV show. What Rachel Ray has done for cooking on TV, Barbara Corcoran just might do for real estate. She is currently a fan favorite in the popular ABC television series *Shark Tank*.

STRATEGIES FOR SUCCESS

- ♦ Barbara had a tough time in school because she was dyslexic and considered "stupid"—yet she built, from scratch, a real estate business she eventually sold for $66 million. She *never let adversity get in her way*; instead, she found creative ways to overcome her disadvantages and innovative ways to solve problems.
- ♦ At age twenty-four with no real estate experience, Barbara was undaunted by the prospect of going into business for herself— first with a partner, then on her own. She was eager to *just start*: move to New York, take the real estate exam, set up an office in her apartment, and begin renting and selling.
- ♦ Barbara knew how to *get her business noticed without expensive advertising*: She invested in a glam coat to make her look more successful than she was; she started *The Corcoran Report* to get her company's name in newspapers; she even got publicity for commenting on clients she didn't have, including Madonna.
- ♦ Barbara also *bucked the conventional wisdom, trusted her gut*, found *underserved niches*, and *hit her competitors where they ain't*: She set up a real estate office to market New York City's downtown corridor well before her competitors did, after in-house research revealed rising demand. While everyone else thought it was too early to target residential business there, she moved in, and by the time her competitors woke up to the potential of these new markets, she *owned* them. She also saw the possibilities of selling real estate on the Internet—obvious now, but not when she started—and she created a Web site five years before her competition.

CHAPTER 8

David Steward *(Courtesy of World Wide Technology Inc.)*

David L. Steward

Founder and Chairman, World Wide Technology Inc.

"Risk takers encounter setbacks along the way but don't permit that to defeat them."

—**David Steward**

Davide Steward vividly remembers the turning point of his professional life—the moment when he finally decided to discard the security of his $65,000-a-year corporate job and take a leap of faith to run his own company. At the time, he was a Federal Express senior account executive in his early thirties. All his colleagues had gathered to celebrate the company's leading salespeople. Federal Express CEO Fred Smith, standing at a podium on stage, had just called David's name to honor him as salesman of the year. David walked to the stage and accepted his award—an ice-bucket-style trophy engraved with his initials. As everyone in the room applauded, David held up the trophy and peered into it.

"When I looked inside the bucket, I saw nothing, and to me, that was a defining moment," he recalls. "I asked myself, Is this what I wanted out of life? A pat on the back, and an ''Atta boy, get back out there and get 'em again'?"

To David, that bucket's emptiness was a metaphor for his career. He felt like he'd settled for the path of least resistance, and his future prospects looked an awful lot like his present. "I thought, I don't want to wake up when I'm seventy or eighty and wonder why I didn't do more," he says.

"Few [friends and family members] have the same belief in you that you have in yourself. There will always be someone who wants to rain on your parade, but an entrepreneur can't be swayed by other people's standards."

An African American Success Story

David decided it was time to make a big change. In 1984, he made an offer on a consulting business that served the railroad industry. His offer was accepted, and he embarked on an entrepreneurial path that ultimately led him to launch another company, World Wide Technology, about six years later. Today, World Wide Technology is a leading systems integrator that provides technology solutions—including e-commerce and datacenter expertise—to corporate customers around the globe. Annual revenue approaches $3 billion.

As an African American entrepreneur, David has made history. World Wide Technology, based in St. Louis, Missouri, is the nation's highest-grossing industrial service company owned by a black American. The company's success story has become a cultural touchstone—all because David resolved that day to take a big risk and become an entrepreneur. In doing so, he defied the advice of many people around him. But he recognized that many first-time entrepreneurs face such resistance—it's just another obstacle to overcome.

"Some well-meaning friends and family members are trying to protect you, while others may be jealous that you might succeed," David explains. "Few have the same belief in you that you have in yourself. There will always be someone who wants to rain on your parade, but an entrepreneur can't be swayed by other people's standards. Don't let them put you into a box. If you buy into what's expected of you, you'll be restricted by others' limitations."

David views his father as his first entrepreneurial role model. Watching his father juggle all those jobs and responsibilities showed him "that in spite of all the challenges that people have, if they have a will and determination and they have faith and hope . . . any and all things are possible."

Racial Segregation Influenced His Outlook on Life

Having grown up during the days of racial segregation, David developed an aversion to such limitations early in life. One of eight children, he was born in Chicago but raised in Clinton, Missouri, a town of about 8,000 people, located about fifty miles southeast of Kansas City. "I vividly remember segregation—separate schools, sitting in the balcony at the movie theater, being barred from the public swimming pool," David says.

In fact, David was among a group of black teenagers who—in an act of civil disobedience—decided to jump into Clinton's whites-only public pool in 1967. David was just sixteen at the time. The Civil Rights Movement was gaining momentum, and this was a time of heightened racial tensions. That same year, major race riots took place in Newark and Detroit. So when David and his friends defiantly entered that public pool, they braced themselves for the worst. To their surprise, nothing happened: no arrests, no violence. "From that day forward, the Clinton public swimming pool was integrated," David says.

David acknowledges that living with racial segregation—and witnessing firsthand the social impact of the Civil Rights Movement and the early stages of integration—had a profound affect on him. "I am not one to back down when it comes to taking a stand for what I believe," he says.

In elementary school, David had been the only African American boy in his class. At a young age, he already knew plenty about class differences and discrimination. But his mother taught him to never resent anyone who had more than he had. "Again and again, she said, 'You can do anything you set your heart to, son, and someday you'll have all those nice things, too,'" David recalls.

A Strong Family Work Ethic Leads to Persistence and Tenacity

David's father, Harold, ran a small farm but also worked a variety of part-time jobs. He repaired cars, tended bar, cleaned offices, hauled garbage, and worked as a security guard—he did whatever work he could find. "My dad was always working," David says. "The only time he did not work was on Sunday afternoons."

The family farm included a few cattle and hogs—a modest operation, for sure, but one that helped keep the family fed. David did his share of farming chores before school each day, including milking the family cow, and also took odd jobs to earn extra cash. Sometimes that meant mowing lawns or shoveling snow for neighbors. He even sold Christmas cards door-to-door. His father's example instilled in David a solid work ethic.

David views his father as his first entrepreneurial role model. Watching his father juggle all those jobs and responsibilities "was my first experience of getting a sense and a feel for drive and determination and perseverance," David says. "It shows that in spite of all the challenges that people have, if they have a will and determination and they have faith and hope . . . any and all things are possible."

The family of ten lived in a three-bedroom home near the train tracks. Rail riders would sometimes come to the front porch, asking for a bite to eat. David's mother, Dorothy, would give them whatever she could spare.

"We were poor, but I personally never felt like we were," David says. There was always enough food on the table. The kids would get new clothes before each school year began. And they always had three pairs of shoes: one pair for school, one for play, and one for church on Sunday. The Steward kids knew that many of their classmates weren't as fortunate.

David Steward as a young boy at Easter (second from right) *(Courtesy of World Wide Technology Inc.)*

Though David loved the town of Clinton, even as a boy he knew he wouldn't live there as an adult. His dreams would take him elsewhere. He recalls that as a boy he would sometimes visit his grandfather, who worked as a groundskeeper for a local lodge about twenty miles outside of Clinton. Occasionally, top executives with the Peabody Coal Company would book the lodge for meetings or even hunting trips. David found the business world intriguing, even back then. "I said, 'One day, I want to be like that,'" he recalls.

But as a teenager in high school, David was extremely shy and maintained just a C average. He struggled with a speech impediment—stuttering—and failed in his early efforts to try out for the football and basketball teams. When he tried out for the football team as a freshman, he was too small—5' 7" and 125 pounds. After a growth spurt during his freshman year, he tried out for the basketball team but was deemed too skinny. In his junior and senior years, he finally made the basketball team, but the coach continued to chide him for his lean build.

"About the only thing I had going for me was my perseverance," David says. "I probably just didn't know any better, but once my mind was made up, I had the tenacity of a pit bull."

After graduating high school, David attended Central Missouri State University (now known as the University of Central Missouri) in Warrensburg, about thirty miles from Clinton. There, he played college basketball and earned a degree in business administration with an emphasis in industrial organization. By his senior year, he stood at 6' 5", had added considerable bulk, and was a capable player on the basketball court—a testament to his tenacity. "When anyone asks my mother how I got so tall, she says, 'David wanted to play basketball so badly, he willed himself to grow,'" David says.

A Tough Job Hunt: Four Hundred Résumés in Three Years

After college graduation in November 1973, David worked for a while as a part-time substitute teacher and later accepted a job with Boy Scouts of America. Years earlier, as a boy in Clinton, David had tried to join the hometown scouts troop but was turned away because it was for whites only. Upon learning this, both he and his mother had cried. They didn't give up though. David and a group of his friends, along with their parents, formed their own troop—Troop 225—the first-ever integrated scouts troop in Clinton.

The scouts job paid little, so David continued to send out résumés. A few months later, he landed a manufacturing supervisor's position with Wagner Electric—then he was laid off just a year later. So the job-hunting process started up again, and it was difficult to make ends meet. "All in all, starting from the time I graduated college, I sent out about four hundred résumés and averaged two or three interviews a week for three years," David says. He credits his mother with instilling in him the belief that success comes from hard work. So the tenacious bulldog from Clinton, Missouri, kept at it. He *refused to let adversity or failure defeat him.*

───────────◄◦►───────────

Auditing payments that were due but not being collected was crucial to his start-up company's early success. The strategy allowed Transport Administrative Services to grow without facing formidable competition. "Even a huge multi-billion-dollar company can't offer something for everyone. Many niches are too small for giant corporations to consider."

───────────⚭───────────

Finally, after a series of interviews, he landed a sales and marketing job with Missouri Pacific Railroad Company, based in St. Louis, in February 1976. Committed to hiring African Americans, the company welcomed David aboard and enrolled him in a fourteen-month training program where he learned all about the railroad industry. That training would serve him well at Missouri Pacific Railroad—and years later, after he started his own business. His new position reignited his childhood fascination with the railroad business. Not only had David grown up near the railroad, but one of his older brothers had held a business management position in the industry. His brother's success had helped inspire David to study business in college.

Looking back, David acknowledges that his first couple years after college were fraught with disappointment and financial struggles. But he was able to persevere in large part because his past struggles had made him stronger. "Although I didn't know it at the time, the adversity I encountered as a stuttering, thin-as-a-rail kid toughened me up," he says. "It developed my character so I could stick with the program when I didn't make the freshman basketball team in college. Making the team as a sophomore strengthened my faith. That prepared me for the two years of hard times bounding around job-hunting before being hired by the railroad."

It also helped that during that period of job-hunting travails he met his future wife, Thelma. She proved to be his biggest supporter and confidante—in good times and bad.

The position with Missouri Pacific Railroad Company provided the career launching pad that David had craved for so long. He not only sold railroad freight services but also sold the company's trucking and airfreight services. It was a rewarding job, but he and his wife, Thelma, eventually grew tired of the constant uprooting. A developing merger with Union Pacific Railroad had played a role. It seemed as though they barely had time to unpack their moving boxes before being relocated to a new city. After living in St. Louis, Newark, Milwaukee, Houston, and Los Angeles, David decided to give notice and look for another job in his home state of Missouri. After a year of job hunting, he landed the FedEx position.

"From the time I graduated college, I sent out
about four hundred résumés and averaged
two or three interviews a week for three years."
He credits his mother with instilling in him the
belief that success comes from hard work.

In 1981, David's being named one of the recipients of the Salesman of the Year trophy—there were only six that year out of a sales force of eight hundred people—secured him a spot in Federal Express's Sales Hall of Fame in Memphis. The accomplishment was particularly notable since he had struggled to meet sales goals when he first began working at the company.

Leaving Corporate America and Buying a Business

At the time he quit FedEx to become an entrepreneur, David had logged a full decade working in corporate America. For him, that was enough, and he was ready to *just start* running his own company. He asked a business owner he knew if the man would consider selling his consulting business, which audited freight bill charges. David was familiar with the firm because he'd performed some marketing work for it. The firm's owner, who'd recently turned sixty-five, agreed to sell so he could retire.

"I leveraged his assets to give him a down payment and to create cash flow for the business so I could move the business forward," David explains. The plan was to make payments from future earnings—a strategy that was quite a leap of faith in itself. But as a devout Christian, David believed that if he applied biblical principles to how he ran his newly acquired business, the company would succeed. (In fact, years later David wrote *Doing Business by the Good Book: 52 Lessons on Success Straight from the Bible,* in which he describes how the Bible inspired him in building his hugely successful and highly ethical business.)

David quotes scripture frequently when discussing his philosophy of running a business. For example, he believes that a successful business owner must be willing to be a risk taker, and he cites John 20:29: "Blessed are those who have not seen and yet have come to believe."

"Jesus could very well have been addressing a business leadership convention with this message," David explains. "Although a decision maker believes he will achieve positive results from time and money invested in a business venture, the outcome is not guaranteed. . . . No one of this world is capable of predicting the future with absolute accuracy."

David couldn't predict the future, but he believed he could succeed in his new business. He renamed the firm Transportation Business Specialists and enlisted Jim Kavanaugh, a friend who had worked for electronics manufacturer Future Electronics, to help oversee day-to-day operations. At the time, there were only about ten employees. Most of the company's contracts involved auditing overcharges for customers of railroad freight services.

Expanding the Business by Finding New Niches

Three years later, in 1987, David launched a sister company, Transport Administrative Services (TAS), which tapped an *underserved niche*—identifying undercharges for the railroad companies. TAS's meticulous auditing procedures revealed how much revenue the railroads were losing because of undercharges. "At the time, many companies provided overcharge services informing customers that ship by rail when they were charged too much, but nobody had ever taken our approach and worked the other end of the equation," David explains. He had found an *underserved niche* that he could tap by developing electronic auditing processes that *bucked conventional wisdom.*

David's sales efforts included networking with former colleagues in the railroad business. He contacted his former mentor at Union Pacific, George Craig, to let him know about TAS's new auditing services. Craig, in turn, introduced David to many of the industry's key decision makers. Through such industry networking, David was able to *save his bucks and get noticed without expensive advertising.*

This newly developed niche prompted Union Pacific Railroad to hire TAS to audit three years' worth of freight bills. That meant managing $15 billion worth of rate information for a single client. To perform this monumental task, David had his own local area network (LAN) built to link data electronically from all of the railroad's operations. At the time, it was the biggest LAN in all of St. Louis. In many respects, David was trying to pull the creaky old railroad industry into the twenty-first century. There were plenty of cultural barriers to overcome. "You've got unions, you've got a culture that has kind of limped along for years, doing the same old thing the same old way, and you have a lot of nepotism," he explains.

But David's previous experience working in the railroad business, coupled with his growing expertise in information technology (IT), gave him a competitive edge in a narrowly focused niche. Serving that niche—auditing payments that were due but not being collected by the railroad companies—was crucial to his start-up company's early success. The strategy allowed TAS to grow without facing formidable competition.

"Even a huge multi-billion-dollar company can't offer something for everyone," David explains. "Many niches are too small for giant corporations to consider." Nonetheless, he made sure his company continued to improve its services to thwart any efforts by would-be competitors to copy TAS. That niche service first attracted one large customer, Union Pacific, but three other railroads eventually followed. Four out of seven of the country's biggest railroads became clients.

The company's mission was to offer IT solutions
to a variety of industries, not just the railroads.
That meant marketing to industries in which David
had no track record—a high-risk undertaking,
to say the least. Even many of his friends didn't
believe David stood a chance of succeeding.

In 1989, the company was performing well. David's hefty investments in technology, such as the LAN, had paid dividends. TAS had proven its value, saving its railroad customers boxcar loads of money. Then, one day, David received a phone call from Union Pacific. At the time, he was expecting to hear from the railroad company to begin discussing the terms of a renewed contract. He wasn't at all prepared for what the Union Pacific representative had to say.

"The man explained that everyone was totally satisfied with our auditing services and told me, 'You've saved us a bundle, Dave,'" he remembers. "Then there was a slight hesitation, and he added, 'I'll get right to the point. We have no complaints, and in fact, you did the work so efficiently that we're now in a position to do it internally, so we're not going to renew the contract.'"

Losing a Major Client Forced Him to Launch a New Business

The news was like a punch to the gut, leaving David practically speechless. He simply thanked the man for the opportunity to have served Union Pacific in the past. Union Pacific had represented 70 percent of TAS's total business. Suddenly, the company was in dire straits.

The risks that accompany having too few clients became all too clear. As a first-time entrepreneur, David had gained a foothold in the business world by finding and dominating a market niche. But he now needed to expand his company's reach and think bigger. In 1990, he launched World Wide Technology (WWT), using $250,000 in earnings from Transportation Business Specialists and Transport Administrative Services. The company's mission was to offer IT solutions to a variety of industries, not just the railroads. That meant marketing to industries in which David had no track record—a high-risk undertaking, to say the least. Even many of his friends didn't believe David stood a chance of succeeding.

"When friends and acquaintances asked my wife, Thelma, about our new venture, and she explained what our IT company did, they'd roll their eyes," David recalls. "Once a woman told Thelma, 'Well, you guys must like living on the edge.' We quickly learned to throw conventional wisdom out the window, knowing that what the world thinks is wise, God thinks is foolish."

"I concentrated on what I had to do in order to fix my financial woes. I persevered through these hard times with a belief that what we were doing for our employees and customers was meaningful. . . . Risk takers encounter setbacks along the way but don't permit that to defeat them."

The early days of WWT were filled with peaks and valleys, David says, but he made certain that he never missed a single payroll. During that first year, a representative from the Small Business Administration's office in St. Louis contacted the company to see whether it—as a small minority-owned business—would be interested in performing some work for the federal government. Those early projects provided a needed revenue boost.

But the IT field in the early 1990s was in a constant state of flux as the Internet's influence expanded. WWT required lots of capital to keep up with all the changes. For a start-up company like WWT, that led to trying periods of cash flow problems. At one point, the company was $3.5 million in debt. With a wife and two kids to support, David had never dealt with this level of stress before. Bill collectors visited the house, demanding payment. Bankers took steps to try to shut down the business. Creditors badgered David on the phone daily. One afternoon in 1992, his car was repossessed from the company parking lot. He had to chase down the repo men so that he could retrieve his briefcase from the car trunk.

Somehow, David kept his focus on establishing WWT as an exceptional provider of IT-based business solutions. He *trusted his gut* that all his efforts would eventually lead to success. He resolved to *never let adversity defeat him.*

"I concentrated on what I had to do in order to fix my financial woes," he says. "I persevered through these hard times with a belief that what we were doing for our employees and customers was meaningful." Confident that ultimately WWT would make a positive difference in the lives of its employees, customers, and vendors, he trusted his gut—that voice inside—which told him not to give up. "Risk takers encounter setbacks along the way but don't permit that to defeat them," he says.

Going After Government Contracts

To dig the company out of its fiscal hole, David and his company set their immediate sights on a potential multi-million-dollar contract with the air force. Landing that one contract would take the pressure off and keep the creditors at bay. A successful bid, in fact, would triple the company's revenue. Over the next six months, WWT invested thousands of hours and about $150,000 to better its chances of closing the air force deal. Four other IT firms were competing for the contract. When the air force announced it had narrowed the field to two—and WWT was one of the two in the running—David and his employees were overjoyed. But that just made it all the more disappointing when the other company eventually emerged as the victor. A second-place finish didn't improve WWT's financial standing one bit.

Fortunately, the company's melancholy was short-lived. WWT received an unexpected call from the General Services Administration (GSA), saying the agency was looking for an IT company to assist with a brand-new program. The GSA, based in Washington, D.C., is a centralized federal procurement and property-management agency. On behalf of other federal agencies, the GSA acquires IT, telecommunications, equipment, office space, supplies, and a variety of services. David flew to Washington for a meeting with agency representatives and emerged from that meeting convinced that his company was ideal for the job. From that point on, WWT focused its energies on winning the GSA contract. This time, everyone's efforts were rewarded.

*"I have an appreciation for challenges. You either
go through a challenge or you're stopped by it.
There's always opportunity at the end. If you give
up, obviously, there's no chance of ever having any
hope of reaching that end where the prize is."*

"At the time, our cash flow was so tight, our survival was on the line," David says. "Miraculously, within sixty days, we had a deal signed, sealed, and delivered with the GSA." Normally, it takes six months to a year to prepare for and land such a contract from a federal government agency.

With the GSA contract, WWT's annual sales ballooned from $17 million to $74 million, and the company became a major IT provider to the federal government. The program's success quickly led to more big contracts.

WWT also began introducing IT product lines designed to meet the special security needs of the Department of Defense and its various agencies, including the CIA, National Security Agency, FBI, and branches of the military. This success, in turn, led to more work with such organizations as the Federal Communications Commission, the Department of Agriculture, and the Transportation Security Agency.

Gradually, WWT diversified its client base, securing contracts in the private sector as well and initially gaining a number of new clients in the telecommunications field. In time, Fortune 500 companies from a variety of industries, including corporations in the health-care and financial sectors, came onboard.

"These days, World Wide Technology is deeply entrenched in the Internet industry, the fastest-changing industry ever," David notes. He never stops *reinventing his company* to adapt to changes in technology and customer needs. In this field, there's always another challenge around the corner.

"I have an appreciation for challenges," David says. "You either go through a challenge or you're stopped by it. There's always opportunity at the end. If you give up, obviously, there's no chance of ever having any hope of reaching that end where the prize is."

A Belief in Giving Back

In 1998, the company's sales totaled $202 million, and David received the Ernst & Young Entrepreneur of the Year Award. Sales surpassed the $1 billion mark in 2003. In 2008, sales reached $2.5 billion, and the company had more than 1,000 employees. Providing employment for talented, hardworking people has always been a principal goal of WWT. For David, that's the greatest reward of building a hugely successful company.

"While it is true that I prosper from the success of my company, my goal is to build a business to benefit current and future employees—men and women who will work at this company when I am no longer here," he says. "In years to come, the prosperity of those people will rest, in part, on the foundation of integrity we build today."

WWT's success has also allowed David to donate his money and time to organizations that serve the community. He has served on the boards of such groups as United Way of St. Louis, the Boy Scouts of America Greater St. Louis Area Council, and Variety the Children's Charity of St. Louis.

When queried about whether the American Dream is still possible today—and whether success is still attainable for the cash-strapped start-up companies of tomorrow—David answers emphatically: "More than anywhere else on the planet, America nurtures and rewards the entrepreneurial spirit—our ability to be able to create and be innovative, our ability to have the freedom to think outside the box and have the courage to do so," he says. "Where else can a guy like me, from a small country town, own and operate and develop a company of this size? America is the greatest country in the world for opportunity."

∽

STRATEGIES FOR SUCCESS

♦ Despite what seemed like an interminable job search, David stayed optimistic and *refused to let adversity or failure defeat him.* He kept sending out résumés and going on job interviews until he landed a well-paying job with the railroad.

♦ When David decided to leave corporate America to become an entrepreneur, he *just started* by offering to buy a business owned by an acquaintance nearing retirement. He found an *underserved niche* when he discovered his company's electronic auditing procedures could help railroad companies identify freight undercharges and recoup the money owed to them. This was a specialized service that *bucked conventional wisdom.*

♦ By networking with former colleagues in the railroad business, David managed to *get his company noticed without expensive advertising.*

♦ When his company's principal client decided to replicate the auditing procedures in-house instead of renewing its contract, David set out to *reinvent his company* by offering a variety of IT services to a broader range of customers in the public and private sectors.

♦ When World Wide Technology suffered a cash-flow problem and the bill collectors came knocking, David *trusted his gut* that the financial troubles would be short-lived. He *never let adversity defeat him.* That faith paid off when WWT landed a major contract with the General Services Administration. David continues to *reinvent his company* to keep pace with changing IT technology and customer needs.

CHAPTER 9

Maxine Clark *(Provided by Build-A-Bear Workshop)*

Maxine Clark

Founder, Chairperson, and Chief Executive Bear, Build-A-Bear Workshop Inc.

"Not dreaming big enough is one of the biggest mistakes entrepreneurs make."

—Maxine Clark

In 1995, Maxine Clark was one of the retail world's most powerful women. As president of Payless ShoeSource, she oversaw a $2 billion–plus discount footwear chain with more than 4,400 Payless stores and 630 Payless Kids stores. Given her indisputable track record as an innovative thinker and retail visionary, her success came as no surprise to those who had followed her twenty-plus-year rise to the industry's upper rung.

In early 1996, however, the retail industry *was* surprised when Maxine decided to leave Payless ShoeSource to start her own company. Why walk away from such a powerful position with all its accompanying rewards—seven-figure salary, stock options, bonuses, and retirement plan? Why risk losing her retirement fund by embarking on a new, unproven venture? The answer was simple: She just wasn't having enough fun, she says.

But as founder of Build-A-Bear Workshop, Maxine has made millions *selling* fun. The company has taken the toy industry by storm since 1997, when the first store opened in St. Louis, Missouri, offering children the chance to make their own teddy bears. Today, Build-A-Bear Workshop is a public company operating more than four hundred stores in the United States, Puerto Rico, Canada, the United Kingdom, Ireland, and France. There are also franchise stores in Europe, Asia, Australia, and Africa. Total sales reached $468 million in 2008.

These days, Maxine is having plenty of fun. "Starting this business and seeing what it's become—it's just been beyond my wildest expectations," she says.

As Maxine worked to launch and later expand her company, she continued to involve Katie Burkhardt, the daughter of a close friend: "Kids are worth listening to, and their opinions are very important. You never know how a child's words might inspire you."

Creating a Dream Come True for Kids

When you step inside a Build-A-Bear Workshop store during a big birthday party, you encounter equal parts toy store, theme park, and summer camp crafts day. A giant sign on the wall displays the pledge every child makes before departing with a newly assembled bear: "My bear is special. I brought it to life. I chose it. I stuffed it. Now I am taking it home. Best friends are forever. So I promise right now to make my bear my #1 pal."

Further inside the store, you see rack after rack of little bear clothes—everything from leather motorcycle jackets to princess gowns and cell phones. Elsewhere, kids line up at various stations, each representing another stage in the bear's construction. Children who have already completed the process are seated at a bank of computer monitors and keyboards, where employees and parents help them register the name of their newly formed bear and make the Bear Promise. With parental approval, they're adding their names to a customer database that will enable the company to return any lost bears to their owners. Before leaving, these kids will receive a Cub Condo carrying case—because a shopping bag just wouldn't do for your number one pal—and a special birth certificate for each stuffed animal signed by Chief Executive Bear Maxine Clark. The kids also receive a code to bring their furry friend to life in the company's online virtual world, Build-A-Bearville. Clever product packaging has *always* been central to the company's branding. "We sell the brand *experience*—not the product," Maxine explains. "Our guests say they pay for the experience, and the stuffed animal is free."

A Build-A-Bear Workshop store *(Provided by Build-A-Bear Workshop)*

You can be sure that many of these kids will return to the store soon to expand their bear's family, wardrobe, or cadre of accessories. Each year, the company sells millions of bear shoes alone. About 60 percent of Build-A-Bear Workshop's clientele comprises repeat customers who plan their store visits in advance.

"Starting this business and seeing what it's become— it's just been beyond my wildest expectations."

Maxine believes she and her employees are in the business of entertainment retail—and giving kids a way to express themselves creatively. "Our product—making people smile—is clearly a wonderful product to be in the business of selling," she says.

For a kid, shopping at Build-A-Bear Workshop is kind of like a real-life trip to Willie Wonka's Chocolate Factory, except the people in charge are a lot friendlier and you get to be one of the Oompa Loompas. It's a child's fantasy.

As an entrepreneur, Maxine wanted to recapture that sense of discovery and excitement she had felt during her childhood shopping trips with her mother and little sister. The girls would follow their mother through the bustling aisles of department stores, checking out the latest fashions. They might have lunch at the store restaurant and take in a fashion show. But they rarely left the stores carrying shopping bags. Their budget didn't allow it. The family was working-class, but fortunately, as Maxine's mother was a talented seamstress, she could take mental notes and replicate outfits at home on her sewing machine. Despite the tight purse strings, shopping was a cherished family adventure.

Out of the Mouths of Babes . . . Can Come a Great Idea

After quitting her position with Payless ShoeSource, Maxine relocated from Topeka, Kansas, to St. Louis. Away from the pressures of the corporate world, she had time to carefully consider what kind of company she would ultimately launch. She also had time to just enjoy herself, hanging out with friends and their children.

Clever product packaging has *always* been
central to the company's branding. "We sell the
brand *experience*—not the product. Our guests
say they pay for the experience, and the stuffed
animal is free." About 60 percent of Build-A-
Bear Workshop's clientele comprises repeat
customers who plan their store visits in advance.

Maxine readily acknowledges that the initial idea for Build-A-Bear
Workshop wasn't hers alone; she had a collaborator—Katie Burkhardt,
the then ten-year-old daughter of a close friend. Though Maxine and
her husband had no children of their own, Maxine enjoyed a real
connection with kids. Katie and her brother, Jack, were avid collectors of Beanie Babies, and Maxine enjoyed taking the two on shopping trips in hopes of adding to their collections. One afternoon, the
three stopped in a local toy store, lured by a big sign promising a wide
selection of Beanie Babies. But the sign's boast didn't bear out. Every Beanie Baby on the shelves looked familiar. Disappointed, Katie
picked up one of the dolls, gave it the once-over, and commented to
Maxine, "You know, these are so easy. We could make these." That's
when Maxine got her idea to launch a company that allowed kids to
make their own teddy bears—a concept that *bucked the conventional
wisdom* that stuffed animals must be mass-produced.

Maxine wanted her animals to be huggable and
lovable toys that would endure a lifetime. She
aimed to reinforce the relationship between
owner and stuffed animal. That connection is a big
part of the reason for the company's success.

Maxine and Katie then began the journey that led to Build-A-Bear
Workshop. They talked about what the bears would look like. Katie
suggested the bears shouldn't have names, allowing guests to name
their own bears—now a key step in the bear-making process.

As Maxine worked to launch and later expand her company, she continued to involve Katie and others like her. After all, Katie embodied the company's target demographic: girls who live in the suburbs and enjoy playing with real and imaginary friends, including stuffed animals. Maxine had identified this *underserved niche* and created the brand identity by tailoring her marketing message, product, and delivery to this very targeted group.

While Maxine developed her business plan, she thought about what Build-A-Bear Workshop could offer little girls. For example, Katie and her friends loved pretending and acting out their own stories, so Maxine decided that company stores would never rush kids through but let them feel welcome to play at their leisure. Because Katie and her friends loved dressing up and playing make-believe, the stores would also sell wardrobes, like wedding gowns and superhero outfits, for the teddy bears.

Maxine continued to involve Katie, valuing her feedback. The message from Maxine on this is very clear: "Kids are worth listening to, and their opinions are very important. You never know how a child's words might inspire you."

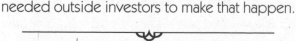

Maxine credits much of her Build-A-Bear Workshop success to her willingness to "dream big," without placing restrictions on her vision for the company. She envisioned a multi-million-dollar business with hundreds of stores, and she knew she needed outside investors to make that happen.

Working Hard to Design an Appealing Product

Even today, approximately 70 percent of Build-A-Bear Workshop customers are girls, and about 80 percent of all customers are under fourteen. Little girls and teddy bears just go together, and they have for a long, long time. Maxine still remembers her childhood bear "Teddy," which she carried around like a security blanket. When she lost the bear at age ten, Maxine never stopped looking for him. "I've never quite recovered from it," she says with a smile. That's what inspired her to insert a barcode tag in every bear to identify its owner. If someone returns a lost bear to any Build-A-Bear Workshop store, the company will make sure it's reunited with its registered owner. By the end of 2008, the company had already arranged more than 5,000 such reunions.

———————◄○►———————

Maxine's passion for her new enterprise didn't hurt either. Her ambitious vision for the new company made a compelling story—one that helped attract investment and publicity.

Maxine also wanted her animals to be huggable and lovable toys that would endure a lifetime. She studied other toy success stories, such as Beanie Babies and Cabbage Patch Dolls, and learned as much as she could from them. Using her research and personal experience, she wanted to be sure to reinforce the relationship between the owner and stuffed animal. That connection is a big part of the reason for the company's success because the customers themselves build their own stuffed animals.

She had *defied the conventional wisdom* wherein most of today's toys are high-tech and "hard-touch." Maxine explains, "We are soft-touch. Our concept is based on entertainment and personalization."

When Maxine talks about the company's appeal for kids, her enthusiasm is palpable, even infectious. She seems like a big kid—well, maybe not that big since she stands just 4' 10''. Maxine wouldn't hesitate to get on the floor to play dolls with a group of giddy seven-year-olds—but she's also one of America's most ambitious businesswomen. The success of Build-A-Bear Workshop stems from her meticulous planning and risk-taking innovation.

Convincing Potential Investors by Putting Up Her Own Life Savings

Maxine credits much of her Build-A-Bear Workshop success to her willingness to "dream big," without placing restrictions on her vision for the company. "Never discount the power of a positive attitude,"

Maxine says. "Not dreaming big enough is one of the biggest mistakes entrepreneurs make."

From the beginning, there was nothing modest about Maxine's goals. She envisioned a multi-million-dollar business with hundreds of stores, and she knew she needed outside investors to make that happen. First, she demonstrated her faith in the venture by investing her own retirement fund, which lent her a high level of credibility in the eyes of potential investors. She showed that she was willing—*eager* even—to risk her own life savings. She *trusted her gut* that her personal investment would eventually pay big dividends. "After all, how can you expect someone else to put money into your company if you're not willing to do the same?" she says.

◄○►

> One of Maxine's strengths is her ability to focus on details that separate Build-A-Bear Workshop from competitors. Most business owners would scoff at assuming these extra costs, but Maxine knows that kids notice and appreciate these details. She knows this because she *listens* to them.

Then she carefully positioned the company as a prime investment opportunity for venture capitalists. She shared her plan with the Committee of 200, a group of female business executives of which she was a member. The members not only offered advice about her new venture but spread word of the company to venture capitalists.

During the course of her retail career, Maxine had cultivated an extensive network of esteemed colleagues and friends. Her contacts in the fashion world proved helpful when developing the bears' wardrobes. Those relationships also came in handy during the company's infancy because venture capitalists at the time focused primarily on technology companies in anticipation of an Internet boom. Networking also helped ensure she had enough capital and resources to respond quickly to customer suggestions.

Maxine's passion for her new enterprise didn't hurt either. Her ambitious vision for the new company made a compelling story—one that helped attract investment and publicity. Even before a single store opened, the business *got noticed without expensive advertising.* During construction of the St. Louis store in the summer of 1997, "Coming Soon" signs at the shopping mall site prompted a *St. Louis Business Journal* reporter to seek an interview with Maxine.

---◄○►---

Maxine's company culture encourages trying
new, creative approaches, without fear of
reprimand if the risk doesn't pay off.

---❧---

The resulting article piqued the interest of Barney Ebsworth, a St. Louis businessman with a private investment firm. During his meeting with Maxine, she shared her vision for the company and unveiled her detailed business plan. When Ebsworth asked her how much money she needed from him to get started, Maxine didn't hem and haw. "Four to five million dollars," she said matter-of-factly. Maxine's enthusiasm and confidence in the project were convincing. "Is next Thursday okay?" Ebsworth asked half-jokingly. A month and a half after that meeting, Ebsworth and his partner, Wayne Smith, committed $4.2 million in start-up money for a 20 percent stake in the company.

Handling Severe Setbacks—with Aplomb and Preparation

Maxine didn't become an entrepreneur until her late forties, but her previous management experience had prepared her well for the challenges she would face. Undoubtedly, Maxine's breadth of experience in the high-stress corporate world helped ready her for a phone call she got one day from the warehouse operation where Build-A-Bear Workshop stored all its merchandise. The company was still in its infancy at the time, running just one store in St. Louis. But sales had already far exceeded Maxine's expectations, and she was feeling pretty good about her new company's prospects.

And then the warehouse operator called to tell her the warehouse ceiling had collapsed, destroying all of the store's merchandise. This was one week before Thanksgiving weekend, a four-day holiday weekend when parents traditionally have extra time to spend with their kids—yes, those teddy bear–loving tots just itching for a trip to the mall. The timing for the debacle couldn't have been worse.

But Maxine suffered no meltdown. She promptly got on the phone with vendors and arranged to have replacement merchandise sent by airfreight from China. Yes, she paid an inflated price for this—about double what she had paid before. But she diffused the crisis, relying on many of the same business relationships she'd forged during all her years in the retail business. When the insurance carrier refused to cover the loss, she still didn't buckle under the pressure. She had wisely raised enough capital to respond to such an unforeseen crisis. She did *not let adversity defeat her.*

Executives don't operate in a corporate-headquarters bubble. "I am a collaborator, and I encourage that style of management at all levels of our company."

The success of the first Build-A-Bear Workshop store at the Saint Louis Galleria also helped stir interest among investors. During the store's first year, it generated $1.7 million—more than doubling Maxine's expectations. In 1998, a venture capital firm based in Cincinnati invested an additional $5 million in the company. Eventually, Maxine would attract more than $11 million in venture capital from multiple sources.

Paying Attention to What Customers Want and What Employees Suggest

One of Maxine's strengths is her ability to focus on details that help separate Build-A-Bear Workshop from its competitors. For example, the bears' sneakers have real tread on the bottoms. The bear binoculars are functional miniaturized binoculars. The buttons and zippers on the bear clothes are real as well. Most business owners would scoff at assuming these extra costs, but Maxine knows that kids notice and appreciate these details. She knows this because she *listens* to them. Each and every letter and e-mail from these customers gets a response.

"I'm on a lot of online buddy lists," she says, "and now I am also on Facebook." Her BlackBerry is always within arm's reach.

Early in the company's history, Maxine assembled a committee of kids, dubbed the Cub Advisory Board, and began relying on the members for advice and feedback. She continues to trust their opinions, especially when it comes to new product launches. Maxine chose not to pay these volunteers because she didn't want them to feel beholden to Build-A-Bear Workshop. In Maxine's world, the brutal honesty of a ten-year-old can influence boardroom decisions. Why risk compromising that honesty?

Maxine Clark at a meeting of the Cub Advisory Board *(Provided by Build-A-Bear Workshop)*

"Since day one, we have used the input of our guests to help us make store decisions—where to open up new stores, what new products to carry, or when to discontinue something," Maxine says.

Maxine listens to her associates as well. In fact, a part-time store employee at the company's first store came up with the idea of holding a ceremony for the placement of the heart inside the bear. One day, when Maxine arrived at the store while a heart ceremony was underway, she was surprised by how captivated and involved the customers became. It was like walking into a revival meeting. "People

―――――――――◄○►―――――――――

Savvy licensing agreements with professional sports
organizations, such as NASCAR and Major League
Baseball, have allowed Build-A-Bear Workshop
to strengthen the brand's appeal for boys.

―――――――――꠸꠸―――――――――

were jumping up and down, rubbing the heart on their elbows, and rubbing it on their foreheads so the bear would be smart," she says.

Company culture encourages trying new, creative approaches, without fear of reprimand if the risk doesn't pay off. Top-performing store managers help develop company best practices. When Build-A-Bear Workshop readies a new stuffed animal launch, management contacts those stores with the best new-launch sales records and asks for input. Executives don't operate in a corporate-headquarters bubble. "I am a collaborator, and I encourage that style of management at all levels of our company," Maxine says.

Build-A-Bear Workshop continues to reinvent itself, introducing new stuffed animal characters, wardrobes, and accessories. A recent store visit revealed that while stuffed bears still predominate on the display shelves, there are also plenty of stuffed puppies, kittens, and even chimps. Savvy licensing agreements with professional sports organizations, such as NASCAR and Major League Baseball, have also allowed Build-A-Bear Workshop to strengthen the brand's appeal for boys. Teddy bears can don the uniform of a local pro sports team or of a soldier or firefighter. The company has also created its own online virtual world, Build-A-Bearville.

―――――――――◄○►―――――――――

She has succeeded in taking an old-school,
low-tech toy—the teddy bear—and making it
as interactive as today's high-tech video games,
bringing a *fresh approach to an everyday product*.

―――――――――꠸꠸―――――――――

Right now, one of Maxine's priorities for the company is developing senior managers who will ultimately take the Build-A-Bear Workshop's helm and keep it on the right course in years to come. She admits that at age sixty, she still has more energy than many of the company's younger associates. But she takes her role as mentor seriously and hopes to instill the kind of commitment that will take the company to even greater heights.

A Build-A-Bear Workshop party, during the heart ceremony *(Provided by Build-A-Bear Workshop)*

Maxine found a way to build a one-of-a-kind business by igniting kids' imaginations and charming their parents. By *bucking conventional wisdom,* she has succeeded in taking an old-school, low-tech toy—the teddy bear—and making it as interactive as today's high-tech video games, bringing a *fresh approach to an everyday product.* "I want this company to go on for hundreds of years after I'm no longer able to work at it," Maxine says. "Great companies are able to go on through many different leaders and evolve and grow. I really want that for this company."

STRATEGIES FOR SUCCESS

♦ Maxine became a risk taker when she *trusted her gut* and walked away from a high-paying corporate job to launch her own business—even though initially she didn't know what kind of business that would be.

♦ When a friend's daughter triggered Maxine's notion of producing a build-it-yourself product, Maxine decided that she *would exploit the competitors' weakness and make it her strength.* Other toys came off the assembly line, and most were high-tech and unyielding to the touch. Maxine's product gave children the opportunity to make a soft, individualized stuffed companion.

♦ She saw that there was an *underserved niche* audience—children like her friend's daughter and that girl's friends, who enjoyed playing with stuffed animals and wanted one that was uniquely their own.

♦ Having decided to *just start* with her project, Maxine *trusted her gut* enough to invest her retirement funds to launch the business. Impressed by her commitment, other investors followed.

♦ The company was still young when a warehouse disaster wiped out all of Maxine's inventory before the Thanksgiving holiday—the prime retail weekend of the whole year. Maxine didn't hesitate. Rather than disappoint her customers, she *didn't let adversity defeat her* and had replacements shipped airfreight from China. She absorbed the additional cost when insurance wouldn't cover her loss.

♦ She *bucks the conventional wisdom* of cutting seemingly insignificant corners because her regular consultations with young customers have shown her that they really do care about details. They notice, for example, that the bear outfits' zippers really work.

♦ The company constantly *reinvents itself* by introducing new products and variations on existing ideas, even making partnerships designed to woo boy customers. The company has also created its own online virtual world, Build-A-Bearville.

CHAPTER 10

John Paul DeJoria *(Photo by Glenn Cratty)*

John Paul DeJoria

Cofounder and Chairman, John Paul Mitchell Systems (Paul Mitchell Hair Products) and Patrón Spirits Company

"Successful people do the things that
unsuccessful people don't want to do."
—John Paul DeJoria

For a stretch in his early twenties, John Paul DeJoria was a jobless single father. He had earlier enlisted in the U.S. Navy hoping to save enough money to attend college someday, but since his release from service, those hopes had dimmed, and his life had devolved into a daily struggle for survival on the streets of Los Angeles. A short-lived marriage had left him with no home, a son to raise, and scant job prospects. One night, with no place to stay, he and his son slept in the car.

"I used to go out and collect Coke and 7UP bottles at night, then cash them in at the corner drugstore for two to five cents," John Paul recalls. "We lived on a very simple diet of rice, potatoes, lettuce, cereal, canned soup, and macaroni and cheese, but we managed."

John Paul DeJoria on a motorcycle, with actor friend
James Coburn *(Courtesy of John Paul DeJoria)*

Today, you're not likely to catch him spending a night sleeping in his car as he owns several residences, including a home in Hawaii. Known as J. P. to his friends and colleagues, he is the CEO and cofounder of John Paul Mitchell Systems, a hair-care giant that boasts more than $900 million in annual salon retail sales. He's also cofounder of Patrón Spirits Company, which produces the world's leading ultrapremium tequila. In addition, he has invested in many businesses, including alternative-energy firms, pet product lines, and a Harley Davidson dealership.

John Paul DeJoria with Nelson Mandela *(Courtesy of John Paul DeJoria)*

Even if you weren't already familiar with John Paul DeJoria's name, you'd probably recognize him if you passed him on the sidewalk. That's because he's been featured in so many of the company's hair-product commercials on TV. He's the exotic-looking bearded guy with the slicked-backed hair and ponytail, sly smile, and apparent fondness for wearing black. J. P. is a serial entrepreneur with a head for business and a heart for adventure and philanthropy, but the success he now enjoys belies the poverty of his youth, and you can trace his transformation back to a series of go-for-broke risks. At a time when he had nothing to fall back on, he wasn't afraid to throw all his money and soul into a business venture that could easily have failed.

Learning the Value of a Dollar from His Hardworking Mother

John Paul DeJoria was born in 1944 to immigrant parents and grew up mostly in Los Angeles's Echo Park and Atwater districts—about twenty-five miles from his Malibu home, where he vacations today. As a boy, he and his family lived in a neighborhood teeming with European immigrants. "They both came over on the boat to Ellis Island," he says of his parents. "My mother was told that the streets were paved with gold, so when she got off the boat, she went looking around for all the gold and couldn't find any. But she found a great country anyway."

―――――◄○►―――――

A short-lived marriage left him with no home, a son to raise, and scant job prospects. One night, with no place to stay, he and his son slept in the car.

―――――✧―――――

J. P.'s mother was Greek, his father Italian. The family quarters were cramped, probably measuring a mere two hundred square feet, he says. After his parents split up when J. P. was almost two, his father was no longer a part of his life. All the financial responsibilities fell on his mother.

"My mother, she worked, designed hats, took the streetcar to downtown Los Angeles every day," he remembers. The family had no extra money, but neither did anyone else on the block. "We didn't have anything, but we didn't know it," J. P. says.

For a time, J. P. and his brother had to live with a foster family in East LA because their mother couldn't afford a babysitter while she was at work. The DeJoria family would reunite on weekends. Like so many other kids living in LA's barrios, J. P. joined a street gang while he was still in grammar school.

―――――◄○►―――――

The success he now enjoys belies the poverty of his youth, and you can trace his transformation back to a series of go-for-broke risks. At a time when he had nothing to fall back on, he wasn't afraid to throw all his money and soul into a business venture that could have easily failed.

―――――✧―――――

He still remembers the parade of street vendors pushing their carts each day through the neighborhood, peddling everything from rags (before paper towels became ubiquitous) to fish and vegetables. Perhaps that helped inspire him to take his first sales job at age nine, selling Christmas cards door-to-door. Shortly after that, he and his brother took on a newspaper route. They would crawl out of bed at 4 a.m. and venture out onto the darkened streets to fold and deliver papers each day before school.

> "Patrón is the clear winner of the 2007 Luxury Institute's Luxury Brand Status Index (LBSI) survey of Premium Tequilas, leading by a wide margin, and ranking first in each component index: consistently superior quality, uniqueness and exclusivity, consumption by people who are admired and respected, and making consumers feel special. The brand is also the clear leader in the two critical metrics—being most worthy of a price premium, and being the brand that consumers are willing to recommend to people they care about most."
> —Market Wire (USA), November 28, 2006

In this neighborhood, you learned the value of a dollar early in life. Sometimes, the family didn't even have a dollar to its name, but J. P. showed early signs of the entrepreneurial spirit that would later define his adult life. And his dogged persistence in the face of obstacles clearly comes from his mother's influence.

"We kind of helped contribute to supporting the family," J. P. says. "There was a time between my mother, my brother, and I, we had twenty-seven cents, and my mother made the comment, 'We only have twenty-seven cents. We have food in the refrigerator, and we don't have any bills to pay between now and Monday, so we're fine, and we're happy.'"

The teenage J. P.'s restless energy didn't exactly draw accolades from all his teachers at John Marshall High School. He still remembers being ridiculed when a business instructor caught him passing notes to his friend Michelle Gilliam during a lecture. The teacher "announced to the class that Michelle and I were the two students least likely to succeed in the entire class," J. P. recalls. "He wasn't entirely right. Michelle became Michelle Phillips of the Mamas & the Papas, and she's in the Rock and Roll Hall of Fame, and I did all right eventually."

―――――――――――◄○►―――――――――――

"I focused on the fact that I once successfully
sold encyclopedias door-to-door. If you
can do that, you can do anything. It restored
my determination and self-belief."

―――――――――――❧―――――――――――

Unemployed and Homeless but Determined to Turn His Life Around

After high school, J. P. enlisted in the navy. Upon completing his service, he returned to Los Angeles and later married. The couple had a son, and J. P. held a series of jobs, including selling encyclopedias door-to-door. But after just three years of marriage, his wife split, leaving him with sole custody of their two-and-a-half-year-old son and a pile of unpaid bills. Broke and between jobs, he couldn't scrape up enough money to pay the rent. He and his son suddenly found themselves homeless and living out of J. P.'s car; this was in 1969 or so.

"It's amazing what you do when you're destitute," he explains. "I could have asked my mom to loan me some money, but I was too proud."

That's when J. P. started collecting discarded soda bottles at night to turn them in for food money. The experience tested his faith in himself, but he resolved to battle back and turn his life around. "So I focused on the fact that I had once successfully sold encyclopedias door-to-door," he says. "If you can do that, you can do anything. It restored my determination and self-belief."

He *didn't let adversity or failure defeat him.*

———————————◄○►———————————

J. P. favored a lean organization, which his corporate
bosses didn't agree with. "They fired me because I
wanted to do a big job with few people. I ran two
divisions with four people and two secretaries.
They said, 'That's not our way of doing business.'"

———————————◄○►———————————

Building a Successful Sales Career

J. P.'s fortune changed when he ran into one of his friends from junior high school, Lee Meyers. The two had long shared a love of motorcycling. When he learned J. P. and his son were homeless, Meyers invited them to stay at his home in North Hollywood. That enabled J. P. to resume his sales career, and he began selling everything from life insurance to magazines. Eventually, he was promoted to publishing giant Time Inc.'s circulation manager for the Southwest. Later, he landed a sales position at Redken, a major manufacturer of hair and beauty supplies. In 1971, while attending a beauty-industry trade show, he first met celebrated hairstylist Paul Mitchell.

J. P. spent four years with Redken, holding jobs as field sales representative, district manager in Texas, and national chain and school manager. But the more managerial responsibility he got, the more he clashed with upper management over staffing needs. J. P. favored a lean organization—"fewer moving parts," as he put it.

"They fired me because I wanted to do a big job with few people," J. P. explains. "I ran two divisions with four people and two secretaries. They said, 'That's not our way of doing business.'" He landed another job, but that firm eventually fired him as well.

In both instances, J. P. was convinced that keeping his staff smaller would produce better results. His intent wasn't just to cut personnel costs; he had a philosophical difference with upper management. "So many companies, when they grow, they sacrifice their image and culture for volume," J. P. explains. "And when you do that, you leave the people aspect behind." The operation inevitably makes more decisions by committee and becomes more resistant to taking risks and pursuing fresh ideas. J. P. was a maverick who didn't really fit in with corporate America.

◄○►

"So many companies, when they grow, they sacrifice their image and culture for volume. And when you do that, you leave the people aspect behind." The operation inevitably makes more decisions by committee and becomes more resistant to taking risks and pursuing fresh ideas.

Going Out on His Own, with a Partner

It became painfully obvious that J. P. needed to work for himself, so he started a consulting business for the beauty industry. After having lived in Texas for a while, he returned to Los Angeles. His consulting clients included his longtime friend Paul Mitchell. In 1980, the two men first discussed going into business together, both recognizing that each brought different assets to the partnership.

◄○►

J. P. and Mitchell's plan was to produce superior shampoos and conditioners, with the unique idea of selling them directly to—and *only* to—salon owners and hairstylists, who in turn would use the products and sell them to their customers. It was a plan that *bucked conventional wisdom*.

An award-winning stylist well-known to the industry worldwide, Mitchell brought top hairdressing skills and name recognition. A native of Scotland, he first came to the United States to train the staff at Vidal Sassoon's first salon in the states. At that time, Mitchell was already considered one of London's leading hairstylists. After leaving

Sassoon's company in the late 1960s, Mitchell invested in some high-fashion salons in major U.S. cities before selling his shares. He then moved to Hawaii but continued to make appearances at major beauty-industry shows, where he performed hairstyling demonstrations on stage. He had pioneered such styling techniques as the "blow-dry look" and the "sculpted look."

Business partners Paul Mitchell and John Paul DeJoria in 1988
(Courtesy of John Paul DeJoria)

During J. P.'s time at Redken Laboratories, he had learned all about the manufacturing, sale, marketing, and distribution of beauty products. He also had the organizational and management skills required to lead a fledgling company in such a competitive field.

J. P. and Mitchell's plan was to produce superior shampoos and conditioners, with the unique idea of selling them directly to—and *only* to—salon owners and hairstylists, who in turn would use the products and sell them to their customers. It was a plan that *bucked conventional wisdom*. But the two partners eventually convinced an investor to sink half a million dollars into the venture, in exchange for 40 percent of the company.

And then the investor backed out, made skittish by rising inflation and interest rates. That setback left J. P. and Mitchell with no capital to speak of, just $700 between the two of them. J. P. was going through a divorce, and Mitchell was short on cash, too. But instead of scrapping their plans—or postponing them until they could convince another venture capitalist to jump onboard—they forged ahead. They *trusted their gut* and *just started*. They *didn't let adversity defeat them.*

They scaled back the initial product run and settled on a black-and-white bottle design in place of a pricey color logo. J. P. offered the pink slip for his vintage Rolls Royce to a cosmetic lab as collateral for that initial product run. The partners needed the product bottles quickly because a major marketing opportunity, the 1980 West Coast Beauty Supply Spring Style Show, was fast approaching.

> "The annual *Advertising Age Marketing 50 Special Report*, published today, includes just one spirits brand this year—Patrón tequila. . . . Distilled and packaged entirely by hand, Patrón accounts for over 70% of the ultra-premium tequila market."
> —PR Newswire, November 13, 2006

The strategy worked. Mitchell demonstrated the Paul Mitchell system on stage at the show, and J. P. explained the system's potential for client sales. Stylists attending the show responded by buying up every single bottle on hand. That revenue helped the partners pay some of their bills, but keeping the business afloat remained difficult.

Initially, J. P. and Mitchell couldn't afford office space, so they spent $18 on a Universal City post office box for the company address. When J. P. needed an invoice or letter typed, he rushed over to a local secretarial service that charged $3 a page.

John Paul DeJoria with his Rolls Royce *(Courtesy of John Paul DeJoria)*

"It took about two weeks from the time we ordered the bottles until they got through the silkscreen and started being filled," J. P. says. "The minute they were filled, I hit the streets knocking door-to-door at the salons, selling them, and my partner did the same."

———————————◄○►———————————

The partners convinced an investor to sink half a million dollars into the venture, in exchange for 40 percent of the company. Then the investor backed out. The partners had only $700, but instead of scrapping their plans—or postponing them until they could convince another venture capitalist to jump onboard—they forged ahead. They *trusted their gut* and *just started.* They *didn't let adversity defeat them.*

———————————⌣———————————

Paul Mitchell Shampoo One was for normal to fine or chemically treated hair. Shampoo Two was for normal to thick or greasy hair. Both were formulated to cleanse with only one lathering and rinse instead of two. They were also designed to eliminate the need to switch shampoo types every three months. Unlike competing products, Paul Mitchell shampoos over time continued to keep hair looking clean and full-bodied. Their effectiveness didn't diminish with continued use. The other two initial Paul Mitchell products were The Conditioner, which users left in the hair, and Hair Sculpting Lotion. The partners promoted the products as a hairstyling system.

"We knew that what we had was the best," J. P. says. "It was just a matter of hanging in there long enough so a lot of people could try it and want to use it again." Through sales calls and demonstrations at salons, along with trade show appearances, the Paul Mitchell brand started to *get noticed without expensive advertising*.

Using His Sales Experience to Jump-Start His Business

During those first months, J. P. tapped his encyclopedia-selling sales experience to make all those cold calls on salon hairstylists—and to continue making them after a steady dose of rejection. "I would walk in and say, 'Hi, my name is John Paul from John Paul Mitchell Systems. We're going to revolutionize the shampoo and conditioning market, and I'd like to tell you why,'" J. P. recounts. The two partners offered a money-back guarantee on all bottles that remained unsold or unused—a major financial risk that demonstrated their belief in their brand.

J. P. also coached stylists on how to promote sales to customers, promising that Paul Mitchell products would always be distributed solely through salons. The stylists' customers would never have the option of purchasing the products through mass-market channels—supermarkets, drug stores, or warehouse stores.

Paul Mitchell has kept that promise to this day, despite others' elaborate efforts to circumvent the policy. In fact, the company has gone to great legal expense to thwart counterfeiters and unscrupulous distributors from selling the products on the gray market.

"Anything you see in any drugstore or supermarket is counterfeit or gray market," J. P. says. "We did not put it there."

With no budget for advertising or a distributor, J. P. and Mitchell worked at a grueling pace during the company's infancy. Their sales pitches often met indifferent stares, but they persevered. Gradually, more stylists and salon owners agreed to give Paul Mitchell products

———————————◄○►———————————

The partners offered a money-back
guarantee on all bottles that remained
unsold or unused—a major financial risk that
demonstrated their belief in their brand.

———————————◅♨►———————————

a try and grew to rely on the extra revenue stream the products ultimately created. On their next salon visit, customers would invariably
ask for more. Nonetheless, for J. P. and Mitchell, keeping their business out of the red was a constant struggle.

"For the first two years, we should have gone bankrupt every single week, by all standards," J. P. says of the time. "I lived in my car for
the first couple of weeks, and we just really stretched the dollar."

J. P.'s home address during that stretch was his old Rolls Royce—
yes, he was homeless again—and he dined each evening on finger food at a local restaurant's happy hour. He showered in parks.
Throughout the 1980s, Mitchell continued to make appearances at
beauty shows to demonstrate the products to professional audiences.
By 1986, the company could afford to launch a high-concept advertising campaign featuring Mitchell, then animals, and then John Paul.
J. P. hired noted fashion photographer Irving Penn to shoot the ads,
which ran in *Vogue*, *Mademoiselle*, and *Glamour*, in addition to the trade
magazines *Modern Salon* and *American Salon*. Over the next two decades, other famous photographers followed Penn, including Herb
Ritts, Richard Avedon, and Annie Leibowitz.

To further promote the products, J. P. and Mitchell developed the
Associates Program to train hairstylists in the Paul Mitchell system.
After training, associates were qualified to conduct their own training
sessions at salons. This program helped fuel the company's growth.

By 1989, John Paul Mitchell Systems had seven hundred associates and fifty employees, who worked out of the company warehouse
and office building in Santa Clarita, California.

Starting a Completely Different Business—Selling Tequila

Also in 1989, J. P. got into the spirits industry. A friend of his, architect
Martin Crowley, made regular trips down to Mexico to buy furniture

and building equipment to sell back to builders in LA at a profit. One day, J. P. suggested that Crowley pick up some homegrown tequila during his next trek across the border. J. P. hoped the quality would be superior to what he was getting in the United States.

Crowley returned with a bottle from a tequila distillery in Jalisco, Mexico. The distillery had been quietly producing high-quality tequila for more than half a century. After a sip, J. P. knew they had discovered a hidden treasure. The two started tossing around the idea of bottling from the distillery and selling ultrapremium tequila under their own brand, Patrón (Spanish for "the good boss"). Crowley, an architect and designer, drew up a sleek bottle design. J. P. knew he and Crowley could help the distillery tweak the tequila taste just a bit to make it even smoother.

> J. P. and Crowley were confident that their idea would work because there was no superpremium brand in the tequila product category in the United States. They had discovered an *underserved niche*.

"The agave we used was more expensive, the process was more expensive," J. P. says. "We thought, 'Oh, let's go for it.' So I ordered 1,000 cases—that's 12,000 bottles—with the idea in mind that if it didn't make it, well, everybody we knew would be getting tequila for their birthday and holidays for the next ten years."

J. P. and Crowley were confident their idea would work because there was no superpremium brand in the tequila product category in the United States. They had discovered an *underserved niche*. They didn't expect, however, how quickly Patrón would become a marketing juggernaut. Clint Eastwood, as a favor to his friend J. P., gave the new tequila brand some valuable screen time in his new movie *In the Line of Fire*. Within a few years, Patrón was part of pop culture. Wolfgang Puck, another friend of J. P., held a tequila-tasting contest at Spago, and Patrón emerged as the winner. More and more fine restaurants and trendy bars began serving Patrón. Patrón was *getting noticed without expensive advertising*.

Patrón is distilled and packaged entirely by hand. Sold in signed, handcrafted glass bottles, Patrón is made from the finest Weber Blue agave plants grown in the highlands of Jalisco, Mexico. The company has captured 70 percent of the ultrapremium tequila market, and the product is now available in more than forty countries. The corporate headquarters are in Europe, but the tequila is distilled in the small town of Atontonilco, Mexico (the U.S. offices are in Las Vegas). The company began expanding its product line in 1992 with rums and liqueurs, eventually purchasing Ultimat Vodka in 2007. The company has continued to *reinvent itself.*

> "The Patrón Spirits Co. . . . started with two tequilas: Patrón Anejo and Patrón Silver. It quickly became the drink of choice for such celebrities as Clint Eastwood, Peter Fonda, Dan Ackroyd and Fran Drescher."
> —*Hawaii Luxury Magazine,*
> August–September 2008

"Our first distributor, by the way, had told us they could never sell more than 10,000 cases a year," J. P. says. That prediction was way off the mark. The truth is, J. P. has made a habit of spurning such play-it-safe advice from so-called experts like that distributor. He rather enjoys *bucking conventional wisdom.* That penchant may have cost him well-paying jobs in the past, but he enjoys his status as a business maverick. And, by the way, he still maintains relatively small staffs, despite the explosive success of both Paul Mitchell and Patrón. Paul Mitchell has just 182 employees.

Fiercely Independent and Protective of His Products

J. P.'s independent spirit has been evident throughout his career. He infuriated many in the beauty industry when he promoted his company's decision to not test products on lab animals. Some competitors just wanted him to shut up and stop drawing more public attention to a common, yet controversial, industry practice. In response, J. P. challenged competitors to follow his lead and stop harming innocent animals.

◄◦►

Students at his schools train using Paul Mitchell products, so they're much more inclined to use them professionally in the future. The schools have helped bolster both salon-industry standards and brand loyalty in new generations of stylists.

〰

J. P. continues to guide John Paul Mitchell Systems and Patrón Spirits Company, but both of his partners have since died. Martin Crowley, cofounder of Patrón, died in April 2003. Paul Mitchell died in April 1989. Patrón's president and CEO is now Ed Brown, a former Joseph E. Seagram & Sons executive.

John Paul Mitchell Systems now has more than ninety hair-and skin-care products distributed in seventy-seven countries. J. P. has never stopped *reinventing his company* through the addition of new products. Annual salon retail sales total more than $900 million. Patrón is the number one ultrapremium tequila in the world. Both companies have established the kind of brand identity that marketing consultants dream about.

J. P. is also expanding the Paul Mitchell brand through education. The company operates 107 cosmetology schools across the country offering a twelve-month program. The schools are known for instilling professional standards and a positive outlook in their students.

"We started the schools without profit in mind," J. P. says. "We started the schools with the idea of creating better hairstylists."

Of course, because the students train using Paul Mitchell products, they're much more inclined to use them professionally in the future. In effect, the schools have helped bolster both salon-industry standards and brand loyalty in new generations of stylists.

To protect Paul Mitchell's customers and the company's reputation, J. P. also continually battles the efforts of product counterfeiters and distributors that sell Paul Mitchell products on the gray and black markets. The company has even been the victim of truck hijackings.

The company has filed dozens of lawsuits to block sales of phony Paul Mitchell products. For years, J. P. has also lobbied for stiffer federal penalties for product counterfeiting and product tampering and decoding. He testified before a congressional subcommittee in 1999. That same year, he hired a private investigator to track down Joseph F. Thompson, the leader of a crime ring that had bottled ten truckloads of counterfeit Paul Mitchell products and sold them to Quality King Distributors in Long Island, New York. Thompson had fled to Mexico after making bail in Los Angeles County on charges of conspiracy and counterfeiting a trademark. While Thompson was a fugitive, J. P. did several news interviews to ensure the story was covered extensively in the media. After eventually surrendering to police and pleading guilty, Thompson was sentenced to sixteen months in jail.

"Successful people do all the things unsuccessful people don't want to do. They'll knock on ten doors, and even when every one is slammed in their face, they're just as excited on door number 11—or door number 582."

"Our company will continue to use every legal remedy available to eliminate the counterfeiting and the diversion of our products," J. P. says. "This is an issue of consumer safety and corporate honesty, not consumer savings and corporate profits." J. P.'s efforts to protect the company's good name have been unrelenting, despite great expense and sometimes frustrating legal outcomes. But that's not so surprising—J. P. owes much of his career's success to his tenacity, whether he's been battling counterfeiters or just trying to convince a stylist to give his product a try.

"Successful people do all the things unsuccessful people don't want to do," he says. "They'll knock on ten doors, and even when every one is slammed in their face, they're just as excited on door number 11—or door number 582."

STRATEGIES FOR SUCCESS

♦ Once a single father so destitute that he paid for food by redeeming soda bottles, John Paul DeJoria didn't *let adversity or failure defeat him*. He persevered, focusing on his past success selling encyclopedias door-to-door.

♦ He parlayed his sales skills into a job and then a management position, but his desire to keep the operation lean clashed with the corporate mentality. So he looked for an entrepreneurial opportunity more suited to his instinct to *buck the conventional wisdom*.

♦ He and business partner Paul Mitchell developed their own brand of professional hair products and devised a unique distribution system for them, selling only to salon owners and hairstylists. When their primary investor bailed out at the last moment, they *trusted their gut* and did what was necessary to meet the deadline to introduce their products at a trade show.

♦ Unlike with competing brands, the effectiveness of their shampoo didn't diminish with repeated use. They *exploited the competitors' weakness and made it their strength.*

♦ His sales background helped J. P. make cold calls at salons and appearances at trade shows to promote the hair products. He was able to *attract notice without expensive advertising*. The company's money-back guarantee helped, too: The partners took that risk financially because *they trusted their gut* that the hair products would win over salon customers.

♦ J. P. identified and targeted another *underserved niche* when he and a business partner developed a superpremium tequila brand, although again he had to *buck the conventional wisdom* that demand would be low. He got Patrón *noticed without expensive advertising* by networking, enlisting the help of celebrity friends including Clint Eastwood.

♦ By adding new products to the hair-care line and adding other spirits and liqueurs to the tequila company, he has continually *reinvented both companies.*

CHAPTER 11

Sara Blakely *(Courtesy of Spanx.com)*

Sara Blakely

Founder and President, Spanx

*"Really trust your gut and stay in tune with
your gut, even as you continue to grow."*

—Sara Blakely

The idea for Spanx first came to Sara Blakely in 1998, while she was preparing for an open-mic appearance at a comedy club. A twenty-seven-year-old sales manager who moonlighted as an amateur comic, Sara was planning to wear a pair of white slacks and sexy sandals on-stage. She worried that her panty lines would show through her pants.

Performing standup comedy is nerve-racking enough without added anxiety about exposed panty lines. So she opted for a do-it-yourself approach: She grabbed some scissors, cut the feet out of a pair of control-top panty hose and slipped them on. "That's when I had my epiphany," she remembers.

That epiphany ultimately made Sara Blakely a multimillionaire. Today, she heads a company called Spanx, with estimated retail sales somewhere around $350 million in 2008.

> "Sara Blakely is a superhero, and she has the tights to prove it. The 34-year-old has scaled the side of a hot air balloon at 10,000 feet. She was named Georgia Woman of the year. She conquered the male-dominated hosiery industry, and she even made women across America look 10 pounds slimmer."
> —*Atlanta Journal-Constitution*, July 24, 2005

Instead of placing her clever product idea into a mental storage locker, where it would sit undisturbed until someone else came up with it, Sara quickly took action. She researched and wrote a patent for footless pantyhose. She used her irreverent sense of humor to think up an attention-grabbing brand name and slogan for her product packaging: "Spanx—we've got your butt covered." And with just $5,000 in savings to invest in her business, she designed a new product that, by the end of 2000, was being sold in such major department stores as Saks Fifth Avenue, Nordstrom, and Bloomingdales.

Failing the LSAT Led to a New Career Path

Sara had always pictured herself as an entrepreneur in the making. While growing up in Clearwater, Florida, she learned the value of a dollar early—at her father's insistence. She remembers passing out flyers to parents on Clearwater Beach to drum up babysitting jobs. She also organized roller-skating parties at her home and charged admission. She dreamed of someday running her own law practice, hoping to emulate her father, a trial attorney.

———————◄○►———————

Instead of placing her clever product idea into
a mental storage locker, Sara quickly took action.
She researched and wrote a patent for footless
pantyhose. And with just $5,000 in savings to invest
in her business, she designed a new product.

◄◡►

At Florida State University, Sara studied legal communications. But her plans for a legal career were derailed when she failed the Law School Admission Test—not once but twice—and law school was no longer an option. It was a devastating blow, but an experience she now partially credits for her success today. She didn't *let adversity or failure defeat her.*

"I always feel that failure is nothing more than life's way of nudging you and letting you know you're off course," she says.

After finishing college, Sara worked briefly as a chipmunk at Disney World in Orlando. Then she landed a sales job at Danka Business Systems, a major office-equipment supplier, in St. Petersburg. She sold fax machines and copiers to businesses, cold-calling her sales prospects. It wasn't her idea of the perfect job, but she learned how to remain tenacious in the face of rejection. When you peddle business machines door-to-door, rejection becomes part of your daily routine. You develop a thick skin and keep on trying, or you simply quit. Sara didn't quit.

———————◄○►———————

She was confident she was really on to something.
She just needed to develop a prototype and bring
the product to market. She resolved to *just start.*

◄◡►

"They would personally escort me out of buildings," Sara remembers. "And I also had my business card ripped up in my face probably about twice a week."

She wouldn't let that shake her confidence though. She got pretty good at charming would-be customers—even those who initially viewed her as a nuisance—and closing sales.

> "The Spanx name is so synonymous with body-shaping boosts that women who choose another [brand] . . . still refer to it as Spanx. . . . Retail sales are expected to surpass $100 million this year, at least half [going] to Spanx. That compares to a gross $1.6 million in 2001, when *Forbes* first wrote about Spanx. What was then three employees is now 45."
> —*Forbes.com*, October 16, 2006

"I learned that you get about fifteen to thirty seconds to make an impression, and I learned very quickly that making someone laugh or smile pretty much ensures you'll get another fifteen or thirty seconds," the affable blonde explains. "So when you walk in the door of a building with a big sign that says, 'No Soliciting,' you've got to come up fast and you've got to be quick on your feet."

She was eventually promoted to national sales manager and trained other sales reps. She was still working for the company when she launched Spanx.

Seeing a Business Opportunity in a "Eureka!" Moment

The now-legendary white pants—the ones prone to embarrassing panty lines—had been hanging in her closet, unworn for eight months, when she finally decided to don them for a comedy club's open-mic night. The footless panty hose gave her the shape and look she wanted. There were no panty lines, she looked a size smaller, and she was free to wear open-toed shoes.

"Like so many other women, I'd buy clothes and get home and really not know what to wear under them," Sara explains. "Everything shows, or cellulite shows, or you just don't feel like it looks pretty. But the moment I cut the feet out of my panty hose, I thought, 'You know what? This should exist for women.' I'd gone shopping. I'd bought the body shapers. They didn't work."

> "Six years ago, I discovered a miracle product and shared it with the world. . . . Spanx really changed the way I wore clothes. . . . I've given up panties. . . . That's more information than you all need to know, but . . . Spanx started as a simple idea when 27-year-old Sara Blakely cut the feet off of her own pantyhose."
> —Oprah Winfrey, *The Oprah Winfrey Show*, February 1, 2007

Later that night, when the panty hose legs started creeping up her legs, seemingly taking on a life of their own, she knew her project needed some design work. But she was confident she was really on to something. She just needed to develop a prototype and bring the product to market. She resolved to *just start*.

"I was envisioning a totally different life for myself," she recalls. "I knew I could sell, and I knew I could be self-employed, and I knew if I could come up with something for the masses instead of fax machines, I'd succeed."

She received her patent that same year, but she kept her entrepreneurial ambitions a secret. She didn't want friends and family, however well-intentioned, to try to dissuade her from taking the risk.

Before long, she knew she would quit her sales job and sink her entire savings into her business.

────────────◄○►────────────

She had sold fax machines and copiers to businesses, cold-calling her sales prospects. It wasn't her idea of the perfect job, but she learned how to remain tenacious in the face of rejection.

────────────ᘐ────────────

Ignoring Rejections and Plowing Ahead

When she contacted hosiery mills about manufacturing Spanx, they responded less than enthusiastically. The icy reception, however, left her unfazed. "I cold-called for seven years selling fax machines, and I learned to persevere even in the face of hearing 'no' all day long, which helped me when I had to cold-call the hosiery mills," Sara says. "Everybody told me 'no' for a year straight."

> "After giving birth to daughter Apple, now three, Gwyneth Paltrow admitted: 'I wore two girdles. It's a great trick and that's how all the Hollywood girls do it. There are these great things called Spanx which are like bike shorts and they just squeeze you in.'"
> —*Daily Mail* (London),
> November 5, 2007

Time and again, she was told footless panty hose was simply a bad idea. The mills were accustomed to producing hosiery designed to improve the appearance of a woman's legs. But Sara was trying to persuade them to manufacture a product that was completely hidden under clothes. "That was so counterintuitive for them," Sara explains. "They thought I was crazy."

Sara was convinced that hosiery material could create a better body shaper. Other body shapers on the market were made of material that was too bulky. The material found in panty hose, though, is like "second skin," Sara says. Given a chance, she knew she could *exploit her competitors' weakness and make it her product's strength.*

> "Blakely is the creator of Spanx, the hose without toes that flatters a woman's posterior . . . and adds sleekness to the red carpet silhouettes of celebrities like Tyra Banks, Gwyneth Paltrow, Jessica Alba, and Beyonce Knowles."
> —ABC News's *20/20*,
> November 16, 2007

Although her idea *bucked conventional wisdom*, she persisted in presenting her case to hosiery mills: "Please give me a shot and trust me," she'd say. "This is about the butt. This is a new type of underwear. Don't focus on it being hosiery that is supposed to be seen."

In those early days, she also drew inspiration from an unexpected source: Oprah Winfrey. It happened one afternoon while she was feeling particularly frustrated. "I remember verbally saying, 'I'm asking for a sign,'" Sara recalls. "I flipped on the end of *Oprah*, and that day Oprah told the world that she had been cutting the feet off her panty hose for years."

―◦―

"I learned that you get about fifteen to thirty seconds to make an impression, and I learned very quickly that making someone laugh or smile pretty much ensures you'll get another fifteen or thirty seconds."

Perfecting the Product Design and Persuading Retailers

In 2000, Sara finally convinced a mill in Charlotte, North Carolina, to manufacture Spanx. After hundreds of attempts, she also created the prototype she'd envisioned. It was a demanding, trial-and-error process because Sara wanted to make sure the waist- and leg band material was just right, both in comfort and function. In particular, the leg band needed to stay in place but be soft and adjustable. The waistband needed to be more comfortable than that of conventional pantyhose. That meant scrapping the elastic and replacing it with a softer-to-the-touch yarn.

Sara was intent on creating a top-quality product that made women feel good about themselves, even if Spanx wound up costing more than conventional body shapers. When the prototype finally passed muster, she had no doubt that her business would succeed, but others were dubious because of the price point.

"I knew right away when I wore the prototype and I saw the difference it made in my wardrobe," she says. "I knew right away that this was going to be big."

> "Getting a little behind on the latest fashion trends? Then feast your eyes on, well, nothing. They're called Spanx, the secret weapon of women on runways and Main Streets alike. And they promise to make the most—or should we say the least—of one's assets. . . . Spanx are Sara Blakely's million-dollar baby. She's a 30-something undergarment entrepreneur who, truth be told, doesn't look like she's ever needed much help bringing up the rear."
> —*CBS Sunday Morning*, March 30, 2008

As soon as she had a prototype, Sara turned her attention to department stores for product distribution. In a meeting with a Neiman Marcus executive in Dallas, she gave her own before-and-after demonstration. "During the meeting, I had no shame. . . . I asked her to follow me to the ladies room where I personally showed her the before and after in my cream pants," Sara says. "Three weeks later, Spanx was on the shelves of Neiman Marcus." This was in 2000—only two years after she'd first come up with the idea for Spanx.

◄○►

Time and again, she was told footless panty hose
was simply a bad idea. The mills were accustomed
to producing hosiery designed to improve the
appearance of a woman's legs. But Sara was trying
to persuade them to manufacture a product that
was completely hidden under clothes. "That was so
counterintuitive for them. They thought I was crazy."

Using Word-of-Mouth Marketing and Do-It-Yourself Publicity Efforts

Knowing it was time to get the word out, Sara made sure Spanx *got noticed without expensive advertising*. She focused on word-of-mouth buzz and media coverage and stuck with her do-it-yourself approach. The homegrown public relations campaign even included a thank-you gesture for Oprah: Sara sent her a basket full of Spanx.

"I believed so much in my dream that the idea of someone pitching it who maybe hadn't even worn Spanx just completely freaked me out," she says. "So I decided to try the PR myself for a while." The strategy worked. Sara's wit and enthusiasm won over TV news producers and print media editors.

And then, everything changed. Sara received word that Oprah had decided to include Spanx in her "Oprah's Favorite Things" list for 2000, and she wanted Sara to make a show appearance. For a novice entrepreneur, this was like a first-time lottery player winning the state jackpot. At the same time, however, Sara's fledgling company wasn't the least bit prepared for the exploding demand.

In a meeting with a Neiman Marcus executive, she
gave her own before-and-after demonstration. "I
had no shame. . . . I asked her to follow me to the
ladies room where I personally showed her the
before and after in my cream pants. Three weeks
later, Spanx was on the shelves of Neiman Marcus."

"I had to build a Web site in a week, without any prior experience in that," Sara recounts. "Neiman Marcus and Saks Fifth Avenue,
which I had cold-called, said they would try Spanx, and it started selling out like crazy. They were calling me, saying, 'We need more. We
need more.' I had no fulfillment centers, so the hosiery mill was sending huge boxes of Spanx to my two-bedroom apartment."

> "I'm sold! After two weeks of
> wearing my Spanx All the Way
> pantyhose and bandless trouser
> socks, I have to say they are the most
> comfortable hosiery I've ever put on
> my body. And my butt? No bumps,
> ridges or VPLs . . . you could say
> it's as 'smooth as a baby's bottom'
> once again! Thank you, Sara."
> —Customer Stephanie,
> www.spanx.com testimonials

Sara was learning on the fly how to operate a major business and
understandably struggling to fulfill all the orders. But she was determined not to squander the sudden burst of media interest. In addition to the *Oprah* segment, Spanx got exposure in women's magazines
like *Vogue* and business magazines like *Forbes*, as well as on TV shows
like *Good Morning America*. Oprah Winfrey wasn't the only celebrity

touting the slimming and firming attributes of Spanx either. Fashion icons including Gwyneth Paltrow also chimed in with their praise.

Sara assumed the public role of inventor/model and embarked on a promotional tour while the buzz was still fresh. "I went on the road and stood in department stores all day long, every day, lifting up my pant leg and shaking my backside for every woman that would walk by," she says.

———————————◄◊►———————————

"Neiman Marcus and Saks Fifth Avenue . . . said they would try Spanx, and it started selling out like crazy. They were calling me, saying, 'We need more. We need more.' I had no fulfillment centers, so the hosiery mill was sending huge boxes of Spanx to my two-bedroom apartment."

———————————◡◡◡———————————

Expanding and Bringing in Experienced Help

In 2001, Spanx moved from the back of Sara's apartment into an office complex in Decatur, Georgia, and expanded its product line. The company introduced control-top fishnets and Super Spanx, which offered extra control and a tummy panel. That led to more introductions: Power Panties (a no-leg-band shaper for the tummy and mid-thighs), Mama Spanx (for expectant mothers), and Two-Timin' Reversible Tights (sold on QVC). Sara never stopped *reinventing her company.* Under her direction, Spanx continued to take bold risks to expand its customer base and keep the brand in the public's consciousness.

For the company's control-top fishnets, Sara concocted another attention-grabbing ad slogan: "No more grid butt!" Her knack for keeping Spanx in the pop-culture lexicon was uncanny. That bawdy tagline was later featured in a Trivial Pursuit question.

But Sara could no longer oversee every aspect of the company's operations. In 2002, she hired Laurie Ann Goldman, a Coca-Cola executive and mother of three, to serve as Spanx's CEO. The Spanx team also expanded to eleven employees. Like Sara, Goldman was young, sassy, and ambitious—and she was eager to help Sara come up with strategies for further expansion.

Before long, though, Sara recognized that Goldman brought a different set of skills to the company and needed the freedom to use them. So Sara sought to focus her own energies on marketing and product development, her strengths as a business leader.

> "Spanx is the most wonderful thing you can wear. You can still have that bare leg feeling but everything looks very smooth. They're very comfortable and easier to put on than hose."
> —Jeannette Longoria, customer quoted in *San Antonio Express-News*, January 17, 2008

"When you start out and have no money, you're every department," Sara explains. "I learned very quickly what I was good at and what I wasn't as good at. When it's your baby, you control every aspect. It's very hard for an entrepreneur to relinquish some control to someone else, but it is a critical thing to do for the growth of the company."

Sara walks through the Spanx offices and randomly asks her employees, "What have you failed at lately? What risks have you taken?" She's prodding them to think more like entrepreneurs—more like innovators rather than order takers overly fearful of making a mistake.

Sara talks regularly with Goldman and stays involved in all major company decisions, but she isn't consumed with the minutiae of

Spanx's day-to-day operations. This freedom allows her to be more creative, even when traveling on one of her promotional tours.

"I will dream up an idea for a product sitting on a plane, call the office, and everybody will start executing it," she says. "Those are the areas where I'm still most helpful or inspired to contribute."

In 2003, Spanx moved its offices again, this time to the upscale Buckhead community in Atlanta, and the stream of new product introductions kept flowing. Customers gobbled up new lines of Spanx socks, bras, and tights. The company's distribution also expanded to plus-size retailers.

"When you start out and have no money, you're every department. I learned very quickly what I was good at and what I wasn't as good at. It's very hard for an entrepreneur to relinquish some control to someone else, but it is a critical thing to do for the growth of the company."

Taking a Risk on TV to Get More Exposure

In 2004, Sara was approached about participating in a Fox TV reality series, *Rebel Billionaire: Branson's Quest for the Best*, starring Virgin founder Richard Branson. In the program, a group of entrepreneurs would compete in demanding challenges staged around the globe. At stake were money and a stint as president of Virgin Enterprises, but the prize details were kept secret from the contestants.

Participation in the series was a risky proposition. If the program ultimately portrayed Sara as a likable character, the exposure could bolster the Spanx brand. But if the TV audience judged her harshly, the exposure might damage the brand. Also, participation in the show meant Sara would have to take a two-month hiatus from Spanx during a crucial time in the company's growth.

"I had no guarantee of how they were going to edit me or if they were going to be authentic to who I was," Sara says. "A lot of my advisers begged me not to do it. They said, 'You are the face of the brand.

You've worked for five straight years to create this. Why would you jeopardize it for this reality show?' I listened to all of their advice, and then I went quietly and *listened to my gut*. My gut said, 'Do it. It's the right thing to do.' But I was so scared."

Though the show wasn't a ratings monster, it nonetheless gave Spanx added exposure and—at least briefly—made a reality show star out of Sara. She was the resourceful, plucky blonde who quickly became an audience favorite, a woman who tackled every challenge thrown her way—whether it was whitewater river rafting or climbing a rope ladder to the top of a massive hot-air balloon.

Sara placed second in the competition and walked away with $750,000 in seed money to launch her charitable foundation. The Sara Blakely Foundation focuses on funding education and entrepreneurship for women on a global scale. The foundation's first project benefited a group based in Johannesburg, South Africa, that helps send African women to college.

If she had deferred to the experts, if she had conceded that footless panty hose was a bad idea or that Spanx's price point was too high to compete, her company never would have succeeded. That is a message she's eager to share with new entrepreneurs.

"From day one, I realized what a spunky girl she was," Branson says of Sara. "I knew she had a fear of heights, so I took her 10,000 feet up in a hot-air balloon, made her climb a 150-foot rope ladder to the top of it, and then made her have a cup of tea with me. She didn't overcome her fear of heights, but she had the courage to do it. She stood out. She's also full of good ideas, she really cares about people, and she's putting that energy into doing a lot of good things."

In 2005, the company launched two new "intimate collections": Hide & Sleek and Slim Cognito. The following year, Spanx introduced a new brand of body shapers at Target stores nationwide to provide better shape wear to even more women. The product carries the kind of double entendre brand name that Sara's made famous: Assets. The brand's distribution has quickly expanded to include retailers such as David's Bridal, Avenue, Belk, and an e-commerce site, www.loveassets.com.

Today, Spanx holds five patents with five more pending, generates somewhere around $350 million in annual retail sales, boasts more than 150 styles, and employs seventy-five people. Sara continues to take risks and encourages her employees to do the same. She believes a risk that ultimately fails is still better than complacency or just playing it safe. After all, it took hundreds of Spanx prototypes before she finally got it right. In essence, that's hundreds of failures.

> "You might not look like Jennifer Lopez, but you'll be the closest thing to it. . . . I think Spanx are very empowering. . . . When you take that last look in the mirror and see everything is tucked in, you just feel like, wow, ready to conquer the world. Spanx really gives you that sense of confidence."
> —Xitlalt Herrera, public relations spokesperson for Neiman Marcus, quoted in the *San Antonio Express-News*, January 17, 2008

Sometimes, Sara walks through the Spanx offices and randomly asks her employees, "What have you failed at lately? What risks have you taken?" She's prodding them to think more like entrepreneurs—more like innovators rather than order takers overly fearful of making a mistake.

Sara has little reverence for the status quo. If she had deferred to the experts, if she had conceded that footless pantyhose was a bad idea or that Spanx's price point was too high to compete, her company never would have succeeded. That is a message she's eager to share with new entrepreneurs.

"Really trust your gut and stay in tune with your gut, even as you continue to grow," she says. "Use it as your number one source—instead of a board of advisers."

—◦✎◦—

STRATEGIES FOR SUCCESS

♦ After improvising a terrific solution to a wardrobe problem that plagues many women, Sara Blakely didn't just pat herself on the back. She *just started* to work out a way to patent—and then perfect—her idea.

♦ An early disappointment that forced her to abandon plans for a law career, followed by a stint as a cold caller, taught her *never to let adversity defeat her.*

♦ Sara believed she had found a large but *underserved niche*: women seeking a great undergarment for pants. She could *exploit her competitors' weakness*—they all used the wrong kinds of material—*and make it her strength* because she had found a superior alternative.

♦ When the manufacturers she approached said her idea wouldn't fly, she decided to *buck the conventional wisdom, trust her gut,* and keep searching.

♦ When she finally had a sample, she did her own public relations and *got her product noticed without expensive advertising.* She acted as a before-and-after model for retail executives, pitched her story to TV and print media, launched a Web site in a week's time, and went on a promotional tour. She also won over Oprah Winfrey, who chose Spanx for her annual "Oprah's Favorite Things" list.

♦ When Sara was offered the chance to appear on a Richard Branson reality show about entrepreneurs, she *trusted her gut* and took a hiatus from work. The resulting media attention expanded Spanx's recognition, and she was able to use her winnings from the show to fund a charitable foundation.

♦ Sara continues to *reinvent her company* by introducing related products that reinforce her brand's reputation as an innovator. Spanx now boasts more than 150 styles.

CHAPTER 12

Andy Berliner *(Photo by Christopher Chung/*
© The Press Democrat, Santa Rosa, CA)

Andy Berliner

Cofounder and CEO, Amy's Kitchen

"I just had this thought that there have got to
be other people like ourselves out there that
sometimes want a convenience meal but still
want to eat organic, healthy, natural foods."

—Andy Berliner

Andy Berliner, cofounder of the Amy's Kitchen brand of organic
frozen meals, uncovered that goldmine of an *underserved niche mar-*
ket quite by accident. One day in 1987, he made a trip to his local

health-food store in search of healthy prepackaged meals. Normally, Andy and his wife, Rachel, made their vegetarian meals from scratch, often relying on ingredients from the organic garden at their home in Petaluma, California. But Rachel, pregnant with their daughter Amy, wasn't feeling much like laboring away in the kitchen at the time, so Andy went searching for a convenient, but healthy, alternative.

Andy Berliner and Baby Amy at Expo '88 *(Courtesy of Andy and Rachel Berliner)*

"I bought a few things, and they were *horrible*," Andy remembers. That experience, instead of simply leaving a bad taste in their mouths, ultimately spawned a life-altering entrepreneurial project. Just months later, the Berliners launched their own healthy frozen meal brand and named it after their newborn daughter, Amy. Today, Amy's Kitchen makes more than 160 organic, vegetarian products; generates annual revenues of $270 million; and employs 1,500 people in Santa Rosa, California, and Medford, Oregon. Those employees make about 600,000 meals each day—everything from black bean enchiladas to macaroni and cheese. And none of those meals contains hydrogenated fats or oils, additives, preservatives, meat, or poultry. All vegetables, grains, and fruits are grown organically.

―――――――――――――◄O►―――――――――――――

Andy realized he had found an underserved niche, decided to buck the conventional wisdom, and went on to create a major new product category. He identified his competitors' weakness— taste—and made it his company's strength.

―――――――――――――⨠―――――――――――――

Discovering a Market Need—by Accident

When most people can't find what they're looking for in the market-place, they grouse and move on. But Andy realized he had found an *underserved niche*, decided to *buck the conventional wisdom*, and went on to create a major new product category. He *identified his competitors' weakness*—taste—*and made it his company's strength*. He leaped into the right market niche at the right time. In the past decade, organic food sales have more than quadrupled. "I just had this thought that there have got to be other people like ourselves out there that sometimes want a convenience meal but still want to eat organic, healthy, natural foods," Andy explains.

At first, Andy resisted starting a new business and instead tried to sell the idea to established health-food companies. But one weekend, while he and Rachel were relaxing at their mountain cabin in Yosem-ite, Andy decided a change in strategy was in order. "It was actually one of those early-morning realizations where I just had this feeling that this was too good of an idea to let go," Andy recalls. "I told my wife, 'I think we should do this ourselves.'"

An Earlier Venture in Entrepreneurship

A graduate of Purdue University, Andy had always had an adventurous spirit and a mind for business. After college, he had spent some time living in Australia before returning to the United States and landing a commercial real estate sales job in California. But his career took a sharp turn when he took a sales job at a small herbal tea company and bought an interest in the fledgling business. Magic Mountain Herbal Tea, which sold directly to supermarkets, was a burgeoning success. But after a few years, the business's small group of owners sold out to a larger company in 1974. Looking back years later, Andy regretted that decision. Instead of thinking big, he and the other owners had hedged their bets. They didn't believe in the business enough to give it their all and raise the capital for major expansion.

Rachel and Andy Berliner *(Courtesy of Andy and Rachel Berliner)*

"We sold it very early because the financial pressures were great," Andy recalls. "Not just myself but the other people involved were not oriented toward mortgaging houses and doing all the things that you normally do to keep a business going at that point. So we sold it too early, and the people we sold it to gradually destroyed it."

At first, Andy resisted starting a new business and instead tried to sell the idea to established health-food companies. But then he changed his mind. "I just had this feeling that this was too good of an idea to let go. . . . I told my wife, 'I think we should do this ourselves.'"

Determined not to make the same mistake with Amy's Kitchen, Andy was ready to *trust his gut* and *just start.* "Somewhere along the line, I got this confidence where once I felt something was right, I didn't really worry too much about the success or failure of it," Andy says. This time he was willing to make the sacrifices—both personal and financial—and assume the risks required for long-term success.

A Family Business, Involving Anyone Available and Willing to Help

Amy's Kitchen was incorporated in 1988. Andy hoped to build a family business that could ultimately generate $3 million in annual sales. To raise capital, he sold his gold watch for $4,000 and some gold coins. He and Rachel also borrowed a couple thousand dollars from a relative and took out a loan using Rachel's car as collateral. That gave them $20,000 in start-up money.

Keep in mind that at the time Andy was a forty-year-old first-time father. New parenthood isn't typically the kind of life change that normally invites go-for-broke risk taking. But Andy saw Amy's Kitchen as an opportunity for real financial security for his family. Running his own business also gave him more flexibility to spend time with his daughter. "From the beginning, because I was an older parent, I wanted to be very much a part of her life, so I worked a lot from home," Andy says. "I set up an office in the barn so whenever she needed me, I was there. She could come and hang out."

Andy was ready to *trust his gut* and *just start*.
"Somewhere along the line, I got this confidence
where once I felt something was right, I didn't really
worry too much about the success or failure of it."

Amy's Kitchen's first product was a vegetarian pot pie. From the start, the business was a family affair. When she wasn't busy keeping Amy occupied, Rachel spent her time designing product packaging. Rachel's mother, Eleanor, worked on creating the right mix of vegetables. Andy was responsible for the sauce. A family friend zeroed in on finding the right combination of spices. The goal wasn't to appeal to the typical TV dinner eater; it was to win over people who normally prepare their own healthy meals but occasionally don't have time to cook. The emphasis was on health *and* taste.

Outsourcing Production of Their Recipes

After perfecting the pot pie recipe, Andy approached Alvarado Street Bakery, a local organic bakery in Sonoma County, about manufacturing the pot pies. The bakery agreed and launched manufacturing operations inside a building next door to the main bakery.

From the outset, signs indicated that Andy's hunch was spot-on, that Amy's Kitchen filled an *underserved niche*. Andy made the company's first sale while attending a northern California health-food show. "We probably wrote thirty store orders at that show," Andy says.

Under the Berliners' supervision, bakery staff members produced the pies for three months—then gave the couple a thirty-day deadline to make other arrangements. The pot pies were selling, sales orders were flooding in, and the bakery couldn't accommodate the long-term demands of Amy's Kitchen. The bakery staff was already making 2,400 pot pies a day—and that number was bound to climb.

———————◄○►———————

"I had thirty days to find another copacker or to go into production ourselves. I wasn't manufacturing oriented." But he realized he needed to start his own production operation, despite any misgivings.

———————◅◡▻———————

"So I had thirty days to find another copacker or to go into production ourselves," Andy says. "I wasn't manufacturing oriented. It wasn't something that I envisioned doing."

At first, Andy tried to find another manufacturer willing to take the job while adhering to the Berliners' quality standards for organic ingredients. That proved futile. It wasn't long before he realized he needed to start his own production operation, despite any misgivings.

With No Alternative, Do-It-Yourself Production

"With two weeks left on my deadline, we decided to go into production," he recalls. "We started stumbling along, producing our own food. I'd say that was the biggest challenge, just getting started."

Andy wasn't willing to compromise on food ingredients, but the company managed to cut corners in other ways. "Our freezer was a freezing truck at the loading dock," he says. "We would mix the raw materials and freeze things in there." That first year, the company struggled to make payroll for the five employees and to buy and maintain the processing equipment.

Andy Berliner at an early trade show *(Courtesy of Andy and Rachel Berliner)*

In retrospect, Andy says, the bakery's rejection was the best thing that could have happened to Amy's Kitchen "because no one would have gone to the steps that we go through to make our food." By bringing production in-house, the company never had to compromise on quality to appease a business partner. The Berliners maintained full control over quality and all production processes.

Andy resolved to learn all he could about manufacturing frozen foods on a large scale. That required plenty of phone calls. He even called Swanson's headquarters for advice. "I told them who I was and what I was doing," Andy says. "They said, 'Well, this is no competition.' So they talked openly to me about their manufacturing process."

Hand-Selling Products and Trusting Customer Response

During the business's early stages, the Berliners often traveled the country, attending regional health-food trade shows and making sales calls on food distributors. The brand was starting to *get noticed without expensive advertising*. Rachel's father also helped out, making an annual cross-country trip and stopping at small-town health-food stores to make sure they stocked Amy's Kitchen products. During that first year, the company was happy just to break even. "We weren't making money, but we weren't losing money," Andy recalls. "Our sales were growing, and we added a broccoli pot pie, macaroni and cheese, and an apple pie all within fourteen months of starting."

In the Berliner home-kitchen with the first pot pies
(Courtesy of Andy and Rachel Berliner)

The Berliners stayed patient, maintaining their optimism because of the fervid customer response. "We never seemed to have money, but the letters that we got were so appreciative," Andy says. "That kept us going."

―――――――――◄◊►――――――――――

Andy resolved to learn all he could about
manufacturing frozen foods on a large scale. He
even called Swanson's headquarters for advice. "I
told them who I was and what I was doing. They
said, 'Well, this is no competition.' So they talked
openly to me about their manufacturing process."

New Product Development and (Old-Fashioned) Market Research

Over the years, Amy's Kitchen kept adding new meals to its product line—pizzas, burritos, pies, lasagna, veggie burgers, bowls—assembled by hand in the company's 100,000-square-foot plant in Santa Rosa, California. Ideas for new meal offerings often came from customers. "We've never done anything based on market research," Andy says. "In fact, we read all of our consumer letters personally and a lot of ideas, requests, and needs come from them."

As a privately held company, Amy's Kitchen has always had the freedom to try new product offerings without the burden of endless rounds of research and development and market testing. That's not to imply, however, that introducing a new product is easy. The development process can take months. That was the case with the company's rice-crust pizza, for example. A great recipe created in a home kitchen doesn't always translate into an easily mass-produced meal. More often than not, labor-intensive trial-and-error is involved. Also, there are produce-supply considerations. "If we want to create a new product that wasn't planned, we have to see if we can find the ingredients or have [them] grown quickly enough," Andy says. "It helps that we're in California."

―――――――――◄○►―――――――――

During the business's early stages, the Berliners often traveled the country, attending regional health-food trade shows and making sales calls on food distributors. The brand was starting to get noticed without expensive advertising.

―――――――――――――――――――

Growing and Expanding Nationally and Internationally

In its sophomore year, the company had twenty-four employees. But just five years later, Amy's Kitchen had eighty-seven employees and fifteen different products. In 1995, the staff doubled to 175, and Andy was making sales outside of the United States. Finally, all that attention to quality translated into profits—more profits than the Berliners had envisioned. Like so many risk-taking entrepreneurs, they *trusted their gut* instincts (and taste buds) more than they trusted market studies and business-textbook formulas. They discovered a market niche that all the food industry experts had overlooked, and they didn't bail out on the company before it had a chance to succeed.

―――――◄○►―――――

The bakery's decision to stop handling production was the best thing that could have happened. By bringing production in-house, the company maintained full control over quality and all production processes.

―――――◄○►―――――

"We never analyzed it from the point of view of how much do we need to make, and then how much can we spend on the product, but rather we took it from the point of view of how much does it cost to make a good product, and then how can we still do it and make a little money," Andy explains. That approach kept the profit margin at a paper-thin 3 percent but helped generate loyal customers and positive word of mouth.

In time, Andy's sales efforts extended well beyond the network of U.S. health-food stores. He made sales to major supermarkets and to distributors in such countries as the United Kingdom and New Zealand. By the end of 2003, the Berliners knew the time was right for a major expansion in operations. Now offering more than one hundred products, Amy's Kitchen was seeing sales grow at a 20 percent annual rate. Consumer interest in organic foods in general was surging, and Amy's Kitchen was positioned to ride the wave because Andy had *spotted a new trend and pounced.*

―――――◄○►―――――

"We've never done anything based on market research. In fact, we read all of our consumer letters personally, and a lot of ideas, requests, and needs come from them."

―――――◄○►―――――

Rave Media Reviews for Amy's Kitchen

"With a line of nearly 30 products ranging from non-dairy enchiladas to chocolate cake, 110 employees, and national distribution in health food stores and supermarkets, Amy's Kitchen has in the past eight years established itself as a major player in the health food business."
—*Sonoma Independent*, August 22–28, 1996

"The boxes of Amy's Kitchen frozen foods look like other company boxes: a pretty photograph of cannelloni or pizza and back-of-the-box prose about how tasty the food is. The difference is that Amy's really is delicious."
—*Atlanta Journal Constitution*, April 24, 1997

"The first time I heated up an Amy's Kitchen frozen burrito, my kids began circling the table like vultures, asking for a bite here, a bite there. Before I knew it, it was gone. I was thrilled. Nothing pleases a mom more than watching her kids scarf down nutritious food. Delicious, healthy frozen meals? No MSG? No preservatives? Rachel and Andy Berliner . . . have pulled it off. And am I ever glad."
—*Miami Herald*, August 27, 1998

"What is it they say about little acorns and mighty oaks? Whatever it is, it surely applies to . . . Amy's Kitchen. . . . [Nationally syndicated food columnist Carolyn] Wyman, a self-proclaimed junk food fanatic predisposed against both organic and vegetarian items, confessed her attraction: 'Taste is the reason. These are the most flavorful sandwiches I've ever eaten, frozen or not.'"
—*Sonoma County Independent*, March 11, 1999

"Marketing tasty vegetarian dishes has Rachel and Andy Berliner rolling in dough. . . . A hit from the start—six months after the company's inception, its first item, a vegetable pot pie, was outselling meat pies in health food stores nationwide—Amy's is now a $90-million-a-year enterprise commanding 70% of the organic frozen-food market. 'The Berliners are pioneers,' says Mike Gilliland, founder and CEO of the Wild Oats organic-food chain. 'They've made comfort food that's healthy.'"
—*People* magazine, December 18, 2000

"Amy's Pot Pies . . . offer a big mouthful of flavor under a tough whole-wheat crust. Recommended by an editor from *Vegetarian Times*, who called them 'addictive.'"
—*Newsday* (Melville, NY), March 29, 1989

When word spread of the company's expansion plans and the Berliners' frustrations with the spiraling costs of conducting business in California, officials from other states came calling. Amy's Kitchen had a sterling track record as an employer and tax-revenue generator, so there was plenty of reason for other states to try to lure the Berliners away from their home base of California. Ultimately, this Battle for the Great Corporate Citizen had two major competitors: Oregon governor Ted Kulongoski and California governor Arnold Schwarzenegger. Both governors personally made their cases to the Berliners. In the end, Amy's Kitchen opted to keep headquarters in Santa Rosa but build a new $60 million, 176,000-square-foot plant near Medford, Oregon.

Andy and others sit down to test snacks *(Courtesy of Andy and Rachel Berliner)*

The decision to expand operations in Oregon, rather than in California, promised a $4 million savings in energy costs, workers' compensation costs, and other operational expenses. Oregon's Economic and Community Development Department assisted the company with site selection, business financing, infrastructure planning, and workforce training. The state and local governments provided financial incentives worth more than $1 million. When the new facility broke ground in White City, Oregon, Governor Kulongoski joined Andy and Rachel for the ceremony. The plant opened in October 2006.

◄○►

"We never analyzed it from the point of view of how
much do we need to make, and then how much
can we spend on the product, but rather from how
much does it cost to make a good product, and then
how can we still do it and make a little money."

Step inside an Amy's Kitchen plant, and you'll witness hundreds
of employees cooking, preparing, and packing a variety of foods—
garden vegetable lasagna, Mexican casseroles, veggie burgers, and so
on. The aromas are enticing. The operations have a notable human
touch. This isn't an automated food-processing facility controlled by
computers and timers. "When food industry people tour our plant,
their jaws drop because of all the handwork and care that we put into
production," Andy says.

Today's Amy's Kitchen products are carried by major supermarkets like Whole Foods and Safeway, along with warehouse stores such
as Costco and Walmart. "Two out of every three organic meals sold are
Amy's—80 percent of the pizzas and 70 percent of the handheld food,"
Andy says. The brand is also a hit on college campuses. More than five
hundred U.S. colleges carry Amy's Kitchen in on-campus stores.

Continuing to Expand the Product Line

The Berliners have never stopped *reinventing their company*. Amy's
Kitchen continues to expand its line of frozen foods creatively. For
children, the company has rolled out kid-size macaroni-and-cheese
and gluten-free baked-ziti offerings. The brand has also ventured into
the canned soup business, introducing such customer favorites as
black bean vegetable, chunky tomato bisque, and fire-roasted South-
western vegetable. When Andy first suggested the move into canned
soups, a chorus of protests greeted him. "Everybody said, 'No, we
don't know how to do that.' But we tested what's out there, and there
was just so much room for improvement," he says. "I knew we could
do a lot better—and we have."

Again, he *trusted his gut*, despite pleas to stay within the proverbial
comfort zone, and the risk paid off. Without that level of faith in their

own ideas, Andy and Rachel never would have launched the company in the first place. But Andy readily admits he never expected Amy's Kitchen to grow into the major success it has become.

———————◄o►———————

The Berliners have never stopped *reinventing their company*. Amy's Kitchen continues to expand its line of frozen foods creatively. Andy *trusted his gut*, despite pleas to stay within the proverbial comfort zone, and the risk paid off.

———————ᗯᗯ———————

"We thought this was going to be a $3 million business when we started," Andy says. Today, it generates $270 million per year.

Rachel, Amy, and Andy Berliner (*Photo by Jim Morris, Courtesy of the California Farm Bureau Federation*)

One of the company's biggest tasks today is locating and purchasing enough high-quality, organically grown ingredients to make its meals. "Now that organic foods are spreading into the mainstream, it is definitely more challenging, and we have to devote more people and more attention toward it," Andy says. "We've had little dips in the availability of certain raw materials some years. The tomatoes weren't quite as sweet because of weather variations one year. But overall, we have absolutely kept up with the supply and quality."

More Rave Reviews from Happy Customers

"Dear Amy, Just a note to say how much your products improve my quality of life—I'm pregnant and your meals are an easy way to make sure I'm eating something nutritious."

—Abbey

"Dear Amy, I must say the food is very nourishing and filling. Even my kids love it, especially the cheese snacks! The pizza and Indian dishes are totally delicious. There are so many varieties now I don't know what to try next."

—Nita

"Dear Amy, I wanted to drop a note to say THANK YOU for offering products with 'real food' ingredients. It is refreshing to sit down to a 'quick' meal with my family and have everything taste 'homemade' and just like grandma made it! So thank you, Amy's Kitchen staff, for making my life just that much better!"

—Tammy Snyder

"Dear Amy, Thank goodness my campus stocks your frozen burritos and microwave meals in the convenience shop! On days when I don't have anything to pack for lunch, your convenient meals save me from cafeteria fast food! Thanks for creating something so yummy and so healthy!"

—Emma

"Dear Amy, I cannot tell you how amazed I am at the quality of your meals. I eat them every day for two to three meals and I never get tired of them! I am a college student, so I don't have much money or time to spend cooking a full meal all of the time. This way, I get a delicious, wholesome, healthy meal in about five minutes! Thank you so much, Amy's!"

—Randi

"Dear Amy, I wanted to just thank you guys at Amy's for wonderful food. I've thoroughly enjoyed sportin' the Amy's Burrito in my hand at Northwestern College."

—Jordan

While navigating the choppy waters of the food business, Amy's Kitchen has clung to the notion that taste trumps cost, especially in new-product development. Throughout the years, Andy's mission for the company has remained the same: offering healthy, organic convenience meals for consumers who don't always have time to cook. "There's nothing like fresh food, taking the time and cooking for yourself," Andy admits. "But when you don't have time, at least we want people to feel good eating convenience foods."

STRATEGIES FOR SUCCESS

- When vegetarians Andy Berliner and his pregnant wife, Rachel, couldn't find prepackaged frozen meals that were both healthy and tasty, Andy realized he had found an *underserved niche*.

- Having played it too safe with a previous business, Andy decided this time to *trust his gut* and *just start*—even if that meant selling his gold watch, using Rachel's car as collateral, and forging ahead at age forty, just when he had become a first-time father.

- To *exploit the competitors' weakness and make it their company's strength*, he and Rachel decided to make sure all their brand's meals were organic, vegetarian, and tasted great—not bland.

- Demand for their first product, a frozen vegetarian pot pie, climbed to more than 2,400 a day, which overwhelmed the production capacity of their subcontractor. Andy decided to *reinvent his company* and become a manufacturer.

- Andy and Rachel traveled to trade shows and made sales calls in person around the country, building their business through face-to-face meetings and *getting noticed without expensive advertising*.

- *They had spotted a new trend*—organic food—*and pounced*, so their business just kept growing, both in the United States and overseas. And they expanded it. *They trusted their gut*, rather than relying on market research, when expanding their menu with products like kids' sizes and gluten-free items. They *bucked the conventional wisdom* when they added a line of canned soup.

CHAPTER 13

Joe Liemandt (© 2007 *Kirk Tuck, www.kirktuck.com*)

Joe Liemandt

Founder and CEO, Trilogy Inc.

"You have to sort of jump off a cliff
and believe you're going to be able to
overcome whatever that unknown is."

—Joe Liemandt

Back in 1990, nobody would have mistaken Joe Liemandt for an entrepreneurial role model. The young college dropout was flirting with personal bankruptcy, relying on credit card cash advances for all his living expenses. He could have finished his senior year at Stanford

University like his father wanted and earned his economics degree, or he could have looked for a real job. Instead, he was usually found in his cramped apartment, hunched over a computer keyboard and staring intently at the monitor. He was focusing all his energy on developing a sales software system that he and a handful of friends hoped to sell one day to Fortune 500 companies. Never mind that corporate giants like Bell Labs and Hewlett-Packard had already attempted, and thus far failed, to create the kind of system Joe had in mind. In truth, not even Joe's family had faith that his goal was attainable. Nonetheless, he *trusted his gut* that all his hard work would soon make him extremely successful.

> The story of Trilogy illustrates how quickly a pipe-dreaming "loser" can transform into a revered business leader—once all his high-stakes risk taking finally pays off. Joe Liemandt was worth an estimated $500 million before his thirtieth birthday.

Despite the calls to grow up and abandon their overly ambitious plans, Joe and his friends persisted until they finally built what's called a sales configurator. Today, Joe is the CEO and controlling shareholder of the company they founded back in 1989, Trilogy. A private business, Trilogy doesn't release financial information, but the company's market-leading software solutions are ubiquitous in the Fortune 500 realm. Clients include such corporate giants as Ford Motor Company, Nortel Networks, and Xerox. Headquartered in Austin, Texas, Trilogy also has operations in Detroit, Michigan; Bangalore, India; and Hangzhou, China.

Pioneering a New Technology

Just what exactly is a configurator? It's a software system that allows customers to order highly customized products electronically. It can process and manage multiple product lines that feature a range of different options. As a result, clients can easily custom-configure their orders based on their own individual needs.

If you've ever ordered a computer online from a company like Dell or Apple, that experience might make the concept behind product-configuration software easier to grasp and appreciate. Think about the variety of options from which you can choose—memory capacity, colors, software programs, a host of peripherals, and so forth. With the click of a mouse, you can configure your new computer exactly the way you want. Yet the ordering process is surprisingly simple and quick. Pricing information is just a mouse click away. You can instantly add or delete any of the available options. And then days later, that made-to-order computer arrives at your door. Despite all the options, despite all the variables at play, your order is easily placed and processed. That's the value of sales- or product-configuration software.

Trilogy was a pioneer in the development of configurators—a high-tech product category that continues to grow in importance. The story of Trilogy illustrates how quickly a pipe-dreaming "loser" (one hopelessly immersed in algebraic algorithms, no less) can transform into a revered business leader—once all his high-stakes risk taking finally pays off. Joe Liemandt was worth an estimated $500 million before his thirtieth birthday.

"Entrepreneurship . . . is something you need to
do in your career. This is the experience of starting
your own company. The work intensity. A time
that is both the best and the worst of your life."

In October 2005, Joe returned to the Stanford University campus where he had majored in economics fifteen years earlier. While a student there, guest lecturers such as Apple Computer's Steve Jobs, Microsoft's Bill Gates, and Sun Microsystems's Scott McNealy had inspired him to become an entrepreneur. But now, he was the one addressing students at the Terman Auditorium speaker's podium, and his audience wasn't quite sure what to make of his advice. "I am going to try to convince many of you to drop out and start your own company," he said. The audience responded with a smattering of laughter.

"Entrepreneurship, whether you drop out or not, is something you need to do in your career," he continued. "This is the experience of starting your own company. The work intensity. A time that is both the best and the worst of your life."

———————◄◦►———————

"[Configurators] would be worth hundreds of millions of dollars, but no one had ever built one that was any good. Sitting there reading about that, I thought, Wow, this is a big market opportunity."

———————⚭———————

With his boyish looks and casual, rapid-fire speaking style, Joe both engaged and challenged the audience. He seemed to be *daring* the students to take an unthinkable leap of faith—one sure to horrify their parents. Joe peered out at the rows of auditorium seats. Everyone stared back. The students weren't throwing their textbooks into the air and sprinting to an exit to start a new business just yet, so he resumed making his case. "I also would recommend that you do it now because it's the least-risk time, right? Are most of you guys undergraduates? Most are? When you're an undergraduate, you don't have a lot to lose."

That's not entirely true. If you review Joe's entrepreneurial path, you can see he risked losing plenty during Trilogy's protracted launch—the respect and support of family and friends, financial solvency, and a healthy long-term credit rating. But his story is like a cautionary tale in reverse. It's anybody's guess how his life would have turned out if he *hadn't* dropped out of Stanford ten months before graduation to start his own enterprise software business.

Dropping Out of College to Develop a Revolutionary Product

Joe grew up in a family with high expectations. His father, Gregory Liemandt, was a financial wizard. For years, Joe's dad worked as a strategic planner for General Electric CEO Jack Welch. That exposed Joe to the high-pressure world of business and finance—a world that fascinated him even as a child. Lucky for him, his father encouraged that curiosity. "I was learning stretch goals when I was eight years old," Joe says.

Joe also shared his father's interest in computer software. After high school, he decided to attend Stanford University, not just because of its academic standing but also because of its proximity to Silicon Valley—the epicenter of the computer industry and home to so many digital-age entrepreneurs.

For three years, Joe dutifully attended class, maintained his grade point average, and seemed bound for graduation. But all that changed one day in an artificial intelligence/expert systems class. That day, he learned about the potential demand for product- or sales-configuration software. "[Configurators] would be worth hundreds of millions of dollars, but no one had ever built one that was any good," Joe recalls. "Sitting there reading about that, I thought, Wow, this is a big market opportunity."

Most incipient enterprises face a turbulent, uncertain beginning. "There's nothing harder than the start-up stages of a company. Every bad decision you make, you might go out of business."

Previous attempts at developing such a system had all come up short because of the complexities involved. "People had been trying to build configurators since the midseventies," Joe says. "People had tried to build them but hadn't built a good one. We thought we could."

Joe decided to *just start* working on developing a superior configurator that would fill that *underserved niche*. He *trusted his gut* that he and his friends could complete the project within a year if they worked diligently. He was just ten months away from graduation, but otherwise his future after college was a big question mark. If he and his friends developed the configuration engine, they could cash in on a major market opportunity and also create their own high-paying jobs. That promise of ready-made job security helped convince four of his friends—John Lynch, Christina Jones, Chris Porch, and Tom

Carter—to sign on to the project. After Joe's junior year, they spent the whole summer writing computer code.

When the fall quarter started, Joe and John Lynch focused almost entirely on the configurator project and rarely attended classes. Eventually, they decided to drop out of Stanford in order to finish the configurator by their self-imposed deadline. The truth is, Joe chose a path taken by some of the computer industry's most iconic figures. Bill Gates dropped out of Harvard to start Microsoft. Microsoft co-founder Paul Allen dropped out of Washington State University in his sophomore year to work as a programmer for Honeywell—and later convinced Gates to leave Harvard so they could launch Microsoft. Apple Computer's Steve Jobs left Reed College in Portland after just one semester. Oracle's Larry Ellison dropped out of the University of Illinois in his sophomore year, then dropped out again after a quarter at the University of Chicago. Michael Dell dropped out of Texas University to run his own computer business. They all saw a market opportunity and pursued it full speed ahead, without benefit of a college diploma.

One reason a group in their early twenties
succeeded in developing the configurator,
when experienced teams at Bell Labs had
failed, was that they didn't fully understand all
the hurdles they faced at the outset, and they
didn't view the challenge as insurmountable.

Surely, Joe's parents would recognize this Silicon Valley tradition and commend him for his entrepreneurial spirit, right? Joe knew they wouldn't, so he never mentioned his decision to leave school. For months, he managed to finesse his way around the subject like a crafty politician during a congressional hearing. "I don't know what I was thinking because they were going to find out someday. So I *forgot* to tell them," Joe says.

When the spring quarter neared its end, Joe got the inevitable phone call from his proud parents. They wanted to know what time to show up for their son's graduation ceremony. That's when Joe broke the news that they needn't worry about getting seats close to the stage. The conversation quickly turned ugly. His father called him a moron. Joe tried in vain to convince his parents he was on the cusp of developing a groundbreaking product. He was sure he was about to make computer-industry history.

"It didn't work," Joe says. "No amount of enthusiasm would get them excited about that idea."

Rave Reviews for Trilogy Inc. and Joe Liemandt

"Trilogy Development Group has landed on the cover of *Forbes*. . . . [The] seven-page profile . . . examines the six-year-old Austin software company and its founder, Joe Liemandt. The verdict: 'Move over, Bill Gates and Michael Dell, computerdom's newest magnate is just 27. Joe Liemandt is out to change the way we buy and sell things.'"
—*Austin American-Statesman*, May 20, 1996

"28-year-old Austin software mogul Joe Liemandt has moved fast in his young career. He dropped out of Stanford University in 1990 to start a software company before the competition could beat him to it. Liemandt's speed in forming Trilogy Development Group has earned him a spot as the youngest self-made member of the 1996 Forbes 400 list of wealthiest Americans. *Forbes* listed Liemandt's net worth at $500 million, good for No. 333."
—*Austin American-Statesman*, October 1, 1996

"At 29, Mr. Liemandt might be the youngest self-made member of the Forbes 400—and the only one who lives in a rental apartment."
—*New York Times*, November 30, 1997

Graduation ceremonies came and went, and the year-long project remained unfinished. Many of Joe's friends at Stanford left town to tour Europe or start new jobs, while the configurator team continued working fifteen-and sixteen-hour days. However, they were all running out of money. Joe's parents declined their son's pleas for seed money to maintain the company and its research-and-development efforts.

Trilogy needed a quick financial strategy. With little cash for rent, a short-term strategy was bumming off friends. They slept on friends' sofas and converted friends' garages into makeshift apartments.

"This is where having friends is very important," Joe deadpans. "Building networks at Stanford was critically important because we had to have a place to live after we lost student housing, right?"

Trying to Find Money to Finance Their Work

But keeping the project on track required more than just an occasional hot meal and a comfortable couch. So in the early 1990s, the Trilogy team developed a slide-show presentation for venture capitalists and took to the road. The VC road show, however, didn't go well. None of the venture capitalists were all that eager to throw wads of cash at a group of guys barely old enough to drink and with no management experience. During one meeting, a venture capitalist pointed out that Bell Labs had been trying to develop a configurator for years, all for naught.

> "We decided to completely remake our business from what had worked the first ten years because we didn't believe it would work the second ten years. We had built this entire company around technical excellence, and we had to retool it around delivering guaranteed business value."

With few options left, Trilogy adopted the kind of capital-raising strategy that would make Suze Orman break out in hives. "We definitely needed some money," Joe says. "That's when we realized that being a senior at a university was a great thing because at the time—the late eighties and early nineties—there was a new innovation called preapproved credit cards. 'Dear Graduate: You need credit.' We were getting stacks of them."

When they didn't have enough money to cover a card's minimum payment, they got a cash advance on another card. "At the time, back then, the sophistication of credit scoring was nothing," Joe says. "I don't think you could do now what we did then. But we actually had thirty credit cards and were pyramiding them the whole way."

Meanwhile, the team members were making progress on the configuration engine, but they kept encountering more problems than they had anticipated. When friends and family inquired, they responded that the project was three months away from completion. But three months later, the project still wasn't finished.

The one-year project entered its second year—and then its third in 1992. Not only had the configuration engine strained Joe's relationship with his parents, but he was starting to hear from the worried parents of other Trilogy team members: Who was this Joe Liemandt? And why had he lured their children into career suicide with a toxic combination of cryptic computer code and delusions of entrepreneurial grandeur?

Joe tried his best to allay their fears and convince them that Trilogy was on the brink of something great. "Three months away" remained their mantra, but only the Trilogy team members still believed it. Even their friends began to doubt them. The configurator had become almost mythical, the unattainable golden fleece for computer geeks. It was a time of great stress. But, Joe acknowledges, most incipient enterprises face a turbulent, uncertain beginning. "There's nothing harder than the start-up stages of a company," he says. "Every bad decision you make, you might go out of business." But Joe and his team *never let adversity or failure defeat them.*

The Phone Call That Launched Their Business

Then, one Friday in 1992, Joe received a phone call from Silicon Graphics Inc. (SGI). Trilogy had performed a rough demo for the company a couple of weeks earlier. The woman calling was a bit frantic. The company had experienced a major configuration error costing millions of dollars. She needed Trilogy to convince SGI brass that the bleeding could be stopped. An executive meeting was scheduled for Monday.

"But we're not done yet," Joe told her. "We're three months away, not three days."

She responded by issuing a challenge. "She says, 'This is your shot. You've got to make it happen,'" Joe remembers. "So we stayed up all weekend, hard-coding everything in there."

Trilogy already had a set of demo tricks in its arsenal. When the computer crashed during a demo—the outcome roughly 60 percent of the time—that was team member Tom Carter's cue to mutter sheepishly, "Oops, I just pulled the power cord. Sorry. We know you're busy executives. We don't want to waste your time. We'll show your team later on how it works."

"For ten years, we made a lot of money doing stuff
the old way, and it was hard to let go of that. We
tried to have a very smooth transition and get there
incrementally. But one day we just . . . stopped trying
to hold onto the cash flow and the profit margins of
the old business and moved to the new one. Then, all
of a sudden, our progress accelerated to light speed."

After arriving at the meeting, Joe made his usual "three-months-away" disclaimer for the demo. But one of the SGI executives would have none of that. "He said, 'I'm not willing to see a demo. I want to put in real values,'" Joe recounts. With that pronouncement, Joe and the rest of the team braced themselves for some professional humiliation and hoped for the best. The executive typed in the values and clicked "go," and the Trilogy team held its collective breath. But the crash didn't come.

"It worked!" Carter yelled. Heads turned, and Carter turned his enthusiasm down a few notches to mask his incredulity. "Uh, I mean, of course it worked. It works every time."

"When you're doing a start-up, it is so much better to be lucky than right," Joe says in retrospect. "That was a perfect example. We expected it to crash. We expected the whole meeting to go terribly, and we were super lucky."

That sense of triumph was short-lived, however. Trilogy got $100,000 for its SGI work, but the client wouldn't spend any more because of the team's inexperience. Like nearly all Fortune 500 companies, SGI had a policy against hiring start-ups. But about a month later, SGI called back. Trilogy had no real competitors. No other product on the market could deliver what Trilogy's configurator could, so SGI was willing to make an exception to its no-start-ups rule. Joe welcomed SGI back and tripled the price tag to $300,000. The company agreed. Having no competitors has its rewards. "We were, like, holy cow!" Joe says. "We were learning our pricing in real time."

That sale led to an inquiry from Hewlett-Packard, which cut a check for $3 million. Six months later, AT&T called—another $7.5 million. No more credit card debt. No more "three months away." The five Trilogy founders were rich. Their parents were no longer fretful and suspicious.

By 1992, attracting venture capital wasn't a tough sell either, and the company continued to grow. To save costs, Joe moved Trilogy to Austin, Texas. That same year, Trilogy introduced SalesBuilder, a software program for cataloging inventories and reconfiguring product lines to reflect up-to-date pricing. Meanwhile, revenue kept flowing—no, gushing—in.

"In 1994, IBM wrote us a check for $25 million," Joe says. "At the time, that was the most expensive, biggest enterprise software deal done to date."

Creating an Incubator for New Ideas

In 1994 Joe launched Trilogy University, a sort of entrepreneurial boot camp designed to develop Trilogy's future innovators. The company training program *bucks conventional wisdom*. Trilogy recruits a hundred or so overachievers from such esteemed universities as Stanford, Harvard, the Massachusetts Institute of Technology, and the Universities of Pennsylvania and Michigan. Trilogy University is a three-month marathon of caffeine-fueled fifteen-hour (sometimes longer) workdays, including weekends.

The value of Trilogy University is that young talent is free to experiment and challenge convention. During their university term, these young employees are isolated from the rest of the company, protected from the forces of office politics, and unconstrained by established expectations. Joe understands that one reason a group in their early twenties succeeded in developing the configurator, when experienced teams at Bell Labs had failed, was that they didn't fully understand all the hurdles they faced at the outset, and they didn't view the challenge as insurmountable. Trilogy University essentially re-creates the environment in which Trilogy was born.

In 1996, a Trilogy University team developed the company's Selling Chain software, allowing clients to build an automated system that linked all the steps in the entire sales process—from initial customer inquiry to product delivery. Clients could finally create links between disparate sales and marketing functions, and this new capability translated into higher profits.

Restructuring the Company to Meet New Customer Needs

In 2001, Trilogy underwent a major restructuring and downsizing. Major corporations were trimming their technology budgets, and Joe decided Trilogy needed to narrow its focus on core business and the Internet. This was one of the most difficult times in Joe's career. About 340 employees got pink slips. To cut costs, Trilogy moved its computer-programming operations and Trilogy University to Bangalore, India. At Austin headquarters, Trilogy set up a special conference room, named after Garfield the Cat, for videoconferencing between Austin and Bangalore employees.

In 2006, Joe decided to completely *reinvent the company*. Trilogy exited the traditional enterprise software business to focus on delivering strategic, high-growth Internet value services, or vServices. "We decided to completely remake our business from what had worked the first ten years because we didn't believe it would work the second ten years," Joe says. "Basically, we did a complete 180 and changed the strategy to head toward what we thought was a new, better vision. We had built this entire company around technical excellence, and we had to retool it around delivering guaranteed business value."

Trilogy introduced a new business model that tied its own revenue directly to clients' return on investment. In effect, the company chose to guarantee the business value of its software products, taking the risk out of client investment. The new strategy represented a bold departure—and a major risk for Trilogy.

"For ten years, we made a lot of money doing stuff the old way, and it was hard to let go of that," Joe says. "We tried to have a very smooth transition and get there incrementally. But one day we just said, 'You know what? We are done with that business.' And at that moment, we stopped trying to hold onto the cash flow and the profit margins of the old business and moved to the new one. Then, all of a sudden, our progress accelerated to light speed."

―――――――――◄○►―――――――――

"You have to sort of jump off a cliff and believe you're going to be able to overcome whatever that unknown is. . . . No one had ever built [a configurator] before, and everyone told us we couldn't build one. We woke up every day and said, 'We have to be able to do it.' It took us a lot longer than we expected, but we were able to do that."

―――――――――◦―――――――――

Bucking conventional wisdom, Trilogy is paid a prearranged percentage of the business value it delivers to a client. That means Trilogy focuses on providing solutions whose value can be measured monetarily. "In our business model, the only thing that matters is whether or not we put real dollars in our customers' pockets, dollars that they can clearly see on their P&Ls," Joe explains.

Of course, adopting such a payment structure is a risky proposition, one that most companies wouldn't even consider. But Trilogy's success has always relied on high-stakes risk taking.

"You have to sort of jump off a cliff and believe you're going to be able to overcome whatever that unknown is," Joe says. "For us, when we started, no one had ever built [a configurator] before, and everyone told us we couldn't build one. We woke up every day and said, 'We have to be able to do it.' It took us a lot longer than we expected, but we were able to do that."

And the payoff for all that risk taking eclipsed Joe's expectations. It's no wonder he has the gall to tell an auditorium full of college students to take a similar leap of faith while they still have the chance.

∿

STRATEGIES FOR SUCCESS

◆ In a college classroom, Joe Liemandt learned about a potential bonanza: creating a sales configurator for Fortune 500 companies. To date, no one had come up with a good solution, and Joe decided treasure awaited him if he pursued that *underserved niche.*

◆ He decided to recruit other undergraduate partners and *just start.* The group set themselves a deadline to finish their project that eventually conflicted with the demands of schoolwork. Like the others, Joe knew his parents wouldn't approve. But *he trusted his gut* that his focus and determination would pay off, and he dropped out of school to devote himself to his business.

◆ His parents weren't inclined to support him when he failed to get a diploma, and he and his cash-strapped associates nearly wore out the welcome mats at friends' apartments. When they attempted to raise venture capital, they were advised that even Bell Labs had failed to solve the problems they were working on. But Joe and his team *never let adversity or failure defeat them.*

◆ After years of persistence, they finally completed the configurator and all became rich. But ensuring the long-term success of Trilogy became a priority. In 1994, the company *bucked conventional wisdom* and launched Trilogy University, a business boot camp of sorts designed to develop Trilogy's future innovators.

◆ After ten years, Joe decided to completely *reinvent the company,* changing Trilogy's focus from technical excellence to business value. He had *spotted a new trend and pounced on it:* corporate America's greater focus on measuring return on investment. Although this was a big change, Trilogy had always *bucked the conventional wisdom,* and as it turned out, the new model accelerated Joe's company's growth.

CHAPTER 14

Mal Mixon at the Invacare Plant in Elyria, Ohio
(Courtesy of Invacare Corporation)

Mal Mixon

Chairman and CEO, Invacare

"Clearly, you either shy away from
competition or you thrive on it."

—Mal Mixon

Mal Mixon is living proof that it's never too late to slam the brakes
on a ho-hum career to *just start* running your own company, your own
way—even if all you've got in the bank is $10,000. Mal's unbridled
determination overcame the most daunting of financial hurdles, allowing him to build the world's leading manufacturer and distributor

of wheelchairs and home-health-care equipment: Invacare, based in Elyria, Ohio.

Since acquiring Invacare three decades ago at the age of thirty-nine, Mal has led the company to grow its annual sales from $19 million to $1.8 billion. He has also emerged as a committed advocate for both the home-health-care industry and its customers—people of all ages intent on increasing their personal mobility and quality of life. "Our products aren't just about illness," Mal explains. "They're about mainstreaming. Most spinal injuries affect eighteen- to twenty-five-year-olds who have been in accidents. Our vehicles become an important factor in how they feel about themselves, so we pay attention not only to technology but to color and design."

"My father taught me to question everything, to dream of the possibilities in life, and to take intelligent risks."

When we first met Mal, he was holding court in one of his favorite restaurants in Cleveland. While he sipped whisky at a table surrounded by friends and family, he commented on the news of the day—speaking his mind and never mincing words. With his booming voice, hearty laugh, and unfiltered candor, Mal commands a room.

He wears tailored suits these days, and he's a fixture of Cleveland society. In addition to heading Invacare, he's chairman of both the Cleveland Institute of Music and the world-renowned Cleveland Clinic Foundation. But his roots are firmly planted in the rural heartland of his Oklahoma youth. Mal is a larger-than-life leader who never backs down from a challenge and excels under pressure. But surprisingly, his early career in the private sector didn't fully showcase his leadership traits.

Bored with Corporate America and Willing to Take a Chance

Back in 1979, just before he took control of Invacare, Mal was a thirty-nine-year-old vice president of marketing for a Cleveland firm that sold medical diagnostic equipment. He was in a career rut. He saw little room for advancement and felt stifled by corporate politics. Having recently battled testicular cancer, Mal felt he had a new lease on life that he wasn't about to take for granted. *Trusting his gut*, he decided it was time to walk away from his job and control his own destiny by running his own company. That's when he set his sights on Invacare, a locally based wheelchair firm. It was a surprising decision, considering that Mal had only $10,000 in personal savings. But he spearheaded a leveraged buyout that provided a glimpse into his take-no-prisoners approach to running a business. "I didn't hold anything back," Mal says.

Looking back, Mal admits that what stirred him to take that plunge into entrepreneurship wasn't so much a belief in Invacare's market potential. Rather, he knew in his gut his own potential as a business leader. If the Invacare deal had fallen through, Mal no doubt would have found another company to take to the top.

------------------◄◦►------------------

He was in a career rut. He saw little room for advancement and felt stifled by corporate politics. Having recently battled testicular cancer, Mal felt he had a new lease on life that he wasn't about to take for granted. *Trusting his gut*, he decided it was time to walk away from his job and control his own destiny by running his own company.

Early Emphasis on Education, Competition, and Risk Taking

Mal may be a Harvard Business School alumnus, but his upbringing in small-town Oklahoma and his service in the marines have figured more prominently in his development as a leader. He grew up in Spiro, Oklahoma, population 1,200, a farming town near the Arkansas River that was home to four generations of Mixons. His late father, Aaron Mixon Jr., worked as a career salesman and remains Mal's role model.

"There, my father taught me to question everything, to dream of the possibilities in life, and to take intelligent risks," Mal says. Spiro engendered its residents with a strong sense of identity and purpose. "Whether it was sports, education, music, or summer jobs, you always felt like you were part of something important in Spiro," Mal says. The Mixon family wasn't wealthy, but Mal's father made a decent living. His mother worked as a secretary to the commanding general of a nearby army base.

In Vietnam Mal became a tested leader and proved his mettle under pressure. "I learned more about leadership in the Marine Corps than I ever learned in Harvard Business School." He learned firsthand the importance of team building.

Though neither of Mal's parents had attended college, his father loved to read and often challenged Mal with brain-teasing games and puzzles to sharpen his language skills. "I remember as a child he used to give me ten difficult words to use in sentences and he paid me ten cents a word," Mal recounts. "So I got a whole dollar bill if I took each of the words and used them in ten different sentences."

Mal excelled in school, earning mostly As, but he also found time to play football, basketball, and baseball in high school. His father instilled in him a competitive drive that would later define his business career. When Mal was a sophomore in high school, his father told him he would cease picking Mal up from school until he made the varsity basketball team's starting lineup—meaning Mal had to walk a mile and a half home during Oklahoma's windy, chilly fall days. Aaron Mixon's extra incentive worked: Mal's commitment and focus as a player sharpened. By the second game of the season, he was a starter, and his dad had resumed the car rides home. In his senior year, Mal helped lead Spiro High School to the Oklahoma state semifinals in both basketball and football.

Weekends were often devoted to music—an interest that nurtured Mal's creativity. His parents "used to drive [him] to Fort Smith,

Arkansas, every Saturday to get a piano, voice, and trumpet lesson," Mal says.

Growing up in a deeply patriotic family—Mal's father had served proudly during World War II—Mal dreamed of someday attending the Naval Academy. But when he applied, he just barely missed the cut in 1958, though he was given the principal appointment for 1959. This would have required him to attend another school for a year before admission to the Naval Academy. Mal didn't know until later that his father had secretly applied for him to attend Harvard College. "Lo and behold, I was accepted at Harvard," Mal says. "I remember going out to see the superintendent of schools because I had to take the college boards and he had never heard of them. So I was the first student ever to take the college boards from my high school."

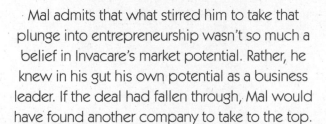

Mal admits that what stirred him to take that plunge into entrepreneurship wasn't so much a belief in Invacare's market potential. Rather, he knew in his gut his own potential as a business leader. If the deal had fallen through, Mal would have found another company to take to the top.

When Mal arrived at Harvard, however, he found himself at a disadvantage. At first, he struggled to keep pace with students who were accustomed to a more rigorous academic regimen than Spiro had to offer. "I remember calling my dad and saying, 'Dad, I'm in deep trouble. I just sat through a French class taught in French and didn't understand a word.' So I had a lot of catch-up to do," Mal says. "But through the process, I learned I could compete."

Learning About Leadership in the Marines and Vietnam

While a student at Harvard, Mal joined the Naval Reserve Officer Training Corps. After college graduation, he joined the marines and trained as an artillery officer. In 1965, just as American involvement in the war was growing more intense, he shipped off to Vietnam. His responsibilities required split-second decision making in life-and-death situations: leading a fire direction center on the ground, spotting enemy positions from a light observation aircraft, and calling in air strikes and artillery fire, among them. By the time Mal returned home, he had earned several Air Medals and a citation honoring his "exceptionally valorous actions" in combat. In Vietnam Mal became a tested leader and proved his mettle under pressure. "I learned more about leadership in the Marine Corps than I ever learned in Harvard Business School," he says.

Mal Mixon in the U.S. Marine Corp.
(Courtesy of A. Malachi Mixon, III)

In particular, he learned firsthand the importance of team building and the mutual pursuit of excellence. "Every marine who finishes officer training or boot camp knows the price of excellence," he explains. "In sixteen weeks, you are taught that you are the very best—the

―――――――――――◄○►―――――――――――

"I felt I was ready to run a company, and [Invacare]
just happened to be the one I found. I felt I was
ready, and my current employer was not ready
to give me a division or company to run."

―――――――――――▽―――――――――――

Mal Mixon while serving in Vietnam
(Courtesy of A. Malachi Mixon, III)

benchmark against which other military units are measured. You are also taught that the only way to remain the best is to keep working to be better."

While still stationed in Vietnam, Mal began planning for his future and dreamed about an eventual career in business. "I typed out my application to Harvard Business School in a tent in Chu Lai, South Vietnam," he recalls. And he was accepted.

Ready to Run His Own Company, via an LBO

After earning his MBA from Harvard, he and his family then relocated to Cleveland. Eventually, he found himself working as a vice president for Technicare, a medical equipment company. It was a career path in which he excelled but never quite reached his potential as a business leader. Mal's experience in the military, at Harvard, and in the business world had taught him that he thrived in a competitive environment and was a proven leader under pressure. But his job at the time didn't challenge him in the way he desired. So finally, after eleven years in the industry, he decided to purchase Invacare.

"You may find this strange, but I felt I was ready to run a company, and [Invacare] just happened to be the one that I found," Mal recalls. "I felt I was ready, and my current employer was not ready to give me a division or company to run. I talked to my wife and said, 'You know, honey, I'd like to have a little piece of the rock, and here's an opportunity, I think.'"

———————◄o►———————

He talked to the company's customers—home
medical equipment providers—and to the
wheelchair consumers themselves to find ways to
prop up customer satisfaction and market share.

———————ꕥ———————

Once he'd made up his mind, Mal doggedly pursued the financing to acquire Invacare, which carried a $7.8 million price tag. He borrowed $40,000 from two friends and signed a $100,000 note from Invacare. He convinced two real estate brokers to buy Invacare's building for $2 million and lease it back to the company. Mal rustled up a group of investors who purchased common and preferred stock, and Mal also signed a personal guarantee on a $4.3 million bank loan. He ended up owning 15 percent of the million dollars in common stock after investing $150,000 into the company—all except $10,000 of which he had borrowed.

Listening to Customers and Building a Stronger Sales Team

Once at the helm, Mal wasted no time lifting employee expectations and remaking the company culture. He talked to the company's customers—home medical equipment providers—and to the wheelchair consumers themselves to find ways to prop up customer satisfaction and market share. He replaced sixteen members of the eighteen-person sales team and then raised the pay scale. He instinctively knew that the team's annual sales average of $1 million per salesperson fell well shy of the ideal target. He needed to assemble his own sales team, recruiting ambitious sales professionals who thrived in a competitive, pressure-cooker environment.

Mal recognized that his sales managers needed enough drive to challenge and ultimately beat Invacare's principal competitor, Everest & Jennings—the wheelchair market leader at that time. Mal sought sales professionals who relished taking risks, brought a sense of passion to their work, and could establish a rapport with clients. He aimed to build the most talented, committed, and best-paid sales team in the industry, bar none—a goal he achieved.

———————————◀○▶———————————

Mal sought sales professionals who relished taking risks, brought a sense of passion to their work, and could establish a rapport with clients. His goal was to build the most talented, committed, and best-paid sales team in the industry.

———————————〜〜〜———————————

"The company had been undermanaged," Mal explains. "I was able to reduce days' receivables, reduce inventories. I got a 5 percent price increase to stick, and we grew the company from about $19 million to $25 million the first year." Though the company was highly leveraged, Invacare managed to generate a $1.4 million pre-tax profit that year.

Mal studied the company's product line and discontinued obsolete or unprofitable products. He also wasted little time in *exploiting his competitors' weakness*—delivery times—*and making that his company's strength*. Mal recognized that when personal mobility is at stake, providers and their customers want a quick turnaround. Mal *bucked conventional wisdom* and expanded his company's warehousing system across the country to speed deliveries to only one day after order placement.

Thriving on Competition and Outsmarting Rivals

At the time Mal took over Invacare, industry leader Everest & Jennings generated annual sales of $124 million and controlled 80 percent of the world's wheelchair market. However, Mal felt confident

Rave Reviews for Invacare

"Invacare is a world leader in the market for medical equipment used in the home and has a well-deserved reputation for innovative products. I am particularly grateful for the opportunity to become associated with a company that devotes so many resources to improving the lives of our nation's disabled veterans."

—Gen. James L. Jones, U.S. Marine Corps (ret.), at the time of his appointment to the Invacare Board of Directors in March 2007. (Jones was previously supreme allied commander of NATO and commander of the U.S. European Command.)

"Overall, I am more than satisfied with the quality, durability, design, and performance of this machine [Invacare XLT Pro hand cycle]. It is an excellent machine for everyone, from the newly injured to the seasoned veterans, and I couldn't agree more with what they say in the bike's promotional material, and that is: 'If you want a great way to exercise, cross-train, or just have fun, the Invacare Top End Excelerator XLT PRO is what you're looking for!'"

—Matt Strugar-Fritsch, a paraplegic athlete writing for AccessAnything.net, August 16, 2007

Invacare could ultimately outsmart and outinnovate them. He gave his company's underutilized engineering department the resources it needed to develop new, cutting-edge wheelchairs and other home-health-care products. "We had engineers at the company who weren't doing anything," Mal recalls. "They were just sitting around waiting for someone to tell them what to do."

"The company had been undermanaged. I was able to reduce days' receivables, reduce inventories. I got a 5 percent price increase to stick, and we grew the company from about $19 million to $25 million the first year."

Expanding the company's home-health-care product line became a priority. A competitor's gravitas helped ignite that effort. "A week after I bought Invacare, I got a call from a guy with the number one market share in beds," Mal recalls. "He wanted to buy Invacare. He said, 'If you don't sell to us, we'll go into the wheelchair business.' He was showing me how wheelchairs fit into his business. What he was also showing me was how beds fit into my business." As a result, Mal *reinvented Invacare* by adding beds and bedside equipment to its profitable line. Eventually, Invacare put that company out of business and became the market leader in home-care beds.

―――――――――◄○►―――――――――

He also wasted little time in *exploiting his competitors' weakness*—delivery times—*and making that his company's strength.* Mal recognized that when personal mobility is at stake, providers and their customers want a quick turnaround.

―――――――――∽∾―――――――――

Mal wasn't finished *bucking conventional wisdom* and *reinventing his company* either. He launched a series of initiatives to make Invacare more attractive to home-health-care providers. Over time, that included offering financing options, volume discounts, cooperative advertising funds, and prepaid freight. Also, Invacare's improved warehousing and distribution network meant that customers always had quick and easy access to Invacare products; the company didn't have to buy in volume and maintain large inventories to keep its customers happy. Of course, that improved client cash flow—a major selling point.

Mal's management style ignited a competitive drive that had been lacking in Invacare. He admits that having competition has always pushed him harder. "Clearly, you either shy away from competition or you thrive on it," he explains. "I've always loved competition and excellence. I've always said, 'Show me a good loser, and I'll show you a loser.' I don't always come in first, but I sure as heck try to get there."

New Ideas for New Products

In 1982, Mal's focus on product development paid off when Invacare introduced a motorized wheelchair with programmable microprocessing controls—an industry first—that made it easier for the disabled to operate and maneuver their chairs. This product rollout signaled that Invacare had become a serious challenger to Everest & Jennings, and that company took notice. "The day I introduced my first motorized wheelchair, they cut prices on standard wheelchairs about 15 percent, trying to run me out of business," Mal recalls. "It didn't work."

◄○►

He expanded his company's warehousing
system across the country to speed deliveries
to only one day after order placement.

Mal continued to fund product development, and Invacare expanded its line with popular items like titanium wheelchairs and oxygen concentrators. Such innovations continued to fuel company growth and fill *underserved niches*. In 1984, Mal decided to take the company public and also began servicing the European market. Invacare acquired two European wheelchair manufacturers that year.

Mal and his family and friends celebrate Invacare's listing on the New York Stock Exchange by ringing the opening bell *(Courtesy of Invacare Corporation)*

Overcoming Setbacks

In 1984 Mal also confronted a series of mishaps that threatened his company's future. During start-up of a new factory, an error in inventory documentation took a heavy toll on annual earnings. What's more, manufacturing defects in Invacare's oxygen concentrator forced a product recall. And if all that wasn't enough, the following year the U.S. government changed its formulas for Medicare reimbursement—a policy shift that threatened Invacare's profitability. Facing this wave of adversity, Mal rose to the challenge and acted decisively. He *never let adversity defeat him.*

"I got a call from a guy with the number one
market share in beds. He wanted to buy Invacare.
He said, 'If you don't sell to us, we'll go into the
wheelchair business.' He was showing me how
wheelchairs fit into his business. What he was also
showing me was how beds fit into *my* business."

He responded to the recall by hiring a quality-control specialist to pinpoint weaknesses in the manufacturing process. He also began requiring the sales force to submit monthly reports detailing customer complaints about any Invacare product. Using the information culled from those two efforts, the company corrected its quality problems. Invacare also began sending out representatives to inspect suppliers' plants. Mal's commitment to quality was so great that he even authorized the company to purchase some equipment that duplicated NASA precision-testing procedures. The equipment was used to test the electronic control systems on Invacare's motorized wheelchairs. NASA had previously used the same equipment to test controls on the space shuttles.

Mal also helped organize industry lobbying efforts to educate Washington legislators about the home-health-care field and successfully pushed for reform legislation to resolve some of the Medicare reimbursement issues. He remains active in politics today, advocating for his industry and people who rely on Invacare wheelchairs and home-health-care products.

The year 1986 brought a new challenge. Manufacturers in Taiwan began selling their wheelchairs in the United States at a price about 20 percent below the prevailing price. "It scared the hell out of us, but we decided we were going to meet them head-on," Mal remembers. He opened an additional manufacturing plant in Reynosa, Mexico, to cut production costs and thwarted Taiwanese efforts to gain a foothold in the U.S. wheelchair market. "We were able to adjust our pricing, and they never really landed on the beach here," Mal says. "They made no infrastructure investments and were shipping products through distributors." But that short-lived threat foreshadowed future competition from China in the 2000s.

Phenomenal Growth and Expansion

In 1986, the company's profits reached $3.4 million on revenues of $111 million. Invacare was the undisputed industry leader. The early 1990s ushered in a period of phenomenal growth. In 1990, the company introduced fifty-three new products. Invacare produced the broadest line of home-health-care products on the market, distributed by more than 10,000 providers throughout the world. Invacare also became an innovator in wheelchairs for paraplegic athletes (another *underserved niche*), creating more flexible wheelchairs using lighter composite materials.

Throughout the 1990s, the company's expansion plans included pursuing tactical and strategic acquisitions, both in the United States and abroad. Among them was the purchase of Denmark-based Scandinavian Mobility International, one of the largest European manufacturers of bed systems and mobility products for the home- and institutional-health-care markets.

Exploring Other Business Ventures and Giving Back

By 2000, Mal had overseen the acquisition of thirty-five companies since taking the helm of Invacare. Earnings in 2000 were a record $59.9 million. The following year, Invacare hired legendary golfer Arnold Palmer to act as a company spokesman and introduce a new company tagline, "Yes, we can," which reflected the can-do attitude

of the disabled people who use Invacare's products. It also reflected
Mal's willingness to *buck conventional wisdom* and reshape the home-
health-care industry.

"Our best idea was to identify the home-care market perhaps before anyone else did and to put all these product lines together into
one force," Mal says. "When I entered this industry, there were a lot of
one-product companies out there: a wheelchair company, a bed company, a patient-aid company, an oxygen company. We were the first
ones to envision putting all those under one umbrella, bringing them
together under one sales force, delivering them all at one time."

Throughout the years, Mal has pushed Invacare to new heights
through entrepreneurial risk taking. The company today offers more
than two hundred products sold around the world—customized and
computerized wheelchairs, ambulatory aids, respiratory devices, oxygen systems, and much more. Under Mal's direction, Invacare has
continued *to reinvent itself* and its industry—developing new products,
identifying and serving new niches, and advocating for the rights of
Invacare product users. For years, Mal lobbied for the passage of legislation like the Americans with Disabilities Act, and he has been an
ardent supporter of the Wheelchair Games sponsored by the Department of Veterans Affairs and the Paralyzed Veterans of America.

———————————◄◦►———————————

"Clearly, you either shy away from competition or
you thrive on it. I've always loved competition and
excellence. I've always said, 'Show me a good
loser, and I'll show you a loser.' I don't always
come in first, but I sure as heck try to get there."

———————————◊———————————

Invacare has established itself as a global leader in products for
paraplegic athletes. At the 2008 Paralympics in Beijing, China, athletes using Invacare Top End sports wheelchairs and hand cycles
brought home more than 122 medals, 50 of which were gold.

In addition, Mal has long served as an advocate and role model
for aspiring entrepreneurs. In the early 1980s, he helped a friend purchase Royal Appliance, the maker of the Dirt Devil vacuum cleaner.

"After cashing out on that IPO, I became involved in some venture capital projects and launched my own LBO firm, MCM Capital, which has bought and sold some forty companies," Mal says.

Mal also spearheaded development of the Minorities with Vision Pinnacle Capital Fund, the largest private equity fund in Ohio that invests in promising minority-owned businesses. Mal raised $24 million among private investors and personally invested the first $1 million in the fund. He is also active on the President's Council in Cleveland, a group promoting entrepreneurial and economic development within the African American community. "My focus has been to create more capital for African American businesses, which eventually will create more African American wealth to give back to the community," Mal says.

"Our best idea was to identify the home-care market perhaps before anyone else. . . . There were a lot of one-product companies out there: a wheelchair company, a bed company, a patient-aid company, an oxygen company. We were the first ones to envision putting all those under one umbrella, bringing them together under one sales force, delivering them all at one time."

Meanwhile, Mal continues to confront a range of new challenges as CEO of Invacare. In recent years, the company has faced stiff competition from lower-priced Chinese imports—a reality that spurred Mal to shift some manufacturing operations to China and open a purchasing office in Hong Kong to cut costs. Operating from the Hong Kong office, Invacare can make purchases out of China, Hong Kong, Vietnam, India, and Taiwan. "It's an incredible office and runs like a Swiss watch," Mal says. "In 2008, we'll probably buy $300 million in parts and components that we ship to all our factories around the world. Our factories have become assembly operations as opposed to integrated manufacturing operations. And we've probably saved 20 to 25 percent on those purchases."

The company's potential customer base keeps expanding as baby boomers age. In 2004, U.S. government data indicated there were about 36 million Americans over the age of sixty-five. "That's the last official government data that we have," Mal notes. "It is projected to grow to 72 million by 2030." And that's just talking about the United States. Today, Invacare markets in eighty countries. "Worldwide, we've got a 23 to 25 percent market share," Mal says. "We should grow it to 50 percent in the next ten years."

Now that Mal is in his late sixties, some wonder why he hasn't sold the company yet. Despite his thirty-year tenure as CEO, he insists he still has no immediate plans to place Invacare on the block. "I could have sold out anywhere along the line, except I still believe we're building an incredible company," Mal explains with a smile. "I like being the acquiring company rather than being the acquired company. We're one of the largest medical device companies in the world, we're growing stronger, and we're still having a lot of fun."

༄

STRATEGIES FOR SUCCESS

◆ The challenges of competing at Harvard, where he initially felt out of his league, and serving his country in battle in Vietnam taught Mal Mixon *not to let adversity or fear defeat him.* He also learned to lead.

◆ Dissatisfied with his career after a bout with cancer, he decided it was time to *just start* running his own company. Certain he had the potential for great success, he *trusted his gut* and took the next opportunity that came along: A wheelchair manufacturer was for sale. Starting on a shoestring, he made the deal happen.

◆ Then he set about invigorating the company. Initially, he focused on *exploiting his competitors' weakness and made it his strength:* Aware that immobilized customers want quick delivery, he promised to fulfill orders within a single day. He accomplished this by expanding the company's warehousing system.

◆ He *bucked conventional wisdom* by bringing the full spectrum of home-care products under one brand and one sales force. In addition, he offered retailers more financing options and other incentives, such as volume discounts and co-op advertising funds.

◆ When a product recall and Medicare reimbursement cutbacks dealt blows to the company, again he *didn't let adversity defeat him.* Instead, he instituted better quality control and helped bring about legislation that resolved some of the issues. Subsequently, he dealt successfully with competition from overseas manufacturers.

◆ Mal continues to *reinvent his company,* introducing new products that reflect technological innovations. Some products, such as paraplegic athletic equipment, also target additional *underserved niches.* Today, Invacare offers more than two hundred products, including specialized beds and oxygen systems.

CHAPTER 15

Tova Borgnine *(Photo by Davis Factor)*

Tova Borgnine

Founder, Tova Corporation

"I had learned the valuable lesson that you
didn't have to slavishly follow tradition."

—Tova Borgnine

Talk about *bucking conventional wisdom.* How can you explain Tova
Borgnine's decision to sell her company's flagship product, Tova Signature fragrance, on cable television's QVC channel? On the surface,
it makes as much sense as trying to sell a woman a new pair of shoes
she's never even seen, much less tried on. Sure, fragrances are often

advertised on television, in hopes of luring consumers to the local shopping mall to sample the scent and then plop down their credit card. But *selling* a fragrance directly on TV is an entirely different matter. There's no such thing as a scratch-and-sniff scent-a-vision. Viewers' olfactory discretion isn't a factor; first-time sales are made on a viewer's leap of faith and the convenience of a toll-free number.

But sales numbers prove Tova is a savvy risk-taking entrepreneur, however counterintuitive her strategies may seem. Tova Signature fragrance has sold an astonishing 10 million bottles, and Tova Borgnine is viewed as a direct-marketing pioneer in the $5 billion fragrance industry. In 1999—twelve years after her first appearance on QVC—she sold her Tova brand to the cable TV network for an eight-figure price. She remains involved in all the brand's major decisions and continues to make appearances on QVC.

Tova Borgnine markets her signature fragrance *(Photo by Gordon Munro)*

So how do you explain all this? It's easier to understand once you've seen Tova Borgnine at work in front of the television cameras. The picture of Beverly Hills–style beauty, glamour, and sophistication, she looks every bit the former model she is, with her perfectly styled auburn hair and creamy complexion. During a Christmas season appearance, she sits on a sofa in an elegant living room–style studio set, addressing the camera like she's sharing beauty secrets with a group of her dearest friends. As she's done countless times before, she sings the praises of Tova Signature fragrance. "It's soft and sensual and clean," she says. "Men *love* it because it's like you just stepped out of a spring shower."

Tova Signature fragrance has sold an astonishing 10 million bottles, and Tova Borgnine is viewed as a direct-marketing pioneer in the $5 billion fragrance industry. In 1999—twelve years after her first appearance on QVC—she sold her Tova brand to the cable TV network for an eight-figure price.

And then viewer after viewer calls into the show to share stories on air about the compliments she's garnered while wearing Tova fragrances. One recalls the time she was waiting in line at a bagel shop when a stranger came up to tell her how good she smelled. Another caller remembers the time she was in an elevator and a man she didn't know asked her what perfume she was wearing so he could buy it for his wife. Tova's eyes light up. "That's why I keep doing this!" she responds.

A Unique American Success Story

The success of Tova Signature fragrance, as well as the scores of other Tova beauty products sold on QVC, is inextricably tied to the larger-than-life personality of the brand's founder, Tova Borgnine. Through television, she has found a way to build a rapport with millions of customers. It's not a one-way relationship either; she talks to them during her live on-air appearances. Tova represents classic Hollywood glamour—she's even married to actor Ernest Borgnine, although she was already running her own business before she met him—and many of her customers admire her and want to be just like her.

Tova's story underscores how powerful electronic media can be in establishing a loyal customer base and generating large-scale word of mouth. Early in the game, she *spotted a trend*—direct marketing over cable TV—*and pounced*, giving her a decided advantage over competitors. She also *hit 'em where they ain't*—she made it possible for women to shop for high-quality fragrances and beauty products without ever leaving home. And over the years, Tova never stopped *reinventing her company*, continually introducing new fragrances, skin creams, and other beauty products.

> "Despite their toned dancers' physiques, many of the girls were ruining their skin with pore-clogging pancake makeup worn under hot lights, compounded by poor diet and erratic sleep. I seized the opportunity to service their needs."

Her longtime career in the beauty industry took many twists and turns and suffered a few setbacks. But all those experiences equipped Tova to make her company, Tova Corporation, succeed on a massive scale. It's a classic American business success story that actually begins in Oslo, Norway. The breakup of her parents' marriage after the end of World War II, when she was just seven years old, spurred Tova's journey to the United States. "My parents' marriage was one of the many casualties of a war that had devastated Norway and our beloved Oslo," Tova recalls. "Cruel as it now seems, I was given the choice of remaining in Oslo, to be raised by my father's family, safe in the bosom of familiar friends and surroundings, or to venture off to a far-away land with my mother where I could have bubblegum every day. There was no way I could ever leave my mother's side, but I adored my father and was heartbroken over my choice."

Tova and her mother arrived in New York with just $70. Tova's mother, who had previously held a prestigious job at the American

Embassy in Oslo for years, was forced to take a job as a live-in house-keeper. In those early days, before Tova learned to speak English, she felt especially alienated. "My ignorance of the English language left me isolated and lonely, unable to express even my most basic thoughts," she says. She spent her childhood living in the home of her mother's employer, often longing for her idealized life back in Oslo. But that lonely childhood fueled an ambition that surfaced in her young adulthood.

Making a 180-Degree Turn—from Modeling to Behind the Scenes

For a while, she tried fashion modeling and acting in New York City. During that time, however, she made a surprising discovery: She found the work of the makeup artists more fascinating than her own work in front of the cameras. Eager to learn all she could about the trade, she took her acting coach's advice and began working as an assistant to several makeup artists based at the Makeup Center in New York City. "I had recognized my true calling for the cosmetic arts," Tova explains. "Finally, I had found something that gave me a true sense of fulfillment."

After marrying, Tova opened up a small makeup boutique, dubbed Tova's Touch, in Sea Gert, New Jersey, to pursue her passion for cosmetics. It was the mid-1960s, and female entrepreneurs were still a rarity. In fact, her own husband wasn't really sold on the idea and merely tolerated this business pursuit, dismissing it as a hobby. She ran the shop for four years. When the marriage ultimately failed, Tova sold the business and left for the neon lights of Las Vegas.

Tova was convinced she could make a career out of providing quality cosmetics to the casino showgirls who performed on the Las Vegas Strip. Too many of the performers knew little about skin care and nutrition—and the effect the wrong cosmetics and lifestyle can have on the aging process. Tova was intent on remedying that. "Despite their toned dancers' physiques, many of the girls were ruining their skin with pore-clogging pancake makeup worn under hot lights, compounded by poor diet and erratic sleep," Tova recalls. "They couldn't get hold of high-quality cosmetics in the rough-and-tumble desert, and now that I was single again, I seized the opportunity to service their needs."

————————<o>————————

Merle Oberon showed Tova a jar of the special
skin cream from Mexico that she credited for her
luminous look. Tova set out to locate the maker
of that skin cream. She *trusted her gut* that the
formula could be a big seller in the United States.

————————⬃⬂————————

Tova opened two small makeup concessions in the beauty salons
at Caesar's Palace and the International Hotel (now the Hilton) and
gradually built a clientele. While operating her business, she became
friends with a number of celebrities, including comedian Marty Allen
and actress Merle Oberon. As fate would have it, Marty and Merle
would eventually play pivotal roles in Tova's life—roles that she could
never have anticipated. It was Marty Allen and his wife, Frenchie, who
arranged a blind date for Tova with actor Ernest Borgnine. At the
time, Ernest was going through a bitter divorce from his fourth wife.
Like Tova, he was nursing a broken heart. "We dined at the much
missed Chasen's restaurant in Beverly Hills," Tova says of that first
date. "That two battered hearts would soon fall deeply in love defied
all odds." The two eventually married and, more than thirty-five years
later, are still together. Ernest would prove to be Tova's leading business supporter.

Tova and Ernest Borgnine, New Year's Eve *(Courtesy of Tova Borgnine)*

Creating a New Product from a Special Ingredient

Merle Oberon, an Oscar-nominated film actress who began her career in the 1930s, was also one of Tova's clients in Las Vegas. The actress was known for her radiant skin, which belied her true age. When Tova inquired about her skin-care regimen, Oberon kept mum. She wouldn't give away her secret. But over time, Tova began to gain her client's trust and friendship. Finally, one day in 1972, Oberon showed Tova a jar of the special skin cream from Mexico she credited for her luminous look. The cream contained elements derived from desert cacti, a natural botanical antioxidant. Despite Tova's pleas, Oberon wouldn't reveal the source of the cream, but Tova's curiosity was piqued. Like a hard-nosed detective obsessed with solving a mystery, Tova set out to locate the maker of that skin cream from Mexico. Her husband, Ernest, was a willing accomplice. They both *trusted her gut* that the formula could be a big seller in the United States.

> "I was sure that there was great potential with the
> products, and I dreamed of selling them in all of
> the major department stores. I quietly distributed
> samples to our friends in Beverly Hills, certain
> that would create enough of a buzz that Saks
> Fifth Avenue would beat a path to my door."

"Whenever my husband had a break during on-location film shoots south of the border, I dragged Ernie halfway across Mexico in search of a supplier," Tova says. "I finally located a family that still prepared the cactus extract in the ancient, traditional way, bought the rights, and trademarked Cactine."

Now that the formula was in her hands, Tova set out to make improvements and develop new applications. Her natural curiosity made such tinkering and experimentation unavoidable. Tova knew she was on to something special, and she wasn't about to squander a promising opportunity.

"I began to experiment with my own homemade creams, a facial toner, and an invigorating, clay-free Cactine masque," Tova says.

> When Tova told the family members she
> needed them to produce two tons of masque
> formula in twelve days, they promptly started
> to walk out of the meeting. Tova grabbed a
> handful of $100 bills and tossed them down
> on the table. That needed no translation.

"I was sure that there was great potential with the products, and I dreamed of selling them in all of the major department stores. I quietly distributed samples to our friends in Beverly Hills, certain that would create enough of a buzz that Saks Fifth Avenue would beat a path to my door."

Great Word-of-Mouth Marketing and Publicity Led to a Distribution Challenge

Saks Fifth Avenue didn't come calling, but within just a couple of years, word spread in Hollywood circles about Tova's skin-rejuvenating masque. Celebrity friends of the Borgnines, including Anne Bancroft and Ali MacGraw, became regular clients. Meanwhile, Ernest continued to encourage and champion Tova's efforts. During an interview with a reporter from the *San Francisco Examiner,* when asked how he managed to look so young, Ernie credited his wife's miraculous antiaging masque used by him and his famous friends. To their surprise, the reporter wrote about Tova's "facelift in a jar." The story spread through the wire services to newspapers across the country. Tova was shocked when she went to the post office one day to retrieve her husband's fan mail and was greeted with thousands of letters addressed to her. Each one contained a check and an order for Tova's beauty potion.

Saks Fifth Avenue might not have been interested in Tova's beauty products, but plenty of consumers were. Faced with a mountain of orders, Tova scrambled to enlist the help of friends and family to fill them.

"Imagine the situation I found myself in," Tova says. "I had $56,000 of other people's money sent in by trusting souls from all across the country who believed in my husband's testimonial to a product that didn't even exist. At the very least, I was facing possible federal prosecution for mail fraud if I failed to deliver a product within thirty days. I knew that this was an extraordinary opportunity, but was I ready to take the risk?"

Rave Reviews for Tova's Products from Delighted Customers

"When Margaret from Pennsylvania confided shyly, on a live phone-in, that she had been wearing Tova's perfume the previous evening and she and her husband had had, well, a bit of a 'Tova Night,' Tova was so delighted she used the phrase for the name of her next perfume, a deeper, stronger version of the original."
—*Evening Standard* (London), January 22, 1999

"My skin loves them!"
—Jessica Walter

"Tova 9 has a fresh just-showered feeling!"
—Connie Stevens

"I have not had a face lift. The only reason I look younger today than I did ten years ago is because of what my wife has discovered."
—Ernest Borgnine

As it turned out, she was more than ready to take the risk and *just start.* She learned from the postmaster's office that if she notified clients of a delivery delay within thirty days of an order's placement, she would then have a total of six weeks to fill the order. That was the deadline looming overhead. Tova sent out the delivery delay notices and quickly arranged a meeting in Mexico City with the family who produced the formula. Accompanying her were Ernest, a legal advisor, a business advisor, and an interpreter. When Tova, through the interpreter, told the family members she needed them to produce two tons of masque formula in twelve days, they promptly stood up and started to walk out of the meeting. Tova grabbed a handful of $100 bills and tossed them down on the table. That needed no translation. Negotiations got under way, and a deal was struck. The ancient formula, handed down from Aztec Indians, was about to reach the masses.

Tova hired a design team to help her develop product packaging and a logo, and Tova's new company (then called Tova 9) was up and running. She mailed out 3,147 boxes of Cactine within the legal time frame. Looking back, she admits that at the time she had no idea what hurdles she faced and how impossible that deadline was. But that's partly why she just persisted until every last order in that stack was filled; she didn't know enough about the business to talk herself out of reaching her goal. Once she fully realized the scope of what she'd accomplished, she adopted a new mantra: "It can be done."

‒‒‒‒‒‒‒‒‒◄○►‒‒‒‒‒‒‒‒‒

She admits that at the time she had no idea what hurdles she faced and how impossible the deadline was. But that's partly why she just persisted until every last order was filled; she didn't know enough about the business to talk herself out of reaching her goal.

‒‒‒‒‒‒‒‒‒◅◣►‒‒‒‒‒‒‒‒‒

The company's infancy was a manic, nerve-racking, pressure-filled time—one with more than its share of unexpected complications. But Tova and Ernest always found a way to diffuse every minicrisis they encountered in those early days. When Food and Drug Administration inspectors delayed the processing of the second major shipment of the masque formula, Tova dispatched Ernest to Los Angeles International Airport to reassure officials that the mysterious ointment posed no health risk whatsoever. Ernie charmed them and allayed their concerns, as she knew he would. Eventually, Tova acquired the Cactine formula outright to handle manufacturing within the company, eliminating the potential for such bureaucratic snafus.

Although having a famous husband initially helped Tova market her first face masque and Ernie continued to be her personal cheerleader, the Borgnine name was of little help when it came to fulfilling those first mail orders within the legal time frame. Tova accomplished that feat through innovation and tenacity. She repeatedly relied on those same traits to build her one-time home-based business into a multi-million-dollar enterprise. She always knew her products had to deliver the goods to ensure repeat sales and generate word of mouth; her celebrity name alone could not guarantee success.

By 1982—only about five years after she started her business— Tova Corporation's annual gross reached $5 million. Immersed in a world of chemists, suppliers, labelers, and bottle manufacturers, she was a hands-on CEO, personally coordinating every aspect of her beauty products' production, marketing, and distribution. During the toughest times, her husband's unfaltering faith buoyed her spirits. "Ernie wholeheartedly supported my ambitions and delivered more than one impassioned pep talk whenever my spirits ebbed low," she says.

One of Tova's priorities was making the sales process easy for customers. She wanted to give them more options in both skin-care products and ways to order them. "I had learned the valuable lesson that you didn't have to slavishly follow tradition," she explains, "so I was quick to seek out and adapt to new marketing concepts like toll-free telephone ordering, credit card acceptance, and a corps of handpicked Tova beauty counselors who were on a first-name basis with virtually every one of my customers."

Expanding the Product Line

As the business grew, Tova also decided to branch out into fragrances. Yet again, she *bucked conventional wisdom*. Instead of collaborating with an established fragrance maker, she sought to work with a manufacturer specializing in exotic essential oils. J. Manheimer Inc., based in New Jersey, was a family-run business dating back to 1860. One of its products, a bath oil, was a favorite of Tova's as she found its scent sensual and fresh but not overpowering. Tova wanted to develop a fragrance with those same qualities, so she gave the company a call and arranged a meeting with Steve Manheimer. When she told him of her plans, he agreed to the project. Tova made it hard to say no.

"I was a little skeptical, but Tova had such a passion for what she wanted," Manheimer recalls. "She knew what she wanted. And she gave me the inspiration to try, even though frankly we were not in the traditional fragrance business at that time."

Tova and Manheimer worked closely together on developing the new fragrance, going through many formula-blend iterations using such ingredients as French lavender, absolute jasmine, and sandalwood from India. Finally, Tova narrowed the field down to two contending formulas. She had a tough time settling on the final formula because she loved both scents.

One evening, Tova and Ernie joined Steve Manheimer and his wife for dinner at Giambelli 50th Restaurant for a classic Italian meal. The popular Manhattan restaurant was packed. After the couples finished eating, they concocted a plan to use the restaurant's guests as a focus group to settle the issue of the fragrance formula. Ernie dabbed one formula on his right hand and the other on his left. He then started walking from table to table, asking restaurant customers to sniff his hands so he could tally votes. Since he was a recognizable TV and film star, everyone in the restaurant gladly joined in. Before long, a clear consensus emerged, and Tova Signature fragrance was born. The product began shipping to Tova's customers in 1982—again, only about five years after she started her company.

Tova Signature quickly gained a cult following among celebrities and the Beverly Hills set. Tova discovered that giving friends her products as birthday and holiday gifts always generated word-of-mouth sales.

In fact, one day she received a phone call from Ronald Reagan during his presidency. He thanked her for sending a box full of Tova products to the White House and then he asked her what was on his mind: "Should I put the masque on before or after the creams?"

To promote fragrance sales, Tova began featuring scent strips in her product catalogs. In addition to newspaper advertising featuring both her and Ernie, she also staged some elaborate sales events that gave attendees the chance to sample her products in a glamorous, partylike atmosphere. One such event, held at the Century Plaza Hotel in Los Angeles, was catered, featured celebrities, and even included a raffle of sapphires. That event drew 4,500 people. Of course, to enter the raffle, attendees had to provide detailed contact information. That data proved invaluable in subsequent marketing campaigns.

Realizing the Need for Greater Exposure and Deciding to Sell Directly on TV

By 1987, Tova had sixty-five skin-care and fragrance products and eighty employees. Company sales, however, had stalled. Tova tried to heighten interest in her catalogs by including ultraluxury items like a $117 million Concorde and an Arabian stallion previously owned by Burt Reynolds, but neither really helped. Fragrance and skin-care product sales remained flat, and the stallion and aircraft went unsold. Tova knew she had to try something new. She spent the money to produce an infomercial and then decided not to buy the air time because the program looked "too canned." Finally, she concluded she needed to pitch her products on QVC, the cable TV network devoted to direct sales.

Tova contacted QVC's Pennsylvania headquarters and left message after message after message. "It took three months just to get someone to answer my call," she says. Eventually, she spoke with a QVC executive who set up a meeting. But, the executive warned emphatically, Tova would have only fifteen minutes to make her pitch to get an on-air slot. Tova agreed. She flew from Los Angeles to New York, took the train to Philadelphia, rented a car, and drove to QVC headquarters in Westchester, where the executive met her in the lobby for their fifteen-minute meeting. "I am not a fast talker, but I was very clear and very quick," Tova remembers. "And that fifteen minutes turned into two and a half hours."

Her first QVC appearance, a one-hour test show, aired live in November 1990. Tova was paired with a sidekick, Marybeth Roe, and the two quickly established an easy rapport and became fast friends. In that first hour, they sold $134,000 worth of Tova products. "I didn't have any idea what to expect of QVC," Tova recounts. "These days, they have guest classes and tutorials—in fact, an entire department devoted to new members. But back then, there was nothing."

Tova quickly became one of QVC's most popular personalities. Before long, she was unloading as many as 33,000 bottles of Tova Signature in just a three-and-a-half-minute segment. "We've stretched QVC," she says. "No one was doing demonstrations when I started, but you must show the viewer how the products are applied."

Today, QVC's Tova products make an on-air appearance on the cable network about once every six weeks, with Tova Borgnine front and center. Though QVC purchased the brand from her in 2002, she remains intimately involved in the decision making and is still the face of the Tova brand. She also appears on the QVC networks in the United Kingdom and Germany. Now, when the Borgnines walk into a restaurant, Ernie isn't the only one recognized.

———————◄o►———————

By 1987, company sales had stalled. Tova knew she had to try something new. She concluded she needed to pitch her products on QVC. Tova had only fifteen minutes to make her pitch to get an on-air slot. "I am not a fast talker, but I was very clear and very quick. And that fifteen minutes turned into two and a half hours."

————————————————

The same year she sold her company to QVC, Tova also successfully battled breast cancer. That fight inspired her to introduce an aromatherapy line designed to foster introspection and calm. She wants the Tova brand to offer clients products not just for the body but for the mind and spirit as well. "It's essential that we find a balance," she explains. "We need to take time for ourselves."

Tova is seen as a pioneer in both direct marketing and beauty products. She recently celebrated her twenty-fifth anniversary in the fragrance industry and her thirtieth anniversary in the beauty business. Tova Signature remains QVC's top-selling fragrance. In 2008, Tova Signature even drew a nomination for the Fragrance Hall of Fame. (Yes, there really is such a thing.)

"I have told the story of how the Tova Corporation was started so many times now that it begins to sound like a fairy tale," Tova admits. But the moral of this story is that sometimes breaking every rule in the book at least once—something that Tova admits to—can lead to a fairy-tale ending if you just *trust your gut.*

∽

STRATEGIES FOR SUCCESS

♦ Tova was liable to prosecution for mail fraud if she didn't deliver her skin-rejuvenating masque to mail-order customers in a timely fashion. More important, she also would have missed a huge business opportunity. Only a true entrepreneurial talent would then *just start* moving so swiftly. She artfully convinced her suppliers to produce two tons of formula in twelve days.

♦ Tova first *got her company noticed without expensive advertising* by giving her products to celebrity friends as birthday and holiday gifts to generate buzz. She later held glamorous, catered events that featured celebrities and gave attendees a chance to sample her products. Raffles helped ensure a big turnout.

♦ She *bucked conventional wisdom* by introducing new marketing concepts such as toll-free telephone ordering and credit card acceptance. When she decided to develop a fragrance, she worked with an essential oils manufacturer instead of a fragrance specialist.

♦ The biggest opportunity came when sales stalled. Tova *spied a new trend*—direct marketing on cable television—*and pounced on it*. She convinced QVC to give her a shot and became a huge success. Yet again, she *bucked the conventional wisdom* by doing demonstrations on television and selling her fragrances to consumers who didn't have the opportunity to smell-test in person—a unique example of *hitting 'em where they ain't*. Through QVC, she *reinvented her company*'s business model and eventually sold Tova Corporation to the cable network. As the brand's spokeswoman, she continues to introduce new Tova products on QVC.

CHAPTER 16

Florine Mark *(Photo by Gregg Campbell)*

Florine Mark

CEO, The WW Group

"I just believed so much in what I was doing.
And when you believe, you can do anything."

—Florine Mark

In 1966, when Florine Mark decided it was time to start a career, the longtime housewife and mother of five reached for her diet pills, hoping to shed some pounds before embarking on her job hunt. An on-again, off-again fad dieter, Florine had struggled with her weight since childhood and viewed her occasional amphetamine use with casual indifference. But this time, her body rebelled, and a life-threatening reaction sent her to a hospital emergency room. After recovering, she vowed to lose weight the healthy way. She joined a Weight Watchers group more than six hundred miles from her home in Detroit, because Weight Watchers didn't yet have operations anywhere near where she lived. The decision transformed her life, both personally and professionally.

Learning to *trust her gut* proved a major part of Florine's personal journey—one that culminated in her using her own weight-loss experience to build her own weight-loss empire. Her business, The WW Group in Farmington Hills, Michigan, eventually grew to include Weight Watchers franchises in twelve states and three countries. In 2003, Florine sold 75 percent of those franchises back to Weight Watchers International for $181.5 million. Still, her company remains the biggest Weight Watchers franchisee in the United States, and she is one of the nation's most popular female philanthropists and inspirational speakers. Weight Watchers helped Florine redefine herself—initially, while she was a client and, eventually, as a franchisee and entrepreneur.

———————◄◊►———————

Learning to trust her gut proved a major part of
Florine's personal journey—one that culminated
in her using her own weight-loss experience
to build her own weight-loss empire.

———————————————————

An Ordinary Kid Becomes an Accidental Entrepreneur

Florine's success as an entrepreneur is all the more remarkable when you consider her background. Early in life, she showed no signs of being a self-assured entrepreneur in the making. That's because she first had to overcome her long-standing pattern of turning to food to cope with stress and feelings of inadequacy. This struggle dated back to her childhood, when she first developed a weight problem and suffered from low self-esteem.

Florine Mark, before and after losing weight with
Weight Watchers (*Courtesy of Florine Mark*)

Florine grew up in a large family, sharing the household with her parents, grandparents, six aunts and uncles, and two sisters. Paying the bills was a constant struggle, and everyone was expected to chip in. At age eleven, she got her first job—selling doughnuts.

Healthy eating wasn't a family tradition. "I came from a family that fried and put sugar in everything," she says. Her childhood weight problem led to playground taunts and alienation. Classmates nicknamed her Fat Flo, and the resulting embarrassment only fueled her dependence on food as a coping mechanism. That led Florine to withdraw socially and focus on her school work. She excelled academically, eventually skipping two grades. As a result, she graduated high school at the age of sixteen.

This was in the 1950s, when women were expected to marry right after high school and start a family. Despite her young age, Florine became engaged shortly after graduation. She even took diet pills to lose fifty pounds for her wedding. Within a year, the couple welcomed a daughter. But that didn't change the fact that the marriage had been a mistake from the start. Despite objections from family—divorce was still a social taboo at the time—Florine asked for a divorce. She then moved back into her parents' home, resulting in feelings of guilt and family tensions. All this further fueled her dependence on food.

◄○►

She knew there were plenty of people in Detroit who needed Weight Watchers as much as she did. She recognized this was an *underserved niche*—frustrated dieters who need help learning how to lose weight and keep it off.

"I graduated in June, got married in August, had a baby in September of the following year, and divorced a year later," Florine recalls. "We were just too young."

Florine remarried, but the overeating issues persisted. She found herself in a continual cycle of dieting—losing a few pounds and then gaining them back. A dependency on diet pills soon followed. After several years of marriage, when her husband's business went through a rough patch, she knew she needed to find work to help pay the household bills. The couple had four more children, so the brood now numbered five kids. Florine feared, however, her weight would discourage managers from hiring her. At the time, she wore a size twenty. Around the house, she wore her husband's old white shirts and any black pants she could find that fit her. When depressed about her weight, she often binged on ice cream—but only vanilla because she figured it wasn't as fattening as chocolate.

A Life-Changing Personal Decision Leads to a New Career

Finally, she reached a moment of reckoning after the drug overdose prompted the emergency room visit. Her doctor warned her that further amphetamine use would be life threatening. Florine knew she had to change her life or risk losing it. After reading about Weight

Watchers in a women's magazine, she contacted the company to inquire about the diet plan. The company advised her to join and attend regular meetings in New York City. She was told that one of the keys to Weight Watchers's success rate was the support group meetings. Participants were encouraged and held accountable by their peers, fellow Weight Watchers members. Florine responded that because she lived in Detroit, attending meetings in New York wasn't an option. "I begged them to send me the diet until they agreed," Florine says. "I tried it for about three or four weeks on my own at home. I didn't gain any weight, but then I didn't lose any weight either."

But instead of giving up on Weight Watchers, she realized she hadn't given the program a fair shot. She needed to attend the meetings and participate fully. "I was desperate, so I asked my mother and dad—who were always wonderful to me—to come over and babysit the five kids," Florine recalls. "I got on an airplane, took my last bit of money, and went to New York because it was my last hope."

She booked a five-day stay at a cheap hotel on Queens Boulevard, within walking distance of the Weight Watchers meeting site. After checking into her room, she started to miss her children and wondered whether she'd done the right thing. She pulled the drapes in the room, expecting to see a New York City skyline. Instead, she saw a slab of concrete—it wasn't a real window. "I will never forget that," she says. "And I cried and cried and cried. But the next day, I went to the meeting."

The walk to the meeting underscored her need to get healthy: She huffed and puffed during the climb up three flights of stairs to get to the Weight Watchers office. When the staff asked her to step on the scale, she begrudgingly obliged. Then she sat down with a group of other people who, like her, had struggled most of their lives with weight issues. They listened to Weight Watchers founder Jean Nidetch talk about the need to maintain a balanced, healthy diet—and the commitment required to lose weight and keep it off.

Nidetch also told her own personal story—one that resonated with Florine. Back in 1961, Nidetch was a forty-year-old housewife living in Queens, New York, and weighed 214 pounds. Determined to lose weight, she attended a diet seminar sponsored by the New York City Board of Health. But over time, she discovered that to stay motivated in her weight-loss quest, she needed a support group. She organized get-togethers with other dieting friends, and they talked openly about their food obsessions and struggle to change their eating habits. Weight Watchers sprung from those meetings.

For the next five days, Florine attended three classes daily. She ate, and learned how to prepare, a range of foods she never ate at home—fresh fruits and vegetables, salmon, liver, and baked white-meat chicken without the skin. She was unlearning a lifetime of unhealthy eating habits.

Nonetheless, as the week drew to a close, Florine was convinced she hadn't lost any weight. When she showed up for Friday's meeting, she was planning to ask for her money back. As she stepped on the scale, she braced herself for the grim news. To her astonishment, the scale revealed she had lost five and a half pounds in just five days. "And then I was hooked," Florine says. "I knew this was going to change my life. So I made a deal with Jean Nidetch."

Florine Mark with Jean Nidetch *(Courtesy of Florine Mark)*

Nidetch agreed that Florine could continue the weight-loss program at home in Detroit as long as she attended four straight days of meetings in New York every month. So every fourth week, she made the trek to New York. She became close friends with the other Weight Watchers members and no longer dreaded the weekly weigh-ins. After just four months of this regimen, Florine had lost forty pounds. That's when Nidetch approached her about starting a Weight Watchers franchise in Detroit. Nidetch realized Florine believed in the program and was an inspirational presence at the New York meetings.

———————◄○►———————

She didn't let a loan officer's snub derail her business plans. She *refused to let adversity defeat her.* Instead, she asked Weight Watchers to loan her the down payment for her franchise, and the company agreed.

———————ᏇᎠ———————

Trusting Her Gut About an Underserved Market

Florine agreed, launching her entrepreneurial career. She knew that plenty of people in the Detroit area needed Weight Watchers as much as she did. She recognized this was an *underserved niche*— frustrated dieters who need help learning how to lose weight and keep it off. She *trusted her gut* that she could run a Weight Watchers franchise and help transform the lives of others, just as Jean Nidetch had helped her.

The sales price for a franchise was $25,000, with a minimum down payment of $5,000. Florine decided to visit her local bank in Detroit to apply for a business loan to cover the $5,000. But the loan officer refused even to consider lending her the money unless her husband agreed to cosign on the loan—an option that infuriated Florine. Feeling newly empowered by her weight loss, she saw launching her business as a personal challenge. "I said, 'You want my husband to sign for me? But I'm the one going into business. No one is going to sign for me.' And then I left the bank. I was really indignant," she recounts.

She didn't let the loan officer's snub derail her business plans, however. She *refused to let adversity defeat her.* Instead, she asked Weight

Watchers to loan her the down payment, and the company agreed. Her franchise was up and running.

This was well before Weight Watchers had become a household name, and the company had no formal training program for new franchisees. As a franchise owner, Florine could use the Weight Watchers name in marketing materials and offer her clients the company's diet plan. But otherwise, she was on her own.

Newfound Confidence and Word-of-Mouth Marketing Help Jump-Start Business

When Florine held her first Weight Watchers meeting on July 12, 1966, family members dutifully showed up to ensure she wouldn't address an empty auditorium. Fortunately, not all the attendees were family and friends. Florine's bare-bones marketing strategy—which consisted of hanging a handmade poster at a local candy store—had lured some other people eager to shed some pounds. Florine had no idea why the candy store owner had agreed to let her promote the weight-loss meeting at his store; she was just grateful he had said yes.

———————◄○►———————

With no experience in either public speaking or running a business, she began to question her decision to become an entrepreneur. Ultimately, she *trusted her gut* that she could improve her clients' lives and lead a successful business. She was able to push those old insecurities aside and *just start.*

———————

Just before the meeting was set to begin, with people still filing into the school auditorium, Florine had a bit of a panic attack. With no experience in either public speaking or running a business, she began to question her decision to become an entrepreneur. She rushed to the restroom, stood in front of the mirror, and had a face-to-face conversation with herself to confront her fears. "Listen, kid, you've got to get hold of yourself. What's the worst that can happen?" she said aloud. She then gathered her courage, walked out, and addressed the group of about thirty people. Ultimately, she *trusted her gut* that she could improve her clients' lives and lead a successful business. She was able to push those old insecurities aside and *just start.* Her weight loss had given her newfound self-esteem.

"All the stuff that was in me before, but was hidden by the fat, was starting to come out," Florine explains. "My self-confidence, my determination, my knowledge, my sense of humor, my everything. I just believed so much in what I was doing. And when you believe, you can do anything."

That evening, Florine discovered she was a skilled salesperson and inspirational speaker. She made an instant connection with her audience. She understood their frustrations, insecurities, and apprehensions. And she was willing to share her own story with unflinching candor.

---◄○►---

"All the stuff that was in me before, but was
hidden by the fat, was starting to come out.
My self-confidence, my determination, my
knowledge, my sense of humor, my everything.
I just believed so much in what I was doing.
And when you believe, you can do anything."

"I just spoke from my heart and told them how terrible I felt before Weight Watchers," Florine says. "I told them that the more I hated myself, the more I ate. And the more I ate, the more I hated myself. It was never-ending. And then I told them about my trip to New York and how Weight Watchers changed my life. Well, I must have convinced them because on the second night, 60 people came. And on the third night, there were 180 people."

To grow her business further, Florine took her message to various shopping malls. Sometimes mall owners would rent her a conference room where she could give her Weight Watchers presentation; sometimes they let her use a room for free. Word of mouth about Florine's inspiring story spread. Soon, churches and synagogues began asking Florine to speak to their members. She also convinced both major

Detroit newspapers to publish lengthy stories about her company. She *saved her bucks and got noticed without expensive advertising.*

Expanding the Business and Buying Additional Franchises

Before long, Florine had to shift much of her focus to employee training to accommodate the additional members and company operations. She was committed to hiring only employees who had struggled with—and overcome—weight issues themselves. "Nobody could work in a meeting with me unless they had a weight problem, sat in my class, lost the weight, and went through the training," Florine says. "By that time, I'd developed written training. When I wasn't teaching classes during the day, I was writing training books and developing a public relations plan. I was doing the bookkeeping, the hiring, etc.—all the things that it takes to run a business."

> "Florine gives you a lot of flexibility. She'd rather you try something and have it fail than not try it at all. I've been with her for 15 years. . . . She's always supportive. She always reminds me of my successes, but I never hear about the things that have gone wrong. The company's 14-member management team meets once a week, and if there's a problem or a question, she wants open communication. That's why our business is so successful. We deal with people from all walks of life, and we're from all walks of life."
> —Carolyn Bough, The WW Group general manager, quoted in *Detroit Free Press*, February 22, 1988

> Florine discovered she was a skilled salesperson and
> inspirational speaker. She made an instant connection
> with her audience. She understood their frustrations,
> insecurities, and apprehensions. And she was willing
> to share her own story with unflinching candor.

Meanwhile, her parents often pitched in to help take care of her children. She eventually hired an assistant to handle everyday errands and drive her and the kids around. By necessity, Florine became a master of time management.

Florine's first franchise territories spanned the regional Detroit area; Toledo, Ohio; and Essex County in Ontario, Canada. Early success spurred her to buy additional Weight Watchers franchises, both new and existing. "Whenever I bought an existing franchise, I never haggled over price," Florine explains. "I'd say, 'It has to be right for you and right for me. What's your fair price?' I'd pay them that price because I always knew I could go in and make their business more profitable."

She even moved to Mexico for almost a year to start a franchise there. Her market research had revealed that many middle-class women in Mexico were hiring pricey diet doctors when they wanted to lose weight. Florine was confident that many of them would embrace Weight Watchers. But the cultural differences she encountered kept hindering her progress. "Everything I did in the United States that made me successful were things that didn't work in Mexico," Florine explains. Her time-tested public relations tricks failed to spark interest. Even her efforts to arrange a phone-line installation came up empty. Finally, she tapped into a winning formula: She gave her Mexican staff members more authority to make business decisions, let them lead the meetings, and returned to her hectic work schedule in the United States.

Strong Customer Feedback Helped Business

Even when running her business was exhausting, the feedback from Weight Watchers members kept her spirits high. Florine recalls,

"People would come up to me and say, 'Oh, my God, Florine. I just love you so much. Thank you, thank you. I feel like a whole new person.' I was a little instrumental in helping people to help themselves. I knew then that this business was going to fulfill my life dreams. I was going to make this into the greatest business in the whole world. And besides that, I was finally healthy. I was feeling good about myself, and I was helping other people feel good about themselves."

Because Florine's employees have conquered a weight problem themselves, they empathize with new members struggling to change a lifetime of poor eating habits. That empathy is a crucial element of Florine's success.

―――◄○►―――

"Whenever I bought an existing franchise, I never haggled over price. I'd say, 'It has to be right for you and right for me. What's your fair price?' I'd pay them that price because I always knew I could go in and make their business more profitable."

―――――

After Florine's second marriage ended, she threw herself further into her work. She also began exercising more, including running and playing tennis. It was on the tennis court, in fact, that Florine eventually met her third husband, Dr. William Ross. He would prove to be the love of her life—someone who fully supported her entrepreneurial efforts and shared her zest for community service and adventure.

Dealing with Critics and Corporate Buyouts

One of the most challenging times for Florine's business was the mid-1990s, when some high-profile critics of the diet industry promoted weight loss through fitness training and low fat intake. Also at this time, pharmaceutical companies introduced a number of new diet pills to the market. "When the no-fat craze hit, people were bingeing on no-fat cookies and ice cream, and they gained more weight," she remembers. "My company had boasted as many as 100,000 members, but during this period dropped as low as 50,000."

Florine received an offer to sell her business at the time but opted to ride out the storm without downsizing or closing centers. The strategy paid off when the public finally wised up to the fact that processed foods labeled "fat free" were not, in fact, *calorie free*. In addition, some serious health risks linked to new diet pills came to light.

Over the years, Florine became a sought-after motivational speaker and a role model for fledgling entrepreneurs, particularly women. She also joined a networking group for the nation's most successful businesswomen: the Committee of 200. To qualify for membership, entrepreneurs must log annual gross sales of at least $25 million. Meanwhile, Florine took steps to give her children a greater stake in The WW Group.

In the late 1990s, the owner of Weight Watchers International—H. J. Heinz Company, which had acquired the corporation in 1978 after a corporate restructuring—placed Weight Watchers International on the sales block. Florine assembled a group of investors and made an offer of $650 million, but she was ultimately outbid by Artal Luxembourg, a European-based private equity company. The sales price was $735 million. The deal closed in July 1999. Though Florine had tried to convince her investors to beat Artal Luxembourg's offer, they didn't want to. Today she has no regrets. "It wasn't meant to be," she says. (Maybe those investors should have trusted Florine's gut more. In 2007, the Weight Watchers brand worldwide generated over $4 billion in sales, including revenue from franchisees and licensees.)

Despite Florine's disappointment over the failed acquisition attempt, she continued to pursue other franchises to further expand The WW Group's footprint. In fact, the new owners of Weight Watchers International became increasingly frustrated with The WW Group's aggressive expansion. Weight Watchers International was finding itself competing against Florine's company to acquire franchises up for sale. In addition, Weight Watchers International issued an initial public offering in 2001. As a public company, revenue from corporate-owned operations took on greater importance. That's what prompted Weight Watchers International to offer Florine such an attractive price for her business.

She decided to accept because of the opportunities that cash would provide her and her five children. Now grown, they all had careers and families of their own. "I said to myself, 'One of these days, when my time is up, they're going to get all this money anyway. Wouldn't it be nice for them to get it right now so I can watch how they handle themselves with all that money?'" Florine explains.

At the time she sold most of her franchises back to Weight Watchers International in 2003, her five children collectively owned a 60 percent share. The family sold franchises in Illinois, Indiana, Kentucky, Massachusetts, Missouri, New Hampshire, North Carolina, Ohio, Pennsylvania, Rhode Island, Vermont, West Virginia, and Mexico. The family retained franchises in Michigan and northern Ontario. The sales agreement included a clause prohibiting Florine's company from buying any more Weight Watchers franchises for ten years.

---◄○►---

When major pharmaceutical companies introduced new diet pills to the market, Florine received an offer to sell her business, but she opted to ride out the storm without downsizing or closing centers. The strategy paid off when the public finally wised up to the fact that processed foods labeled "fat free" were not, in fact, *calorie-free*.

After the sale in 2003, Florine looked forward to spending more time traveling with her husband, Dr. Bill Ross. Trips to Alaska and India were on the couple's to-do list. She also began writing *Talk to the Mirror*, a fun and inspiring book about "being the best you can be every day and taking one day at a time."

But just two months after the sale to Weight Watchers International, Florine's husband was diagnosed with Lou Gehrig's disease, or ALS. As his health declined, Florine spent her days taking care of him and writing her book. It was a difficult time.

After two years of lying completely paralyzed, only able to blink his eyes, Bill Ross passed away. After his death, following twenty-two years of marriage, Florine surrounded herself with family and friends to deal with her grief. "There were always kids around, things to do and people around who I loved and cared about," she says. "And my mother was there for me. So you go on and feel fortunate for everything you have, every single day you have."

Ready for the Next Challenge and Opportunity

Florine continues running her company and contributing her time and money to such charitable groups as the American Heart Association, the Hunger Action Coalition, and the Jewish Federation of Metropolitan Detroit. She has also honored her husband's memory by establishing the Dr. Bill and Florine Mark-Ross Fund for ALS Research.

Today, she limits herself to thirty to fifty hours of work per week, but she makes time to host a television show, *Ask Florine,* and a syndicated radio show called *Remarkable Woman,* spotlighting extraordinary women and their impact on society. Florine's achievements as an entrepreneur, coupled with her philanthropy, have earned her scores of honors, including the U.S. Small Business Administration's Distinguished Entrepreneur Award and Merrill Lynch's Entrepreneur of the Year.

Florine Mark with Hillary Clinton and Don Benyas *(Courtesy of Florine Mark)*

Florine Mark with Sarah Ferguson *(Courtesy of Florine Mark)*

When that ten-year ban on acquiring franchises expires, Florine says The WW Group will see a new growth spurt. She is still as driven to succeed as when she started her business. And she starts each day the same way. "Each morning I get up, look in the mirror, and say, 'Good morning, Florine. It's going to be a great day.' Sometimes I don't believe myself, so I talk faster and louder to make myself believe it," she says.

STRATEGIES FOR SUCCESS

♦ A life-threatening emergency prompted Florine Mark to *just start* really confronting her lifelong weight problem. Ultimately, she made the bold decision to leave her family for a week, fly to New York, and attend a series of Weight Watchers meetings. She lost the weight—and she found a new career.

♦ Jean Nidetch, Weight Watchers's founder, recognized Florine's commitment to the program and suggested she buy a franchise. Florine agreed there was an *underserved niche* in her hometown Detroit area—people who needed to lose weight but lacked a support system.

♦ Even though Florine was ready to *just start* with another bold move, the bank wouldn't give her a loan to buy a franchise unless her husband cosigned. Indignant, she refused—and she also *refused to be defeated by adversity*. She got a loan for the down payment from Weight Watchers itself.

♦ In those early days, franchise owners had no formal training, so Florine had to *trust her gut* that she would be an effective leader. She turned out to have a gift for inspirational speaking and was soon deluged by requests for appearances and newspaper interviews. She *got noticed without expensive advertising*.

♦ She continued to *trust her gut* by buying more new and existing franchises, and she didn't balk at meeting the asking price: She was certain she could make the franchises more profitable. She even branched out into Mexico—*hitting 'em where they ain't* and *reinventing her company* marketing approach to be successful there.

CHAPTER 17

Don Martin *(Photo by Dennis Trantham)*

Don Martin

Founder and Former CEO,
The Cal-Surance Companies

"Do not accept the limits that others place on you."

—Don Martin

In 2002, I sold the insurance business that I had founded forty years earlier to insurance giant Brown & Brown for $64.5 million in cash. When the sale became final, I couldn't help but think back on the role that high-stakes risk taking and gut-level decision making had played in my company's prosperity—and the happenstance that brought me into the insurance industry in the first place. When I started my own business, I had no savings, no investments, no financial safety net. But I was willing to take high-stakes risks that had the potential for high-level rewards. In telling my story, I hope to instill in you that same willingness to believe in yourself enough to take such risks when the right opportunities arise.

Growing Up Poor and Often Hungry

Looking back on my youth, I guess you might say I was an unlikely candidate for such success in the business world. I grew up in the Ohio Valley, where if you were as poor as we were, you had only three options after high school: the coal mines, the steel mills, or if you had the talent and some luck, a sports scholarship that allowed you to go to college. I was too frightened of working underground in the mines and too slight to work in the steel mills. Although I loved sports, I wasn't a gifted athlete either.

My father left us when I was three, and my mother worked to support us. Young, poor, and uneducated, she did the best she could, which meant working days and evenings as a waitress. I was pretty much left to fend for myself in our tiny, century-old house that belonged to my grandfather, a local coal miner.

My most vivid childhood recollections include often being hungry, having to make trips to the outhouse in near-freezing temperatures, and thinking we had landed in the lap of luxury when we moved to a house where we shared the one indoor bathroom with one other family. For several years, my mother put cardboard inside my shoes to cover the holes because she couldn't afford new shoes or the $2 for glue-on rubber soles. During Ohio's frequent rainstorms and heavy snows, I learned to walk to school quickly because the cardboard didn't hold up well in those conditions.

---◄◦►---

Even though I had no role models, mentors,
or money, I had a strong desire to succeed
and a strong belief that I could. To this
day, I have no idea where that came from.
Something in my gut said I could succeed.

Don Martin's childhood home

I was a pretty good student, except during a brief period when my alcoholic stepfather turned his abuse on me. I had no clue about what to do after I graduated from high school, so I sought advice from two teachers whom I respected. One, the football coach, counseled me to enlist in the marines. The other teacher pronounced, in no uncertain terms, that I was not college material. (It probably didn't help that I was dating his daughter.) Fortunately, I ignored both and listened instead to a small inner voice that said, "Go to college." It was then that I learned an important lesson: Do not accept the limits that others place on you.

Moving Cross-Country to an Affordable College

Even though I had no role models, mentors, or money, I had a strong desire to succeed and a strong belief that I could. To this day, I have no idea where that came from. Something in my gut said I could be successful. I couldn't afford college in Ohio, so I convinced my mom to pack up and move to California, where I would have access to the state's affordable junior college system.

My risk taking had begun. I had left my hometown of Martin's Ferry, Ohio (population under 8,000), to go to Los Angeles—where I had no friends, no job, no career, and no idea what I wanted to do.

Back in Ohio, my grade point average had suffered during my freshman and sophomore years because of all the turmoil I dealt with at home. After my alcoholic stepfather moved out, my grades rebounded. I made all As and Bs. But by then, my teachers had already fixed their expectations for me on a lower rung. After I moved to California, only my own expectations mattered. I had wiped the slate and could shape my own fate.

First, I worked a year in shipping at an aerospace facility and saved money for school. I then enrolled at El Camino College, a junior college a half hour's drive from downtown Los Angeles.

I realized within the first few weeks at junior college that I had a problem: I didn't know anyone. Like most college freshmen, I longed for a sense of belonging on campus. I wanted to make new friends, but this was a commuter campus that didn't easily lend itself to socializing. I didn't live in a dorm on campus; I lived with my mother and a friend of hers in a cramped two-bedroom apartment near Los Angeles International Airport. Making new college friends meant I would have to overcome my shyness and take steps to get involved in student organizations on campus.

Back in high school, I had been a leader in both Hi-Y, a YMCA-affiliated group, and DeMolay, a Masonic-affiliated group. Both youth organizations fostered character building and community involvement, and I enjoyed assuming a leadership role in them. My contributions gave me a sense of accomplishment, boosted my self-esteem, and earned the respect and friendship of other members. So, when I read in the El Camino student newspaper that class elections were coming up, I decided that one way to meet people in college was to run for freshman class president.

I was also interested in again taking a leadership role among students. But as a candidate, I had a major disadvantage. The other candidates knew most of the freshman students because they were all from the local high schools. They seemed to have a lot of votes already sewn up, so I devised a strategy to visit the night-school students, who were mostly returning Korean War vets. I went to the school cafeteria every evening, talked to these night students about their problems, and asked for their votes.

I won a close election, but I got 90 percent of the night-school votes. As you can imagine, the losing candidates were asking, "Who is this guy Martin?" In the immortal words of baseball legend "Wee Willie" Keeler, I "hit 'em where they ain't." That was Keeler's response when the 5' 4", 140-pound New York Yankee was asked how such a small guy could get so many big hits. Like Willie, I had simply set my sights on areas that my competition had ignored.

I learned another valuable lesson:
Go where the competition isn't.

I was shy and an introvert. To overcome these limitations, I enrolled as a speech major and joined the debate team. Little did I realize that debate would prove the most valuable skill I learned in my entire college experience. It taught me to think on my feet, to organize my thoughts, and to express myself convincingly—critical skills in sales and business management, as I later learned. What's more, my involvement in student government taught me all about problem solving and the art of negotiation. I was constantly working with different student groups with conflicting agendas.

My involvement in student government also helped me develop social skills. Business relationships are seldom based on profit-and-loss balance sheets; instead, they depend on interactive social relationships. My involvement on campus wasn't just the center of my social life; it was also preparing me for a career. A career in what? That I didn't yet know.

Finding a Job Close to Home—Because I Had No Transportation

Like many college students, I was always short on cash. I decided to look for a job with flexible hours and an easy, convenient location since I couldn't afford a car and had to rely on bus transportation. One day, while waiting at the bus stop near home, I glanced up and happened to notice an insurance agency in the strip mall directly across the street. There was no help-wanted sign in the window—and I knew nothing about the insurance industry—but I decided right then to find out if the firm was hiring. I returned home, put on my only suit, walked into the agency, and asked for a job selling insurance.

As it turned out, the agency was a one-man operation that specialized in insuring taxicab fleets. The owner, figuring he didn't have much to lose, offered me a small salary to get his files in order. To make sure I was available for the job, I enrolled in night classes. I completed a lot of my homework assignments while waiting for my rides at the bus stop. Although short on job experience, I had energy and enthusiasm. With financial help from my mother, I made enough money to stay in school. I then realized that in order to succeed, I didn't have to be the most experienced, just the most tenacious.

While working for the agency, I took every opportunity to learn more about the insurance business—despite my initial role as a mere file clerk. Every chance I got, I studied for the insurance licensing exam, and the agency owner supported my efforts. After passing the test, I began selling policies.

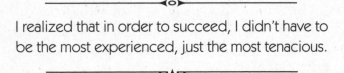

I realized that in order to succeed, I didn't have to be the most experienced, just the most tenacious.

At the same time, I continued taking college courses and stayed involved in student government. Here's what a typical day for me was like back then: I'd arrive at the insurance office at 8 a.m., make some sales calls, catch up on paperwork back at the office, attend college classes, and then catch a meeting or two. At different times, I held a number of leadership positions on campus—commissioner of activities and president of my fraternity to name just two. There was always a meeting to attend or an issue to resolve.

Sometimes the debate team would even meet after business hours at the insurance office to prepare for a competition. On occasion those debate-team sessions had stretched into the early morning hours before I headed back home to study for tests. Rather than becoming overwhelmed by all the responsibilities, I felt more confident and more energized than I ever had before.

I eventually transferred to Los Angeles State College (now known as California State University, Los Angeles) to earn my bachelor's degree. There, I helped strengthen the Greek system on campus, establishing relationships with the national fraternities and acting as president of the interfraternity council. I was also active on the college's debate team, winning numerous awards in national competitions, and was named "Outstanding Man" (one of five) in my senior year. After graduation, I continued selling insurance for the same agency.

Starting My Own Business, with a Partner and a Special Focus

One day I got an unexpected call from an acquaintance at Fireman's Fund Insurance Company. He told me about Don Mehlig, a local independent life insurance agent who was looking for a worthy business partner with experience in property and casualty insurance sales. Like me, Mehlig was in his twenties, ambitious beyond his years, and eager to start his own agency. The acquaintance at Fireman's Fund said he'd thought of me after Mehlig mentioned his search. Intrigued by the prospect of becoming an entrepreneur, I agreed to meet with Mehlig. Two weeks later, we launched our own agency, Cal-Surance.

When I tell this story, many people are amazed that I went into business with someone I'd known for merely two weeks. But after meeting with him several times, I had a *gut feeling* that Mehlig and I could build a successful company together. I just knew he was trustworthy, and I was ready to *just start* our new venture. The year was 1962.

As a foundation for our new company, we acquired the assets of the insurance agency where I'd been working. My boss, struggling financially and in poor health, was eager to sell. Since Mehlig and I had very little capital, the deal was a $35,000 leveraged buyout with a $1,500 cash down payment. Most of the cash came from Mehlig. Each of us brought different areas of expertise to the partnership. Mehlig would concentrate on life insurance and personal lines, and I would focus on commercial policies. Because we would operate in completely different spheres of the business, Mehlig and I agreed to run our divisions as separate companies. We would each lead our own team and profit centers.

Building the Company

Truth be told, when I first began Cal-Surance, I probably envisioned no more than a three- or four-man agency. Over the next few years, however, I became immersed in the inner workings of the insurance industry and tried to learn all I could. Gradually, I began to recognize just how much potential our start-up firm had if we targeted the right *underserved niches*. The more I learned about the industry, the more apparent our competitors' vulnerabilities became to me.

I just knew I could make Cal-Surance a major force if I had a large enough team of committed and talented sales agents working with me. But to recruit such agents, I had to offer them coveted markets and convince them they stood a better chance of making more money with me.

The strategy worked. Over the next few years, I hired several seasoned sales producers. I also persuaded three one-man agencies to merge into Cal-Surance by offering them a small percentage of stock and agreeing to provide them with staffing, accounting, and other administrative services. This freed them to focus solely on sales. It was win-win for all of us. By 1972, ten years after forming Cal-Surance, we had reached sales of $12 million. Three years later, in 1975, our sales grew to $26 million.

Finding Advisors to Help with My Fledgling Business

I trusted my business instincts, but I also recognized that I was a novice at developing an organization. I had been learning management techniques on the job. So, even though the company was privately held, in our tenth year I formed a board of directors consisting of two outside members and four from within the firm to advise and guide me. About seven years later, I changed the board's composition to include only members from outside the organization to ensure that recommendations were objective and not self-serving.

My board members were proven business leaders who brought a wealth of general business or industry knowledge and helped me implement the systems Cal-Surance needed. I paid them a $5,000 retainer for the year plus $1,000 for each quarterly meeting they attended. They were always available for phone consultations during the year. These men didn't join my board for the money; they enjoyed the challenge of lending their expertise to help grow the firm. To fill my board, I approached retired CEOs and presidents from the insurance industry and other industries as well. I respected their candid advice and never made a major decision without their approval.

I was a novice in developing an organization. So I formed an outside board of directors to advise and guide me. These were seasoned business leaders who brought a wealth of knowledge and helped me implement the systems Cal-Surance needed.

Reinventing the Company Through Diversification

Initially, I tried to figure out how I could compete with larger established agencies. Then it dawned on me that instead of competing on their turf, I needed to create new turf that only I owned. My business strategy was to develop a highly specialized organization offering new programs that created an immediate competitive advantage.

The more specialized the program, the better, because that created an edge over the competition. By customizing a program to fit clients' needs, we became more valuable to them. I would have specialized in three-legged giraffes that ate every other Thursday if there had been an advantage in doing so.

Shortly after acquiring the company, I decided to shift our commercial target market away from the taxicab fleet business to more profitable segments with less risk. Eventually, I *set my sights on finding niches* within the trucking industry. I opted to hire a broker with experience in this industry and used his connections to arrange a meeting with the executive director of the California Dump Truck Owners Association. I convinced him he needed an insurance program for his association's members.

Previously, truckers had purchased their policies as individuals. As a result, they weren't getting preferred rates from the insurance companies because they had no leverage as a high-volume collective group. I knew we could cut insurer costs and pass those savings along to the truckers if I administered a program in which the truckers bought insurance through the association from a single carrier. I created this program in 1965, and before long Cal-Surance was insuring a big portion of all the dump truck fleets in California.

I made the company's relationship with the association a top priority—a strategy that paid huge dividends. The association's endorsement lent us instant credibility with a large pool of truck operators. This relationship helped the company *get noticed without having to pay for expensive advertising.*

My vigorous research into the trucking-fleet insurance market also unearthed another opportunity. I realized that insurers had historically used a faulty system for calculating premium rates: They were setting rates based solely on the destination city's loss ratio, which made no sense. The level of risk should also have been tied to the truck's route, trip duration, and other factors such as seasonal weather conditions.

Since the California Highway Patrol had begun raising the frequency of truck safety inspections, I knew that trucks driving within California would be safer because the state frequently inspected their lights, tires, brakes, and load weight. I decided to concentrate our business on intrastate transport—travel only within California's state lines—to further limit risk.

When I pointed out the drawbacks of the old, flawed system of setting rates, the insurance underwriters agreed. We were able to charge much more competitive rates, spurring a growth spurt for our fledgling company. By convincing our insurers to *buck the conventional wisdom* on calculating rates, we had gained a foothold in the lucrative trucking-fleet market, specializing in intrastate transport in California. I negotiated exclusive representation with one particular company and remained the only broker in the country with these low rates for a year and a half until my competitors matched our pricing. During that eighteen-month stretch, I secured 30 percent of the market share. That program came to represent 65 percent of our total revenue. We'd successfully *exploited our competitors' weakness*—premium rate setting—*and made it our strength.*

Developing new programs with the insurance companies was never easy, however. When a program had no history based on which to evaluate potential risk, the insurance company had to depend solely on its instincts in deciding on pricing and whether this new kind of business could turn a profit. The stakes were perilously high: If the executive making the decision guessed incorrectly, he would probably be fired or replaced. Therefore, the safest route for the underwriters was to say no to any new program. This is where my debate-team experience kicked in, and I was able to convince a jittery insurance executive to *trust his gut* and sign on to a new program.

Though the trucking program represented the majority of our total revenue at the time, we recognized that this segment was still highly volatile. In 1979, based on the board's advice, I decided to reduce the company's total revenue from the trucking program from 65 percent to 25 percent, which required me to pinpoint more *underserved niches* and generate a lot more new business. As a result, I devised a new program to insure dredging vessels on a worldwide basis. These are vessels with special equipment that dredge the bottoms of canals, riverbeds, lakes, and ocean coastlines to clear them of debris and sludge. By this time, Cal-Surance was headquartered in Torrance, California, and had about twenty employees. Our annual sales topped $50 million.

We secured the endorsement of the World Dredging Association and drew support from Lloyds of London in insuring the dredgers against loss. Suddenly, we found ourselves taking on competition from Dutch and Japanese companies. The program was a huge, high-risk undertaking for an agency of our modest size, but we gained the trust of underwriters, and the program lasted for several years.

The safest route for the underwriters was to say no to any new program. This is where my debate-team experience kicked in, and I was able to convince a jittery insurance executive to *trust his gut* and sign on to a new program.

I continued to focus on developing new programs that tapped *underserved niches,* which meant viewing the world from an entrepreneur's perspective. You never know what might spawn a great idea for a new program, so your entrepreneurial antenna always needs to be up. One day, while sitting across the desk from the vice president of benefits of a major insurance company, I noticed incredibly tall stacks of papers on his credenza. This was more than thirteen years ago, before computers were commonly used in business.

"What are those?" I inquired. With a deep groan, he replied that those overwhelming stacks were applications from his company's 15,000 agents for their errors and omissions (malpractice) coverage, which he had to collect, oversee, and record.

"What do you do with them then?" I inquired.

"I send them to the insurance company providing coverage to our agents," he answered.

"What do they do with them?"

"I don't really know," he answered in an exasperated tone.

A lightbulb went off in my head, and I asked him, "How would you feel if your 15,000 agents could just be automatically covered by a single master policy without needing to complete any applications?"

"Hugely relieved," he said with a look of real interest.

I knew we could eliminate the paper application process, which no one looked at anyway, thereby sharply reducing the insurance company's processing costs and premiums. I found an insurance company that agreed with my premise and created this exclusive new program for my company. I also convinced other prospective life insurance company clients to collect money directly from their own agents and to try this new concept of *one single policy* instead of thousands of individual agent policies. In that paper-intensive pre-computer era, this program reduced the insurance companies' overhead costs so dramatically that Cal-Surance finally ended up insuring most of the major life insurance company agents in the country for malpractice insurance. The same system worked for property and casualty and real estate agents, and our company's sales exploded. By 1981, Cal-Surance employed over 125 people, and with sales of over $125 million, it ranked sixtieth in revenue out of over 100,000 insurance agencies nationwide.

It was crucial to talk to potential customers and *really listen* to what their concerns and needs were before I devised a new specialized program. Complaints from potential customers often helped identify pathways to competitive advantage. I learned that if I found a way to resolve a problem that was getting under their skin—and resolved it before my competitors did—I'd win a major victory. We always looked for ways to *find our competitor's weakness and exploit it.*

Since our beginnings, Mehlig had continued to run his own division separately. In 1984, he elected to form his own firm specializing in personal investment advising and family wealth counseling. It was an amicable parting of ways after twenty-two successful years of working together.

Building Trust and Credibility

To gain a competitive edge, Cal-Surance willingly participated in a program's actual risk taking—a strategy that bucked industry practice for brokers—to signal that we had "skin in the game" and were more committed to making programs work. This meant that if the insuring company suffered a loss, so did we. On the other hand, if the program became profitable, we would benefit as well. Our willingness to share in their exposure to risk earned us tremendous credibility and trust from the insuring companies. They recognized the integrity of our due diligence and our attention to making the programs efficient and profitable.

It's Never Easy

Of course, it wasn't always smooth sailing with our specialty programs. When you run your own business and take high-stakes risks, you are going to wake up at 3 a.m. some nights with your stomach in a knot. Some crises develop gradually; others sucker punch you.

One day I was on an airplane, heading from New York back to Los Angeles, when I recognized an attorney I knew sitting across the aisle. As we exchanged greetings, he mentioned he was flying to LA to attend a meeting about Transit Casualty Company's impending demise. The newly insolvent firm was shutting its doors. When I heard that bit of news, my heart began pounding like a timpani drum. Transit Casualty was the lead company on our program that insured Farmers Insurance agents against errors and omissions (malpractice).

As soon as we landed, I contacted Transit Casualty and reached someone there who confirmed the grim news. When I explained my

---<o>---

*I always made time to consider possible avenues
for company growth, which meant keeping tabs
on market trends that directly affected our clients.*

---〰---

predicament, he reassured me that as long as Farmers agents paid out any affected claims upfront, they would *eventually* be reimbursed with state funds allotted for such situations. Although that provided a little consolation, I knew it would go over like a lead balloon. The prospect of breaking the news to Farmers and its agents filled me with a sense of dread. Suddenly, the safety net we'd promised our clients looked like it was starting to tear, and the program's future was in jeopardy.

Fortunately, my worst fears were assuaged when Farmers agreed to pay the claims for its agents in the interim. The company was that committed to the program's long-term success. But for about ninety days, I had a lot of sleepless nights until I found another market. I eventually placed the program with The Home Insurance Company, which had been established more than a century before. If you think lightning doesn't strike the same place twice, you're wrong. Unbelievably, two months later, I got a phone call telling me The Home Insurance Company was declaring insolvency. Farmers Insurance expected me to replace that program quickly.

I jumped on a plane to meet with Joe Stinnette, CEO of the Fireman's Fund Insurance Company, in San Francisco. After explaining my dilemma, I asked for his help. Impressed with the program's merits, *that very same day* he gave me the go-ahead to place with his company. Life is a lot easier when you can call the client and say, "Look, here's the problem, but here's the solution." These prestigious clients have remained loyal to Cal-Surance for over twenty years.

Making Hiring and Staffing Innovations

I created services that would support our programs and made it almost impossible for the competition to keep pace. I created a claims operation to service our errors and omissions programs that was superior to any other in this field. This unit, Lancer Claims Services, was incorporated in 1982. The better we were at claims, the more valuable we became to the insurance company.

Our ability to service errors and omissions claims quickly and professionally became the backbone of the program. Most insurance companies use in-house adjusters to negotiate and settle claims. But such adjusters can be at a disadvantage when dealing with attorneys representing claimants. Therefore, I decided to hire only attorneys to settle the claims, clearly *bucking conventional wisdom.* Lawyers would more readily command the respect of the legal departments of the insurance companies, and it's always better if one attorney is dealing with another attorney.

We recognized that attorneys would command higher salaries than the usual insurance adjusters; on the other hand, if they negotiated claim settlements successfully, they would be worth more money. We also found it interesting that attorneys much preferred to work as

Cal-Surance headquarters in Orange County, California

adjusters for a company than to pursue private practice, which would require them to secure their own clients and to work longer hours. We paid high salaries, and this system fit their needs and ours. By 1985, our annual sales had passed the $200 million mark, and we employed 285 people.

Continuing to Create New Products

I always made time to consider possible avenues for company growth, which meant keeping tabs on market trends that directly affected our clients. Occasionally, this also meant shutting my office door, asking my staff to hold all my calls, and taking a moment to *really think* about potential new products and directions for Cal-Surance. To an outsider, it might have looked like I was just wasting time at my desk daydreaming, but those moments of absolute silence were some of the most productive in my career.

The Rewards of My Work to Grow My Business

Forty years after founding Cal-Surance, we ranked fiftieth in revenue nationwide, with annual sales of $250 million. I decided that the time was right to sell. The hypercompetitive insurance business was becoming even more competitive, and I expected profits to taper off over the next several years. We set up a task force within the board structure to help us select the right buyer. We chose Brown & Brown, a New York Stock Exchange company ranked sixth in size out of all brokerage companies in the country. The company paid us $64.5 million on a pure cash basis, with no contingency requirements. Looking back on my professional life, I am proud to have built a high-quality organization that was known nationwide. I'm grateful to have met and worked with so many fine men and women whose careers I helped develop.

The year before, I had been so intent on preparing Cal-Surance for the sale, I'd not had time to contemplate what I would do next. While I knew retirement for me would not mean playing golf five days a week, I believed my life still had a purpose that would be revealed in time. That day arrived after the fateful conversation with my son-in-law's friends who questioned the viability of the American Dream.

Since then, my so-called retirement has been anything but restful. *The Risk Takers* became a whirlwind project of researching, interviewing, and writing about some of the most fascinating—and complicated—entrepreneurs of our time. Renee and I felt compelled to write this book to share my story and those of other successful individuals to motivate and inspire the next generation of entrepreneurs.

Trust me, you have no idea what you're capable of accomplishing until you put yourself out there and give it your all. And if you're like me, you just might have to venture 2,400 miles from your hometown before you really find a home. But taking that leap of faith can make all the difference in the world.

STRATEGIES FOR SUCCESS

- High school teachers, from whom Don sought advice, weren't encouraging about his prospects, so Don told himself *not to accept the limits others placed on him*. Instead, he decided to *trust his gut* and convinced his mother to move to Los Angeles, where he could afford California's inexpensive junior college system.
- He enrolled in college, and to expand his social network there, he ran for school office. Seeing that his competitors relied on their former high school cliques for support, he instead sought votes from the night students, mostly veterans. They helped give him a victory, and he learned an important lesson: "Hit 'em where they ain't."
- When approached by a fellow insurance agent about launching their own firm, Don *trusted his gut* that the two could build a successful enterprise despite their youth and relative inexperience. He decided to *just start* his own business.
- Don went on a hunt for *underserved niches*, knowing that offering specialized programs could give him an edge. This strategy ensured Cal-Surance's success over the course of four decades.
- By nurturing relationships with industry associations, Cal-Surance *saved its bucks and got attention without expensive advertising*.
- By taking steps to reduce premium rates for dump truck fleets, Don was able to *exploit his competitors' weakness and make it his strength*. He repeated that tactic by creating specialized programs at a pace competitors couldn't match.

- ♦ Don *bucked conventional wisdom* by hiring attorneys to settle claims, leveling the playing field since attorneys represented the claimants.

- ♦ He convinced insurance companies they could slash costs by converting to a single master policy for agent malpractice coverage. This *exploited his competitors' weakness*—premium prices—*and made it his company's strength.*

- ♦ When an errors and omissions program twice lost its underwriter to insolvency, Don doggedly pursued other firms to step in and salvage the program. He *didn't let adversity defeat him.* His persistence paid off; he may have lost some sleep during the ordeal, but he didn't lose the program.

- ♦ In a constant search for new products to keep *reinventing his company,* Don was always *on the lookout for new trends.* The quiet moments he took to figure out how to pounce on them were among his most productive.

Renee and Don Martin, 1991

Don and Renee Martin, 2009

CHAPTER 18

Strategies for Success

America has always been a beacon of entrepreneurialism because it is so deeply rooted in our history. Our country was founded and then settled by innovators willing to sacrifice old certainties for new opportunities. The people who came to America a few hundred years ago looking for a better life were risk takers in every sense.

In his 2009 inaugural address, President Barack Obama said, "We are a nation of risk takers." Although high-stakes risk taking has gotten a bad rap recently, thanks to poor decision making in the financial sector, the president understood that a strong economy still requires risk takers. For the economy to rebound, we'll need bold entrepreneurs to recognize and seize opportunities. The American economy became the envy of the world because entrepreneurs were willing to take risks.

Do not mistake being a risk taker with being reckless. Risk takers must also become risk analyzers—evaluating the pros and cons, then trusting their instincts and recognizing and seizing an opportunity to create their own businesses. We, as a nation, must regain our appetite for risk in order to embolden the hearts of our entrepreneurs.

The label of "risk taker" appropriately applies to the entrepreneurs profiled in this book. They earned that label because of the courage they exhibited in many areas. Though most risked loss of money, other inherent risks were equally difficult. They risked ridicule and loss of respect or credibility. However, the rewards of taking high-stakes risks are evidenced in the successful businesses they've built, in the thousands of jobs they've created, and in the lifestyle they've been able to provide for themselves and their families. Hopefully, their journeys will inspire or motivate you to try your own hand in starting a business.

In the preceding chapters, you may have recognized the common traits that bind these entrepreneurs. We don't believe these shared traits are merely a coincidence; we think they are the keys to their success. We hope you'll apply these traits to your own strategy for success for your future or existing business. We've highlighted them in every chapter throughout the book and now present them together, along with examples of their application by our entrepreneurs.

1. Trust Your Gut

Successful, independent-minded entrepreneurs know when to trust their gut. An expanding body of research from a number of fields—including economics, neurology, and cognitive psychology—confirms that intuition is a real form of knowledge. It's a skill you can develop and strengthen—one that's particularly valuable in the most chaotic, fluid business environments, when you must make critical, high-pressure decisions at a moment's notice. At such times, intuition usually beats rational analysis.

Trusting your instincts also emboldens you to carry out new, untested ideas and ventures, even when nobody else believes in them. It's about seeing the need for a product or new service and *just knowing* you can make it happen. You may not have the cash on hand to commission a market study or conduct a focus group, but you're still willing to stake your reputation and money on that idea. Why? Because that's what your gut tells you to do. All of the entrepreneurs discussed in this book listened to and trusted their gut instincts.

Thirty-nine-year-old Mal Mixon felt stifled by corporate politics and recognized he was in a career rut. *Trusting his gut,* he decided to walk away from his job as vice president of marketing and seize control over his own destiny by running his own company.

After Sara Blakely cut the feet out of a pair of control-top panty hose to hide her panty lines and enable her to wear a pair of sexy sandals, she loved the smooth, line-free contour under her white slacks. She had an epiphany and just knew this was a solution to a problem most women faced. She *trusted her gut* and started a company called Spanx.

At first, Andy Berliner resisted starting a new business and instead tried to sell his idea for tasty, healthy, organic convenience meals to established health-food companies. But the feeling that this was just too good an idea to let go began to take hold of him. So, instead, he *trusted his gut* and started Amy's Kitchen.

2. Buck the Conventional Wisdom

Ignore those who say, "It won't work" or "It's never been done that way." Our profiled entrepreneurs succeeded in large part because they veered away from established formulas and ways of thinking. Don't just blindly accept the so-called best practices of your industry. Look at them with a hypercritical eye. Dissect them, slice and dice them, contemplate different what-if scenarios. Challenging convention can open the door to competitive advantage.

Gary Heavin *ignored the conventional wisdom* that profitable gyms must be sprawling, multiroom facilities offering a host of services and filled with pricey (and complicated) fitness equipment. He built his Curves franchise system around sparse six-hundred-square-foot facilities that have no saunas, no tanning beds, no juice bars, and no pools. Gary succeeded because his business model broke the mold and targeted an *underserved niche*—older women who found the traditional gym environment intimidating.

Well-meaning friends and associates warned David L. Steward repeatedly that a black man didn't stand a chance of succeeding in the technology industry. He *shrugged off the conventional wisdom* and built a multi-billion-dollar technology company.

As a college student, Linda Alvarado *flouted the conventional wisdom* when she applied for a campus landscaping job—despite being told that female students were expected to work in the cafeteria or library, not outdoors getting their hands dirty. Later, she pursued a career in the male-dominated construction industry, refusing to let established gender roles restrict her career options.

3. Never Let Adversity or Failure Defeat You

Don't accept the limits that others or circumstances place upon you. The ranks of successful entrepreneurs are filled with men and women who refused to stop believing in themselves, despite the derision of others or heartbreaking failures in their past. As an entrepreneur you'll undoubtedly experience stressful moments that will test your faith, especially in the beginning when you're still trying to establish your brand and separate from the pack. Just remember, the antidotes are persistence and resiliency.

As a kid, Paul Orfalea was a perpetually poor student suspected of being retarded because of his undiagnosed attention deficit hyperactivity disorder and dyslexia. As a teenager, he was unable to hold a job, even while working for a family member. But Paul did not accept the limits others placed on him. He *overcame adversity* and launched Kinko's.

Gary Heavin's first venture into the gym business had provided him with a $1 million financial statement by the time he was twenty-six. Then a series of bad business decisions led to bankruptcy, and Gary lost everything: his marriage, his house, his private plane, his cars, his self-respect. He was $5 million in debt. But Gary *didn't let those failures defeat him*. He took steps to rebuild his life and created his Curves empire.

John Paul DeJoria started selling his first Paul Mitchell hair products while he was so broke he couldn't afford an apartment and was forced to sleep in his car.

After Joe Liemandt dropped out of Stanford University to focus on developing a sales configurator, the skepticism and disappointment of his family (and some friends) never let up. But that didn't stop Joe and the other Trilogy founders from continuing to develop their groundbreaking software product. If they had to live and work in friends' garages to save on expenses until the company turned a profit, so be it. As it turned out, that particular leap of faith was worthy of a gold medal. Today, all of Trilogy's founders are multimillionaires.

4. Go on a Treasure Hunt and Find an Underserved Niche

In the business world, there's nothing more exciting than finding an *underserved niche* representing a lucrative market that everyone else has failed to spot and target. That's like finding gold bullion at a crowded beach—it was there for everyone else to see, but you were the one who took notice of the golden glint in the sand. Even a huge multi-billion-dollar company can't offer something for everyone. Look for ways to fill a niche—a road even small start-ups can take. Many niches are too small for giant corporations to consider.

That's what David L. Steward did after he left corporate America. He observed many companies auditing freight invoices to identify railroad overcharges, but nobody was auditing on the other side of the coin—looking for underpayments due the railroads. Not only did he *fill a niche*, but he developed a way to provide a service with efficiencies that future competitors could not easily duplicate.

When John Paul DeJoria realized no ultra-premium-quality tequila was available in the United States, he decided to produce one to *fill that niche*. His Patrón tequila, distilled and packaged entirely by hand, captured 70 percent of the ultrapremium market.

Maxine Clark figured she could create brand identity with Build-A-Bear Workshops by tailoring her product and marketing to the *underserved niche* she'd identified—little girls who lived in the suburbs and enjoyed playing with real and imaginary friends, including stuffed animals.

Gary Heavin's Curves franchise business actually targeted three *underserved niches*: middle-age and older women eager to get in shape but intimidated by big, sprawling gyms teeming with young, hard bodies; busy working women whose schedules could more easily accommodate the Curves thirty-minute workout; and budget-conscious women who simply couldn't afford the pricey monthly membership dues charged by the major gym chains. Early on, Curves clearly distinguished itself from the pack of gym competitors—its services and clientele were different.

5. Spot a New Trend and Pounce

Often, a shift in cultural or economic trends will create new entrepreneurial opportunities. Sometimes that shift arises from advances in technology. Many of our profiled entrepreneurs recognized emerging consumer needs and desires that signaled new market opportunities.

Robert Stephens was *paying attention to trends* when the home PC market exploded. He figured out that most PC owners had limited technical knowledge. If their hard drive crashed, they were thrown into a state of panic. But unplugging their PC and hauling it off to a repair shop, where it would stay for a week or so, wasn't an acceptable option. So Robert launched his house-call computer repair service, and Geek Squad made millions.

Early on, Tova Borgnine *recognized the growing trend* of women forsaking the malls to make their purchases on new home-shopping cable TV networks. She convinced the fledgling QVC network to let her do a segment on her products, and she was embraced by QVC's devoted audience. She has since sold an astonishing 10 million bottles of her signature fragrance.

After *recognizing a new trend*, the ongoing expansion of the home-care market, Mal Mixon hatched one of his best business ideas: pulling all the home-care product lines under one sales force. There were a lot of specialized providers out there—a bed company, a patient-aid company, an oxygen company. Invacare was the first one to envision putting all those home-care products under one wholesaler umbrella.

6. Hit 'Em Where They Ain't

Casey Stengel, legendary manager of the New York Yankees, loved to tell the story of baseball great "Wee Willie" Keeler, who stood at just 5' 4", weighed 140 pounds, and began a streak of eight seasons with two hundred or more hits. The Hall of Famer's bat was only thirty inches. Once a sports reporter asked him how such a small guy could get so many big hits. Willie replied, "Keep your eye clear, and *hit 'em where they ain't*—that's all." The same holds true in the business world. Whenever possible, set your sights on areas that your competitors have neglected or ignored.

When Xerox copiers were first made available for public use, Paul Orfalea realized that there were no copy centers adjacent to most college campuses. He instinctively knew to *hit 'em where they ain't* and started his Kinko's chain by catering to university students and professors throughout the country and built a billion-dollar company.

Before moving Curves into more populous urban areas, Gary Heavin decided to first *hit 'em where they ain't* and establish a presence in small towns that had been virtually ignored by the big fitness chains. That winning strategy helped Gary and his wife build an international company whose revenues eventually hit the $2 billion mark.

When she diversified into the fast-food franchise business, Linda Alvarado *hit 'em where they ain't* by targeting Denver's inner city, where there were few competitors. At the time, major retail developers had virtually abandoned Denver's inner-city neighborhoods, leading to bargain-basement prices for commercially zoned properties there.

In the late 1970s, Barbara Corcoran recognized that New York City's West Side was receiving very little attention because those neighborhoods had historically lagged behind in property values. Her competitors seemed perplexed when she opened a major Corcoran Group office in the area. But she knew what she was doing. Her own real estate research suggested demand for the area was on the upswing. In effect, she was positioning her company to *hit 'em where they ain't.* Years later, she also anticipated growing demand for the Downtown corridor before her competitors. When Downtown became the hippest market in the city, her competitors had missed the boat. Corcoran's company had established a firm footing, and her competitors never caught up with her.

When Weight Watchers was a brand-new company with limited locations, Florine Mark had to travel from Detroit to New York City to attend regular meetings. After months in the weight-loss program, she shed the excess pounds and began considering bringing Weight Watchers to Detroit as a franchisee. Florine, who'd never run a business before, recognized that Detroit was full of women like her who would benefit from the Weight Watchers program. She started the first of her many Weight Watchers franchises in the Detroit area to *hit 'em where they ain't.*

7. Just Start!

If you have an idea for a business, truly believe it will succeed, and are willing to push yourself harder than you ever have before, then take the risk and *just get started.* If your gut is telling you this business idea is a winner, take action now. The "perfect" time for a business launch will never present itself. More often than not, waiting just gives would-be competitors the opportunity to beat you to the punch. None of the entrepreneurs we interviewed waited for a sign from heaven or until a long-forgotten aunt died and left them $300,000 in seed money.

Many faced tremendous financial hurdles. Nonetheless, they saw a market opportunity and grabbed it.

Much to her surprise and shock, Tova Borgnine one day received thousands of face masque orders, with checks totaling $56,000, after her famous husband mentioned her product in a newspaper interview. Unfortunately, her product hadn't been mass-produced yet for sale on a commercial scale. She found herself in a legal bind: If she failed to fill all the orders within thirty days of receipt of payment, she faced possible federal prosecution for mail fraud. Instead of playing it safe and returning the checks, she rose to the challenge. Recognizing an extraordinary opportunity, she was more than ready to take the risk and *just start*. That was the beginning of her multi-million-dollar business.

Joe Liemandt knew that many established deep-pocket information technology companies such as Hewlett-Packard were working to develop a configuration software system. He knew the proverbial pot of gold awaited the first company to build a reliable one. The race was on. Even though he had no money to match the big bucks of Hewlett-Packard and others, he shelved pursuit of his Stanford University diploma and *just started*. Trilogy was on its way.

While visiting a friend, Paul Orfalea discovered there was not a single copy center near the University of California's Santa Barbara campus. In a real quandary as to what he was going to do after graduation, he had an epiphany that a copy center was a business he could handle and decided to *just start* Kinko's.

8. Save Your Bucks and Get Noticed Without Expensive Advertising

If your start-up business is on a tight budget, there are plenty of ways to get customers' attention without spending money on advertising. Get your creative juices percolating and try something different. And when an opportunity arises to expose your brand to the masses, don't think twice—jump right in. Use your own creativity to make your company stand out in a crowd.

Robert Stephens was a cash-strapped college student when he launched Geek Squad in 1994. With only $200 to invest in his business, he had no budget for advertising. But *without expensive advertising*, using chutzpah and creativity, he still generated enough word-of-mouth referrals to make his computer tech-support company profitable. His attention-getting tricks included outfitting employees in retrogeek uniforms and cruising wealthy neighborhoods with a quirky company car emblazoned with the company logo. He also strategically parked the Geekmobile downtown when a local TV news show started airing live feeds of the area during its broadcasts. Robert made sure his car was always in the video frame.

Liz Lange mastered how to *get noticed without expensive advertising*. She knew the power of celebrity endorsement in the fashion world. She contacted the personal assistants of pregnant celebrities and offered to dress their clients for high-profile events, like award shows, in exchange for a plug. Soon celebrities such as Cindy Crawford, Gwyneth Paltrow, Elle MacPherson, and Kelly Ripa were being photographed wearing Liz's designs and singing their praises.

9. Exploit Your Competitor's Weakness and Make It Your Strength

The sharpest entrepreneurs have a knack for viewing the world from the perspective of their customers. That quality can help identify your competitors' vulnerabilities and shortcomings. If your number one competitor has a reputation for slow deliveries, for example, make certain your deliveries arrive in less time. Engage and listen to customers to identify such weaknesses.

Avid vegetarians, Andy and Rachel Berliner usually made their vegetarian meals from scratch, often relying on ingredients from their own organic garden in northern California. But when Rachel was pregnant with their daughter Amy, she didn't feel like laboring away in the kitchen. Andy made a trip to the local health-food store in search of frozen vegetarian meals they could pop into the microwave. When he and Rachel sat down to eat what he'd brought home, they couldn't believe how horrible the so-called meals tasted.

After surviving that prepackaged culinary disaster, Andy began thinking like an entrepreneur. He realized he'd spotted a market opportunity. Eventually, the couple launched their own line of *tasty* frozen vegetarian meals using quality organic ingredients. Amy's

Kitchen generates annual revenues of $270 million because Andy was successful in *exploiting his competitors' weakness.*

Mal Mixon wasted little time *exploiting his competitors' weakness*—delivery times—*and making that his company's strength.* Mal recognized that when personal mobility is at stake, wheelchair retailers and their customers want a quick turnaround. To speed delivery times, he built a network of warehouse facilities throughout the United States so he could promise delivery within twenty-four hours. That's one of the reasons why his company, Invacare, became the largest manufacturer of wheelchairs in the United States.

Liz Lange *recognized her competitors' weakness*—existing lines of maternity clothes lacked a sense of style. They tended to be ill fitting, unflattering, and just plain dull. That's why she introduced her own maternity line full of boldly creative, yet tasteful and sophisticated, designs.

10. Never Stop Reinventing Your Company

You know the old adage "If it ain't broke, don't fix it"? The problem with that piece of advice is that it invites complacency—and complacency in business is like a slow leak in a tire. You may not notice the damage it's causing until the thing is completely flat and you can't move forward. Top-performing entrepreneurs aren't afraid to take chances and keep expanding their product line. They're not afraid to give their business a major overhaul now and then to keep pace with changes in the marketplace. And sometimes a complete face-lift is in order.

Today's market leaders can become tomorrow's cautionary tales if they respond too slowly or too meekly to changes in the marketplace. Take Levi Strauss, for example. The longtime king of all things denim saw its market share spiral downward in the 1990s because of the company's slow response to competitors. Instead of offering its own fashion-forward designs to stave off competitors such as Calvin Klein and Tommy Hilfiger, Levi Strauss clung stubbornly to its traditions. Meanwhile, the company also began ceding market share to many of its own retailers, as Gap Inc., JCPenney, and Sears launched their own store-brand jeans lines. Eventually, because of its passive approach to competition, Levi Strauss was forced to undergo a very painful reorganization.

David L. Steward started his own company to provide auditing services for the railroad industry. But he eventually *reinvented his business* to offer information technology services to a much broader range of customers, including the telecommunications industry and federal government agencies. With the advent of the World Wide Web, David again reshaped his business model. He's constantly reinventing World Wide Technology (WWT) so that its services and products reflect advances in technology and shifts in customer needs. That's why today WWT is a $3 billion business.

Build-A-Bear Workshops constantly *reinvents itself* by introducing new stuffed animal characters, wardrobes, and accessories, as well as by forming corporate partnerships designed to woo boy customers.

We continually *reinvented* Cal-Surance to create a unique organization that provided every insurance service required by our clients. This enabled us to deliver better pricing, huge savings, greater efficiency, and better service. We outdistanced our competitors who could never catch up.

Create Your Own Strategy for Success

All of the entrepreneurs profiled in this book placed their own personal stamp on these strategies, using them creatively and to great effect. We hope that you will find these traits beneficial for your own entrepreneurial journey and adapt them to your own strategy for success. We hope you can apply them toward a new venture or use them in your existing business.

Believe that growth and opportunity for this nation's economy are inevitable. Look at the world through the eyes of an entrepreneur. Use your imagination to identify market opportunities that others have overlooked. Believe in the power of your ideas and *just start* the pursuit of your own entrepreneurial dream. It's up to you to reclaim the American Dream.

ACKNOWLEDGMENTS

Our special thanks to all the entrepreneurs profiled in *The Risk Takers* who openly shared their personal and professional experiences with us in the hope that their journeys would inspire and motivate future entrepreneurs.

We also want to thank our fabulous team, whose varied contributions made *The Risk Takers* possible:

Beverly Canipe—for her excellent research skills and ability to put her finger on whatever we needed.

Cathy Stephens—for her valuable proofreading, suggestions, and editing.

Heather Chapman—for all the many little things she handled that freed our time to just write.

Bruce Harris—for all his invaluable ideas and direction. He is a first-class publishing consultant.

Roger Cooper and the Vanguard team—for their assistance with, and confidence in, this project.

"The great personal fortunes in this country weren't built on a portfolio of fifty companies. They were built by someone who identified one wonderful business."

—Warren E. Buffett, Chairman and CEO
Berkshire Hathaway, Inc